A
Neutral
Corner

Boxing Essays by
A.J. LIEBLING

Edited by Fred Warner and James Barbour

Foreword by Bill Barich

A FIRESIDE BOOK
PUBLISHED BY SIMON & SCHUSTER
New York   London   Toronto
Sydney   Tokyo   Singapore

FIRESIDE
Simon & Schuster Building
Rockefeller Center
1230 Avenue of the Americas
New York, New York 10020

First Fireside Edition 1992
Published by arrangement with North Point Press

FIRESIDE and colophon are registered trademarks
of Simon & Schuster Inc.

Designed by David Bullen
Manufactured in the United States of America

10 9 8 7 6 5 4 3 2 1

Library of Congress Cataloging in Publication Data
Liebling, A. J. (Abbott Joseph), 1904–1963.
    A neutral corner: boxing essays/by A. J. Liebling.—1st Fireside ed.
        p.   cm.—(Fireside sports classic)
    Collection of fifteen essays, fourteen of which originally appeared in the New
Yorker, 1952–1990.
    Originally published: San Francisco: North Point Press, 1990.
    "Published by arrangement with North Point Press"—T. p. verso.
    "A Fireside book."
    1. Boxing.   2. Boxing—History.   I. Title.   II. Series.
[GV1133.L47   1992]
796.8'3—dc20
                                                                    91-35640
                                                                    CIP

ISBN 0-671-75045-3

Contents

vii   *Foreword, by Bill Barich*

3   *A Hundred and Eighteen Pounds*

16   *The University of Eighth Avenue*

45   *An Old Thuburban Custom*

66   *They Must Tike Me for a Proper Mugg*

84   *An Artist Seeks Himself*

103   *A Reproach to Skeptics*

118   *A Blow for Austerity*

131   *A Space Filled In*

146   *Ad Lib*

162   *Poet and Pedagogue*

175   *Fun-Lover*

181   *The Morest*

191   *The Men in the Agbadas*

213   *Anti-Poetry Night*

227   *Starting All Over Again*

239   *Afterword, by Fred Warner*

Foreword

Boxing has always been the meanest game in town, but you'd never know it from reading A. J. Liebling. While reporting on our most brutal sport for our most genteel magazine, he remained implacably cheerful and wrote of his adventures among the fight crowd as merrily as a man on holiday in the south of France. There was never a hint of judgment in his pieces, no moralizing or pointing of fingers. As a veteran of what he called the "newspaper sweatshops," Liebling prided himself on being unflappable, and if this kept him from making us feel the blood and pain of the ring, as other writers have done, it also saved him from waxing philosophical every time a deserving pug dropped to the canvas.

Because Liebling so enjoyed the world of boxing, he tended to paint fighters and their entourages in the best possible light. His affection for the ragged-edged scene is obviously genuine. He was at home visiting training camps and low-rent bars, happy to play pinochle or eat steak and eggs with men who did not easily convey their intelligence in words. Above all, Liebling was a realist. He understood that human nature can be bestial as well as sublime, so he never blinked when, for example, a great champion began to thumb his opponent in the eye. Quite the opposite, in fact—he seems to have taken special pleasure from the way heroism and duplicity mingle in the ring.

Much has been made of Liebling's style, and its pyrotechnics are in evidence here. He applied a decorous touch to vulgar matters, drawing his references from both the classics and the local gym. His language was grand, and wit was his strong suit. He loved to inflate a sentence, then release it like a helium balloon and watch it skitter across a page.

Who else would accuse Ingemar Johansson, a bon vivant who broke with training tradition to play golf and dance with his fiancée, of "scorning the precepts of the scholastics"? As for Johansson's chances against Floyd Patterson, Liebling believed that "no competent critic hesitated to select him to be annihilated." Johansson went on to win the fight, but he *did* lose a rematch, going down, said Liebling, "like a double portion of Swedish pancakes with lingonberries and sour cream."

When it came to gastronomic asides, Liebling knew whereof he spoke, having weighed in at heavily laden tables from Brooklyn to Paris. His pieces, whether about fisticuffs or food, operated on the principle of inclusion, not exclusion, and unfolded at the leisurely pace of an evening stroll. In the broadest sense, he wrote *about* boxing, circling it as he might a sparring partner, eagerly alert to every intriguing sight or sound. Sometimes he appeared to be less concerned with the main event than with what happened on the way to it, and this can be annoying to a dedicated fan looking for a precise description of Archie Moore's jab. For Liebling, though, to exist is to digress, and an author is entitled to interrupt the narrative flow to comment on Nigerian clothing or Tunisian cuisine.

"The purpose of going to a fight isn't always to see a close contest," Liebling once claimed, and, as if to prove it, he dealt with boxing more as a subculture than as a sport, soaking up its atmosphere. He had an extraordinary fondness for boxers of all types, and spent hours listening to their excuses and their flights of fancy, sharing in the fatalistic humor that characterized their conversations. He viewed them not merely as splendid athletes but as individuals who'd chosen an improbable vocation and now were stuck with it. To his credit, he never gilded a lily. Dumb pugs were dumb, and smart ones were smart. The given of prizefighting (much like the given of journalism) is that everybody gets screwed sooner or later, and Liebling accepted this as a maxim for life and greeted it with a rueful chuckle.

In reading these previously uncollected stories as a group, it's surprising how similar they are to each other in construction. Their effortless quality derives from Liebling's reliance on a number of techniques he perfected over the years. As a working journalist, somebody who lived by the pen, he was perennially short of either time or money, and though he bragged that he wrote as well as anyone who wrote as fast, he must have occasionally wished for an opportunity to expand on his material. In one piece, a poignant moment occurs while Liebling is contemplating Floyd Patterson's diffident, apologetic expression. He decides that it "befits the artist whose accomplishments never measured up to his own opinion of his abilities." And then he adds, as if he were giving himself a kick in the pants, "This includes all artists worth a damn."

The New Yorker was an odd place for Liebling to file his dispatches, since its editors, particularly William Shawn, had a serious distaste for violence, and after his death all coverage of boxing vanished from the magazine for more than three decades. It did not surface again until a naive writer from Out West—namely, me—suggested that an upcoming bout between Ray "Boom Boom" Mancini and Livingstone Bramble might make for scintillating reading. A bleeder and a Rastafarian! Mr. Shawn's dismay can scarcely be imagined. Still, he let me do the piece, but he could never bring himself to run it, and it was not until his successor, Robert Gottlieb, arrived that boxing as a subject, via Mike Tyson's ninety-one-second demolition of Michael Spinks, was restored to its former position of glory.

One can only hope that Liebling, with his generous, democratic spirit, would approve. He had a soft spot for boxing, and his enthusiasm for it was so infectious that he attracted readers who would have fainted at the thought of attending a match in person. His boundless curiosity illuminated many dark corners of the game, and often put its bizarre twists of fate into historical perspective. Because he did not write for "the boys at the quarterlies," his prose is still fresh and alive, and the finest of his pieces have the shapely grace of chamber music. An admirer comes to the last of them reluctantly. They tap us lightly, but they leave their mark.

Bill Barich

A NEUTRAL CORNER

A Hundred
and Eighteen Pounds

In the history of the English prize ring, there came a day when Pierce Egan, its Thucydides, had to write, "Abraham Belasco must be pronounced the only fighting Jew on the boxing list." That was in 1821. Belasco, a hundred-and-fifty-pound man, was a petty epilogue. He could give but not take punishment. The first period of Jewish prizering glory had begun with the rise of Dan Mendoza, in 1788. Mendoza, in Egan's words, "was considered one of the most elegant and scientific Pugilists in the whole race of Boxers, and might be termed a complete artist. His theoretic acquirements were great, and his practice truly extensive." This golden age had ended with the defeat of Dutch Sam by Bill Nosworthy, the baker, on December 8, 1814, eliciting from Egan this noble sentence: "The abdication of Bonaparte, in its proper sphere, was not more electric than the defeat of Dutch Sam in the boxing world." Dutch Sam, returned from retirement at the age of forty-one, weighed a hundred and thirty pounds for that fight. Nosworthy, twenty-eight, weighed a hundred and fifty-four. Nevertheless, to explain the result Egan had to theorize: "His [Sam's] irregularities of life must have dilapidated as fine and strong a constitution as was ever possessed by man." The fight had gone but thirty-eight rounds.

The reasons for the abandonment of the ring by Jews at that moment in history are not now discernible. They subsequently reentered the calling in great numbers, both in England and here. There were good Jewish fighters right up through the nineteen-thirties, and in cities like New York, Philadelphia, and Chicago they were among the best drawing cards. Since the most recent World War, though, there haven't been any new ones, and at Lou Stillman's gymnasium, on Eighth Avenue, where a hundred or so professional boxers train between jobs, a trainer the other day could think of only three Jewish boys who rent locker space—all of them very moderate. This is particularly distressing to the managers and would-be managers who congregate in the space between Stillman's lunch counter and his two boxing rings, because, as one of them said feelingly, "With a good Jew fighter now you could make a fortune of money."

I learned the stark statistics on my visit to Stillman's. Such changes creep up on us by imperceptible degrees; I had taken it for granted that there were still lots of Jewish boys around, even though I seldom happened to see any of them in the ring when I went to fights. The reasons for their disappearance are less obscure than the reasons for the disappearance of Jewish fighters in 1821. Freddy Brown, the fellow who counted off the survivors for me, furnished the explanation. Brown is a partner of an old friend of mine in the training business named Whitey Bimstein, who was also in Stillman's that day. Training is distinct from managing. The firm of Bimstein & Brown trains for any manager with the price, and is therefore in general touch with market conditions. Both Freddy and Whitey are Jews and former fighters.

"When the kids didn't have what to eat, they were glad to fight," Brown, a determined-looking chap with a well-smashed nose, told me. "Now that any kid can get a job, they got no ambition. Fighting used to be the only way to make a dollar, but now it looks like a hard buck. The kids we get now, the most of them, even the Italians, they just want to have a couple of fights so they can say they were fighters. It gives them class. The first time they lay off, we lose them. For instance, they got a rule now that a kid gets knocked out, he can't fight again for thirty days. What does he do? He gets a job. He draws down that fifty, sixty bucks a week, and he can go with girls. So we never see him again."

"The depression killed the gate but it developed fighters," Mr. Bimstein said, delivering a concurring opinion. "Now the kids ain't serious." He has bulging eyes with white lashes, and they looked even more world-weary than usual, because he had worked four corners in Cleveland the night before and had come straight from his plane to Stillman's. "The only ones who work hard are the colored boys," he said, "because for them it's still tough outside. The good white fighters you got coming up, you could count them on your fingers."

"Garbage," said Mr. Brown, waving a hard hand at the roomful of grunting, sweating youth, which included a good number of his own pupils.

Irish boxers are slightly less rare than Jewish ones, I gathered, and there are even a few tolerable postwar developments among them—Billy Graham, Walter Cartier, and Paddy Young, all New York boys but none, unfortunately, blessed with a resounding Hibernian name. There is also Irish Bob Murphy, from the Pacific Coast, a great crowd-pleaser. Still, their numerical advantage over their traditional rivals is only relative—just as the Javan rhinoceros has lagged behind the whooping crane in the race to extinction. They, too, find it easy to get outside jobs. Most of the white boxers using Stillman's now are of Italian stock, but there are at least as many Negroes as all kinds of white boys put together, with a large West Indian group filling in the spectrum between.

"Last week, the Broadway Arena was short a six-rounder," Whitey said. "Fellow got sick on them. They telephoned here but they couldn't fill it. Fifteen years ago, there would of been twenty managers fighting to get boys into the spot."

"Imagine it," said Brown. "The biggest gym in the country and they can't find a guy for a six-rounder. If a kid has had ten fights, his manager wants him to go on top. But the manager wants to name the other guy."

"You can't blame the managers, with the type kids they got," Whitey said. "They got to be careful."

Stillman's is reached from the street by way of a steep stairway. To get in, a spectator must pay fifty cents at a turnstile manned by a fellow called Curley, who is an expert at non-recognition. For years, he has practiced looking at people he knows as if he had never seen them before. The boxers, managers, and trainers who use Stillman's naturally get in without paying admission, and they sometimes bring in their friends. When this happens, an agonized look spreads over Curley's waxlike face. He resents introductions as buildups for future free entries, and makes a point of forgetting them. The striking bags and most of the exercise mats are on a balcony, and the two rings, with a few rows of benches for the spectators in front of them, are the central feature of Stillman's main floor. Earnest pairs of athletes succeed one another within the ring ropes, each boy trying to make an impression as well as sharpen his form, but there is little of that thinly veiled ill feeling that prevails among Sunday-morning tennis players, for example. The professional portion of the Stillman audience was therefore shocked when, on the day of my visit, two boys in a ring started slugging each other viciously, each holding with one hand and hitting with the other. A universal cry of condemnation went up: "Trow dem oudada ring! Trow da bum zout!" Stillman, the master of the revels, rang the electric bell prematurely. The abashed trainers of the uncouth pair climbed through the ropes and pried the solecists apart. Stillman's buzzed censoriously for a good two rounds after their banishment. There were no apologists, such as appear after a rough college football game. "If he wanted to give him a mouthful, he should of went outside!" a trainer named Frank Coco commented indignantly, alluding to one boy's tactic of holding the other by the back of the neck with one hand while he took aim with the other. "What good is it working like that?" a functionalist complained. "No referee will let you get away with it." Freddy had been one of the trainers through the ropes, and Whitey had darted into the locker room on the trail of the angry boys. When they returned, as disconcerted as the sponsors of a pregnant débutante, Whitey said, "I made them shake hands." But he still seemed upset.

Whitey, when he was boxing, in the years just before we went into the First World War, was a bantamweight, I knew, and so was Charley

Goldman, another trainer of my acquaintance. There were, in fact, more bantams than fighters of any other class on view in clubs around New York in the teens and early twenties—little fellows able to get down to a hundred and eighteen pounds. I don't know whether it was because the town swarmed with small men then or whether it was because small men were particularly combative, but you saw bantamweights all over the place. There were flyweights, too, for that matter—fellows able to make a hundred and twelve—but not so many of them.

When I looked Stillman's over that day with Whitey and Freddy, I couldn't see anybody who looked lighter than a featherweight—a hundred and twenty-six—but I didn't completely trust my eyes, because weights will often fool you. So I asked Whitey if there were any good bantamweights around. "Bantyweights?" Whitey said, as if I had mentioned hackney coaches. "I ain't seen one of them little bantyweights around since the war, hardly." It was then that I first realized small boxers are as nearly extinct as Jewish ones. I was aware of the study by the anthropologist Gordon Townsend Bowles, published in 1932, which proved that Harvard students of the day were, on the average, three and a half centimetres taller and ten pounds heavier than their Harvard fathers, but I had never thought of Harvard as a source of bantamweight material in the first place. Even the average Harvard father, as I remembered the data, had weighed about a hundred and thirty-nine. Neither, it seemed to me, had small men in general become less disputatious. Those I knew were, as far as I could recall, as much given to argument as ever.

I asked Whitey what he attributed the dearth to, and he said he didn't know. "It goes in fads," he said. "Sometimes for four or five years most every good boy coming up is a welterweight. Then you get four or five years of nothing but middleweights. Or the middleweight class goes down and your best drawing cards are lightweights. The one thing you could always use more than you got is heavyweights."

"If a manager gets a good, natural bantamweight now, he tries to build him up to a feather, so he can get work," Mr. Brown offered.

"But suppose you had a good kid who couldn't build up—what

would he do for work?" I persisted. "Somebody like Escobar." I remembered that Whitey, in 1935, when I first knew him, had trained Sixto Escobar, a Puerto Rican who was bantamweight champion of the world at a time when the bantamweight championship still meant something at the gate, and that Escobar, whenever he tried to "build up," had merely succeeded in slowing himself down. He was more formidable at "eighteen" than at "twenty-three," as the fancy has it. Boxers and their handlers habitually omit the useless words "a hundred and" when speaking of a fighter's weight.

"A boy like Sixto would have to give away six or seven pounds," Whitey said. "But it's tough." He added, on reflection, that there was one boy using Stillman's who could do eighteen and who was up against exactly that problem. "He's Eddie Walker's kid, Cecil Schoonmaker," he said, "and he's had only one fight in the last three months. He had to go to Cuba for that, and he give the guy eight pounds." For small men, I knew, this is a crushing weight handicap. The lighter fellow, in order to overcome it, has to be far better than his opponent. Schoonmaker, Whitey said, had lost the decision in Cuba. "He's had to go all over the world to get fights," he went on. "It's drove Walker crazy."

I was unable to accept the notion that there were no more bantamweights—or, at any rate, that there were not enough bantamweights left to make one match. But I couldn't turn up another. One manager said a boy called Bill Bossio could do twenty-one. "Could he do eighteen for a big purse?" I asked. "Say, fifty thousand dollars?" "For fifty thousand dollars," the manager answered, "I'd cut his arm off." It happened that I had seen Bossio box, against a featherweight of standard dimensions, at the Westchester County Center, in White Plains, a little while before. A very short boy, with a disproportionately strong torso, he hadn't been quite able to make up for the disparity in reach and weight, and he had lost a close fight. Schoonmaker really did seem to be a lone survivor. Curious to meet a fellow in his situation, I told Whitey I would like to see him, and Whitey said it would be easy to arrange.

That evening, I had a telephone call from Eddie Walker, Schoonmaker's manager. The voice was harsh and indignant. "Cecil's a pretty good fighter," Walker said, "and he's more of a libility than an asset. How do you like that? He win the Golden Glovers, New York and national, and he win easy fifty out of sixty professional fights, and he's a libility. In 1948, he decisioned Dado Marino, the top bantam contender. The California State Boxing Commission recognized him as Number One bantamweight, but they got nobody to fight him. Besides, he don't want to go away from New York no more. He's tired of travelling. He's a New York boy."

I arranged to meet Walker and Schoonmaker at a quarter to twelve next morning, give or take five minutes, on the sidewalk in front of Stillman's. The gymnasium opens at twelve every weekday and closes at three. "That way, we'll have a chance to talk," Walker said. "I got to get away early, because I got a job as checker on the Cunard pier and I got to be over there by one."

When I arrived at the rendezvous, I found two or three young men, evidently fighters, leaning against an automobile parked at the curb, and three older men, who looked as if they might be managers, talking fight in front of a second-hand jewelry store ("Any Ring in the Window May Be Held on a Small Deposit") next door. I asked one of the older men if he was Eddie Walker and I happened to hit it right first time. He was a heavy-set man of neutral coloring, about fifty years old. He had a thrusting underlip and walked with a limp. We shook hands, and he introduced me to one of the boys at the car, who was Schoonmaker.

The fighter did not look unique, nor did he look like a fighter. A slender, very light mulatto with a bushy black mustache, he looked more like a bebop fan than an athlete, wearing a hat turned up in front, a greenish topcoat mottled with purple, a hand-painted necktie, a pink shirt, and well-scuffed loafers. He was tall enough to be a feather, or even a lightweight, and in his clothes he looked as heavy as the boy he was talking to, a fellow with American Indian features under a porkpie hat—Alex Finbreth, a featherweight from Arizona, Walker told me. "My trainer had me drink three bottle ale a day," Finbreth was saying as Walker and I approached. He was giving Schoonmaker a prescription for weight-building. Walker and Schoonmaker and I moved a bit apart from the others, and Schoonmaker said, "I could fight that boy, but his manager won't let him. If a fighter beats a lighter boy, it don't mean anything. And if he gets beat, it looks bad on his record."

"I tell you the truth, this boy is like my deserted child," Walker said to me. "He's had to stay away for years to get work, and now he's come home, I can't do anything for him. I got a couple of other fighters, big fellows, that I get work for them on the docks between fights, but this little bum, what good would he be?"

Cecil did not seem unduly distressed at his disqualification for heavy labor. "If I was heavy enough for the docks," he said, returning, as if magnetized, to his major dilemma, "I would be heavy enough to get fights." We agreed that I should come up and see him box, provided his trainer, Jimmy Brown—no relation to Freddy—could find a sparring partner of appropriate size, and that afterward, when Walker had gone off to the pier, Schoonmaker and I would have a talk.

When the gym opened, the trainer did manage to find a fellow for Schoonmaker to work with. The lad was only a preliminary fighter, however—a tall string bean of a boy, who contented himself with sticking out a tentative left and keeping his right glove in front of his nose, not venturing to become involved in any reciprocal action that might prove too advanced for his accomplishments. As for Schoonmaker, he had apparently been instructed not to damage the other boy. When he appeared in the ring, I could see that he had long legs in proportion to his short, square torso—long from hip to knee as well as from knee to ankle. They were well developed, and so were his arms. His biceps were surprisingly big, and his neck was sturdy. There was just no place for him to put on useful fighting weight. He moved well, flicking a fast left to the face and then getting in under the tall kid's guard whenever he wanted to, or shooting a fast, whipping blow to the ribs. Every time he landed one of these, he would stop the synchronized forward motion of the other shoulder and slide away, instead of throwing a series of punches, as was evidently his style. It was like seeing a child take one piece of candy and pull away from the box.

"I didn't want to hit him but once at a time," he said when he reappeared from the locker room in street clothes. "He's just beginning." We left the gymnasium and headed for a cafeteria at Eighth Avenue and Fifty-seventh Street, where we could talk.

Schoonmaker was born in Greenwich Village, on Gay Street, he said as we walked along, but he wouldn't even know where to find the street now, he had been so small when his parents moved him up to Harlem. There he had started boxing when he was barely visible. His name and his small size, he thought, had combined to force him into at least amateur pugilism. "Schoonmaker's an unusual name," he said, "and not even half the teachers in school could pronounce it. 'Shoemaker,' 'Shoonmaker,' 'Schumacher,' they used to say, and the other kids would laugh and yell in the street, 'Shoemaker, Shoemaker, mend my shoe!' Up there, you got to fight to walk the street. And being small, you get picked on. So I started boxing in the Police Athletic League tournaments for kids. But I did my very first boxing in the gymnasium of St. Charles Roman Catholic Church, on a Hundred and Forty-first Street. The two priests there was very much interested in boxing, but they didn't instruct us personally. In 1938, when I was twelve years old, I won the Police Athletic League championship of Greater New York in the sixty-five-pound class. I only weighed fifty-nine pounds. It was like a prediction of what I would be up against all my life. We boxed just one-minute rounds with big gloves, and the worst punishment we took was being so arm-weary. After I won the championship, there was no holding me. Boxing was all."

We arrived at the cafeteria, and Schoonmaker, going ahead, took two checks from the machine. Walker, he said, had given him a dollar with which to treat me. He took a glass of orange juice and I a cup of coffee, and we sat at a table in the least crowded corner of the room.

"I went to high school and I kept right on boxing," Schoonmaker said. "There wasn't anything else I could do. I was too short for basketball and too small for baseball—and football, it was ridiculous to think of it." His high school, he said, was Seward Park, down on the lower East Side, a long way from Harlem. The course he took there was "academic, whatever that means," and he got as far as the second half of his third year. He had not wanted to go to a vocational school, because he felt he had found his vocation. He kept on entering amateur tournaments, and in 1944 he won the New York *Daily News* Golden Gloves city championship in the flyweight class, a hundred and twelve pounds. He went on to win the regional and national Golden Gloves flyweight titles, and got intoxicated by the publicity with which the *News* rewards participants in its annual promotion stunt. "I really felt I was getting somewhere," he said. Most of his coaching in those days came from his older brother, Winnie, a lightweight, who had preceded Cecil as an amateur and then turned pro. Winnie is a shipping clerk now.

Cecil said he turned pro himself in the summer of 1944 and had nine fights before being drafted into the Army in 1945. He won eight of them. It isn't so hard for a little fellow to get matches when he is just beginning, he explained. There are quite a number of small novices, but they all hope to put on a few pounds, and since most of them are in their teens, most of them do. It's experienced bantyweights that are hard to find.

"I kept on hoping I'd put on weight but I never did," Cecil said. "I'm five feet six inches tall, and the most I get to weigh is twenty-three, when I'm *not* in training. I train a couple of days and I'm eighteen." I tried to tell him of the agonies old-time bantamweights had gone through trying to keep down to weight—a trainer named Ray Arcel, for instance, once brought Charley Phil Rosenberg down from a hundred and fifty-five to a hundred and sixteen for a championship fight— but Schoonmaker was not consoled. "Now I'm twenty-four years old and I guess I'm never going to be heavier," he said. "Sometimes, when I've got to fight a heavier man, I eat and eat to put on beef, but all I do is slow myself up so I can't get out of my own way."

He spent most of 1945 and 1946 with the Army in Germany, he told me. "It was there I got a taste for travel," he said. "Then, when I came back, I found how it was in New York, so Eddie sent me out to the Coast with old Chalky Wright, who used to be featherweight champion. Eddie managed him, too. There were more bantamweights out there, somehow—Filipinos and Mexicans—and I kept pretty busy. I had seventeen fights in 1947, and I got going good. I win my first five fights in 1948—San Diego, Los Angeles, Hollywood—and they put me in with this old Dado Marino in San Francisco. They didn't think I had a chance, but I beat him in ten. He's from Honolulu and a real good fighter. After that, there was the same old trouble—no matches—so I went out to Guam. I stayed out there five or six months and did good."

I said Guam seemed an unlikely place for a prizefighter, but Schoonmaker explained that there had been a boom there—thousands of American civilian construction workers building airfields. "There wasn't much for them to spend money on, so they made a good fight public," he said. "The promoter out there was a fellow named Bill Lujan, a Guamanian. I beat three fellows, and got a thousand dollars a fight. But I broke my hand and never did get time to have it fixed properly. I was going too good, and I couldn't afford to lay off. When they finished the airfields, the construction workers went away, and that was the end of the boxing boom on Guam. I came back and beat a good man, Luis Castillo, in L.A., fifteen rounds, and then I went out to Australia to box the Australian bantam champion, Elley Bennett. I broke my hand again in that fight, and they stopped it in six. It was the end of my winning streak. I didn't have another bout for six months. In 1950, I was out in the Philippines. They put me in with a fellow named Tirso del Rosario. He had about ten pounds on me and he beat me. He's good."

Schoonmaker said he hadn't been to Europe to box yet. There are a few bantamweights over there, but the rate of exchange is not favorable. Anyway, he said, it would be the same as the Philippines, or Cuba, where he fought a fellow named Morasen last summer. "You go to one of those countries where they got a few boys your weight, and you beat them, and then you have to fight some heavier boy anyway, and you got to knock them out to win. You go into one of those countries alone, with nobody even in your corner that you can talk their language, and you pray you won't get cut, because they won't know how to stop the bleeding." He said he thought he had won the fight in Havana, although he had weighed only seventeen while the Cuban had come in at twenty-five, but the home-town judges had given the decision to their own man. "It was so hot that I was a pound lighter than usual," he said.

The only part of the world where bantamweights still draw heavy money is the Union of South Africa. Manuel Ortiz, a Mexican, who won the bantamweight title in 1942 and again in 1947, defended it successfully against Marino, the Hawaiian, and then was induced to visit South Africa and risk it against an Afrikander named Vic Toweel, at Johannesburg, in May, 1950. Toweel beat him, and is the national athletic hero, the only South African ever to hold a world championship in professional boxing. There would seem to be an opportunity for an American bantamweight to go there and pick up some bullion fighting him, even though the decision might be hard to obtain. But South Africa has race laws compared to which those of Mississippi are equalitarian, and there are no mixed boxing matches. "It doesn't matter much," Schoonmaker said. "They have a saying in Harlem, 'Unless you've done it in New York, it isn't done,' and here is where I'd really like to make a showing."

I could have told him that he was a victim of what Bowles termed Increase of Stature as a World Phenomenon, but I felt that it would make him feel worse. In Denmark, Bowles learned, the average stature of Army conscripts increased 3.69 centimetres in a period of fifty-three years, in Italy 2.1 centimetres in forty-one years, and in Norway 2.4 centimetres in thirty-five years, while Akira Matsumura, in Japan, noted comparable changes; moreover, the average weight of male matriculants at the University of Pennsylvania—apparently excluding recipients of athletic scholarships—went up from a hundred and thirty-two pounds to a hundred and forty between 1910 and 1930. Even conceding that children reared in Europe during the war years were restricted in growth by malnutrition, they will not be bantamweights soon enough for Cecil to fight them.

While waiting for something to turn up, Cecil said, he was living on 138th Street, with his mother, his sister, and his shipping-clerk brother, and Walker was staking him to eating money. "It makes me feel bad to take it," he said. "Another bad thing is you live off your manager so long that when you do get a fight, you owe him all the money and you're broke all over again. Also, when you don't get fights it's bad for your form. I *like* to box, but unless I get at least one fight a month, I'm not right. Gym isn't the same thing. A fellow gets only one fight in a long while, he's so anxious to make good that he's bad. He can't do anything. And even if he happens to feel lousy—sick or something—when the offer comes along, he can't afford to turn it down. So he goes in and makes a bum showing. Or he tries to knock the other boy out with one punch, quick, so the club will want him back again. I'm not that kind of a fighter. I hit a fellow one punch once and he stayed down, but I never believed it. He quit. They all talk about the art of self-defense, but you start to defend yourself in some of these clubs and they all holler for action. Being under that need to please them in one shot doesn't give you a fair chance."

I asked him if there was some other job he could turn to, and he said there wasn't. "I dedicated my life to boxing," he said, "and now I'm stuck with it. It would be different if I didn't have any ability," he went on, duplicating the words as well as the tone of a lot of other artists I know. "But I have. You look at some of these big heavyweights, now, and unless they knock each other out with the first punch, it's so dull you could cry. If I weighed eighty, I'd have a million dollars."

February 9, 1952

The University
of Eighth Avenue

In every great city certain quarters take on the color of an industry. Fifty-second Street between Sixth and Fifth Avenues in New York, for example, is given over to strip-tease palaces. In addition to electric signs and posters advertising the Boppa La Zoppas and Ocelot Women inside, it can be identified in the evening by the thin line of nonholding males along the curb who stand on tiptoes or bend double and twist their necks into periscopes in what must surely be an unrewarding effort to see through the chinks in the draperies. This is known as the old college try, since it is practiced largely by undergraduates.

Forty-seventh Street between Sixth and Fifth, for another example, is devoted to polishing and trading diamonds. It is lined with jewelers' exchanges, like North African *souks* with fluorescent lighting, inside which hordes of narrow men rent jumping-up-and-sitting-down space with a linear foot of showcase immediately in front of it. The traders who don't want to sink their funds in overhead stand out on the sidewalk. There is a social distinction even among them: between two-handkerchief men, who use one exclusively for diamond storage, and one-handkerchief men, who knot their diamonds in a corner of their all-purpose *mouchoirs*.

The block on the west side of Eighth Avenue between Fifty-fourth and Fifty-fifth Streets is given over to the polishing of prizefighters. It has a quiet academic charm, like West 116th Street when you leave the supermarkets and neighborhood movie houses of upper Broadway and find yourself on the Columbia campus with its ivy-hallowed memories of Sid Luckman and Dwight D. Eisenhower. It is a sleepy block whose modest shops are given over to the needs of the student body— a couple of hock shops, a pet store and a drugstore which sells bandages and gauze for taping fighters' hands. A careful etiquette reigns in this student quarter, as it is impossible to know if you can lick even the smallest man looking into the pet shop next door to No. 919 Eighth Avenue, which is the Old Dartmouth, or Nassau Hall, of the University of Eighth Avenue.

Old Stillman, as this building is named in honor of the founder, is three stories high, covered with soot instead of ivy and probably older than most midwestern campuses at that. It is a fine example of a post-colonial structure of indefinable original purpose and looks as if it had been knocked down in the Draft Riots of 1863 and left for dead. It hides its academic light behind a sign which says "Stillman's Gym," against a background resembling an oilcloth tablecloth from some historic speakeasy specializing in the indelible red wine of the age of F. Scott Fitzgerald and Warren Gamaliel Harding. Maybe that is where the artist got the canvas; it is an economical neighborhood. The sign also says "Training Here Daily," and in smaller letters "Boxing Instruction—See Jack Curley." This is the university's nearest approach to a printed catalogue. Doctor Lou Stillman, the president, knew when he put out his sign in 1921 that an elaborate plant does not make a great educational institution. In the great schools of the Middle Ages, scholars came to sharpen their wits by mutual disputation. Prizefighters do likewise.

The narrow window of the pet shop is divided by a partition, and the show is always the same. Monkeys on top—which is Stillmanese for "in the feature attraction"—and a tolerant cat playing with puppies underneath, which is Stillmanese for the subordinate portion of the entertainment, as for example a semifinal. Dangling all over the window are parakeets and dog collars. The window draws very good, to stay with the scholastic jargon, before noon when the fighters are waiting for Old Stillman to open and around three, when the seminars are breaking up. A boy wins a four-rounder, he buys a parakeet and dreams of the day he will fight on top and own a monkey. There was a time when a boxer's status was reflected by the flash on his finger, now it is by his pet. Floyd Patterson, a brilliant star on the light-heavyweight horizon, owns a cinnamon ringtail.

Whitey Bimstein, the famous trainer, had one of the pet-shop monkeys hooking off a jab pretty good for a while. Whitey, a small bald man with sidehair the color of an Easter chick, would stand in front of the window darting his left straight toward the monk's face and then throwing it in toward the body, and the monk would imitate him—"better than some of them kids they send me from out of town," Whitey says. Then one day he noticed a cop walking up and down the other side of the street and regarding him in a peculiar manner. "I figure he thinks I'm going nuts," Whitey says. "So I drop the monk's education."

"You probably couldn't of got him a license anyway," Izzy Blank, another educator, said consolingly.

The affinity between prizefighters and monkeys is old; the late Jack McAuliffe, who retired as undefeated lightweight champion of the world in 1896, once had one that rode his neck when he did roadwork. Twenty miles was customary in those days—they trained for finish fights—so the monkey and McAuliffe saw a lot of territory together. "The monk would hold on with his legs around my neck, and if I stopped too fast he would grab my ears to keep from falling off," the old hero told me when I had the good fortune to talk to him. McAuliffe was a great nature-lover and political thinker. When he told me about the monkey he was sixty-nine years old and running in a Democratic primary for assemblyman to annoy his son-in-law, who would give him no more money to lose at the races.

"I went into this contest," he said, "because the taxes are too high, the wages of the little fellow are being cut, and nobody has ever went right down to the basis. There are men in our Legislature today who remind me of Paddy the Pig, who would steal your eye for a breastpin." Not drawing a counter in the political department, he told me about the monkey.

McAuliffe in his glory had been a great friend of John L. Sullivan and of a bantamweight named Jack Skelly from Yonkers. The three were engaged to perform in a Salzburg festival of the Sweet Science promoted by the Olympic Club of New Orleans in September 1892. On September 5 McAuliffe was to defend his lightweight title against Billy Myer, the Streator (Ill.) Cyclone. On the 6th, Skelly would try to win the featherweight championship from the incumbent George Dixon, the great Little Chocolate. And on the third, climactic night, the great John L. would annihilate an upstart from San Francisco named Jim Corbett.

"I thought the monk would bring us all luck," the old man said. "He started good. When I knocked Billy out in the fifteenth the monk was up on the top rope as the referee said 'Ten!' and hop, off onto my shoulder before the man got my hand up. I took him and threw him into the air and caught him again, I was so happy.

" 'Oh, you jool of a monkey!' I said, and when I was on the table after the fight he played in the hair on my chest like I was his brother.

"Then Skelly fought Dixon, and when Dixon knocked him out I thought I noticed a very peculiar look on the monkey's face, like he was glad to see Skelly get it. I said to myself, 'I wonder who you are.' I gave him the benefit of the doubt, but when Corbett stopped Sullivan, I grabbed the monkey by the neck and wrung it like he was a chicken. I've often felt bad about it since. God help me, I had a very bad temper."

I cite this only to prove the ring is a continuum with fixed values and built-in cultural patterns like Philadelphia or the world of Henry James.

Monkeys can fight like hell when properly trained, incidentally, and Jacco Maccacco, the Fighting Monkey, weighing twelve pounds, had a standing challenge to kill any twenty-pound dog in Jane Austen's England. He had a considerably greater public reputation than Wordsworth.

On the second floor of a taxpayer at the northwest corner of Fifty-fourth and Eighth, the International Boxing Guild maintains a brand-registry office for the purpose of preventing managers from stealing other managers' fighters and renaming them. They do not nick the kids' ears or cut their dewlaps, but they keep complete files, so if a rustler lures a boxer under contract to a Guild member from, say, Spokane to Toronto, both out-of-town points, word of the theft goes out. Then no Guild manager will fight him. That is to say, of course, no Guild manager will let his chattels fight him. It is a simpler process than going to law, because the rustler may have an edge in his home town and you cannot carry your own judge with you. It is a handy location, because if anybody smuggled anybody else's fighter into town, Stillman's is where he would be most likely to show up, like a stolen diamond on Forty-seventh Street. It is harder to ring a fighter than a horse, because in order to disguise him you have to change his style, which is more trouble than developing a new fighter.

The whole block is handy to the building called Madison Square Garden, at Fiftieth Street and Eighth, where the International Boxing Club maintains offices and promotes boxing matches on Friday nights when the house hasn't been rented out to Ringling Brothers' Circus or Sonja Henie or the Rodeo. This is of considerable economic advantage to members of the academic community, since they can drop down to the Garden and talk their way into some complimentary tickets without spending an extra subway fare. It is doubly convenient for managers who are discontented with Billy Brown, the IBC matchmaker, a sentiment they usually communicate by sitting around his office and making faces. By walking down from Stillman's, bumming comps and making a face, they effect a double saving. This advantage is purely fortuitous because when Stillman opened his place in 1921 the Madison Square Garden stood at Madison Square. Not even Stillman contends they tore it down and built the present one just to get near him.

The modest entrance to Old Stillman is the kind of hallway you would duck into if you wanted to buy marijuana in a strange neighborhood. There are posters for the coming week's metropolitan fight shows—rarely more than one or two nowadays since television has knocked out the nontelevised neighborhood clubs. There is a wide wooden staircase leading up to the gym. Although Dr. Stillman locks a steel grille across the doorway promptly at three, keeps it locked until five-thirty, when working scholars come in for the poor man's session, and then locks it again religiously at seven, the joint always smells wrong. Dr. Stillman, like so many college presidents nowadays, is not himself a teacher but rather an administrator, and the smell in the hall makes him feel there are limits to academic freedom. He is a gaunt man with a beak that describes an arc like an overhand right, bushy eyebrows, a ruff of hair like a frowsy cockatoo and a decisive, heavily impish manner. He has the reputation of never having taken any lip off anybody, which is plausible, because he seldom gives the other fellow a chance to say anything. In earlier stages of his academic career he used to speak exclusively in shouts, but now that he is in his latter sixties, his voice has mellowed to a confident rasp. The great educator has never, so far as is known, himself put on the gloves; it might prove a psychological mistake. Stillman excels in insulting matriculants so casually that they don't know whether to get sore or not. By the sixth time Stillman has insulted a prizefighter the fighter feels it would be inconsistent to take offense at such a late stage in their personal interrelationship. When that happens, Stillman has acquired the edge.

Dr. Stillman has not been so styled since birth. His original surname was Ingber, but he got into the gymnasium business by working for a philanthropist named Alpheus Geer who ran a kind of Alcoholics Anonymous for burglars trying to go straight. Geer called his crusade the Marshall Stillman movement, and he thought the best kind of occupational therapy was boxing, so he opened a gym, which young Ingber managed. The burglars got to calling Lou Ingber, Lou Stillman, and after they stole all the boxing gloves and Mr. Geer quit in disgust, Ingber opened a gymnasium of his own, farther uptown than this Old Stillman, and legally adopted his present name.

Occasionally Dr. Stillman has a problem student who does not know when he is being insulted, and then he has to think up some more subtle psychological stratagem. Tommy (Hurricane) Jackson, a heavyweight who has to be driven out of the gymnasium at the end of every session because he wants to punch the bag some more, has been a recent disciplinary challenge. Jackson, who is six feet two inches tall and of inverse intellectual stature, would occupy a boxing ring all the time if Stillman let him. He would like to box fifteen or thirty rounds a day, but this would be of no value to his fellow students, even those who worked with him, because Jackson is a purely imitative boxer. He waits to see what the other fellow will do and then does it right back at him until the guy drops from exhaustion. Against a jabber he will jab and against a mauler he will maul; it is the exact opposite of Sam Langford's counsel: "Whatever that other man want to do, don't let him do it. Box a fighter and fight a boxer." Jackson will box a boxer, after a fashion, and fight a fighter, in a way, but he can never decide for himself. Knowing this, most boxers who work with him step in with a right to the jaw, planning to knock him out before he can begin his systematic plagiarism. But he has a hard jaw. Whitey and Freddy Brown, his trainers, who are partners, attribute his lack of originality to an emotional conflict, but it has not yielded to any kind of permissive therapy like buying him a .22 rifle to shoot rats, or letting him drink soda pop on fight nights. "He is not too smart of a fellow," Freddy Brown has concluded.

Jackson, when not exercising, likes to walk around Stillman's with a shiny harmonica at his mouth, pretending to blow in it. A small, white camp follower trails in his wake, completely concealed from anybody in front of Jackson, and plays a real tune on another harmonica. It is Jackson's pose, when detected, that this is an elaborate joke because he could play a tune too, if he wanted to. Dr. Stillman once invited him to play a tune into the microphone with which the president of the University of Eighth Avenue announces the names of students defending theses in the rings. "Give us all a chance to hear you," he snarled invitingly. Tommy backed off, and Stillman grabbed a moral ascendancy. Whenever Jackson is obstreperous now, the good Doctor points to the microphone, and the Hurricane effaces himself.

To gain access to the hall of academe you must pass a turnstile guarded by Professor Jack Curley, the assistant to the president who the sign says is the fellow to see about boxing instructions. The only person who ever did was a follower of Father Divine named Saint Thomas. Curley signed him up as a heavyweight contender before letting him through the gate where the managers could see him. Saint Thomas was a hell of a natural fighter if you believe Curley, but they split on theological grounds such as he wanted Father Divine, *in absentia*, to okay his opponents by emanation. Later he backslid and stabbed a guy, and is now in a place where he has very little opportunity for roadwork. The sign is as sensible as one would be on the door of Yale saying "Instruction in reading and writing, see Professor Doakes." Old Stillman is no elementary school.

There are two ways of getting by Professor Curley. The more popular is to invoke the name of some manager or trainer you know is inside, claiming an urgent business mission. Professor Curley will deny he is there, but if you ask some ingoing fighter to relay the message, the fellow will come out and okay you. Curley will then assume the expression of a baffled witch in a London Christmas pantomime, but he will let you in without payment. The second method is to give him fifty cents, the official price of admission, which he doesn't expect from anybody who looks familiar. Through decades of practice he has trained his facial muscles not to express recognition, but he is violently disconcerted when the other fellow does not demand to be recognized. After you give him the fifty cents he has another problem—whether to say hello. This would be a confession he had known you all along. He compromises by giving you what is known on campus as "a cheap hello," looking over his shoulder as if he might be talking to somebody else.

On the main floor of Old Stillman there are two boxing rings set close together. The space in front of the rings is for spectators, and the relatively narrow strip behind them for boxers and trainers. To get from one zone to the other, the latter must pass directly in front of Dr. Stillman, who stands behind an iron rail leaving a passageway perhaps two feet wide. This is a big help in the collection department, because a boxer who is in arrears can't get into the ring to spar unless the president, who doubles as bursar, gives him an extension. When granted, this is usually on the grounds that the delinquent has a fight coming up.

Boxers pay six dollars a month for a locker and eleven dollars a month for a dressing room, which means a stall just wide enough for a rubbing table. The deluxe dressing rooms have hooks on the plywood partitions. Stillman has a microphone in back of his stand and in the back of his head a rough list of the order in which fighters will go into the rings. Some fighters he knows by sight; trainers have to prompt him with the names of others. Most of the present crop, the Doctor says, he would like to forget as rapidly as possible. When he says the names into the mike they come out equally unintelligible, so it doesn't matter. Most of the spectators know who the guys are anyway, despite the increasingly elaborate headgears which make them look like Tlingit witch doctors.

In the days when 375 boxers trained at Stillman's and the majority actually had bouts in sight, there was considerable acrimony about the scheduling. Trainers were afraid that some of their boys who needed sparring would be crowded out. Now that fewer fellows use the place and are in less of a hurry, everybody gets a chance. The enrollment at Old Stillman is less than a hundred, which is not bad when you reflect that there are only 241 licensed professional boxers in the whole of New York State and this number includes out-of-state fighters who have had to take out a license for a New York appearance.

The main operating theater at Stillman's is two stories high. There is a gallery which, in the halcyon days before television, used to accommodate spectators, but which now serves as a supplementary gym. The light and heavy bags are up there, and so is most of the space for skipping rope. In pre-television times Stillman's had an extensive bargain clientele of fans who couldn't afford the price of admission to regular boxing shows, but now these nonholders see their fights free.

Only knowing coves come to Stillman's these days—fellows who have more than a casual interest in boxing or are out to make a buck, like the diamond traders. Few managers today have offices of their own—there are only a half-dozen such grandees—and the rest transact their business walking around Stillman's or leaning against the radiators. There are seats for ordinary spectators, but managers consider it unprofessional to sit down. Even managers who have offices use them chiefly to play klabiash or run up telephone bills; they think better on their feet, in the mingled aura of rubbing alcohol, sweat and hot-pastrami-on-the-lunch-counter which distinguishes Old Stillman from a gym run by Helena Rubinstein or Elizabeth Arden.

The prevailing topic of conversation at Stillman's nowadays is the vanishing buck. Boxers are in the same predicament as the hand-loom weavers of Britain when Dr. Edmund Cartwright introduced the power loom. Two boxers on a national hookup with fifty major-city outlets can fill the place of a hundred boxers on top ten years ago, and for every two eliminated from on top, at least ten lose their work underneath. The boxer who gets the television assignment, though, is in the same spot as the hand-loom weaver who found work driving a power loom—he gets even less money than before. This is because while wads of the sponsors' tease go to networks for time and camera fees, to advertising agencies in commissions based on the purchased time, to producers for creating the drivel between rounds and even to the promoters who provide the boxers, the boxers themselves get no more than they would have drawn in an off night in Scranton in 1929. Naturally, this is a discouraging technological circumstance, but the desire to punch other boys in the nose will survive in our culture. The spirit of self-preservation will induce some boys to excel. Those who find they excel will try to turn a modest buck by it. It is an art of the people, like making love, and is likely to survive any electronic gadget that peddles razor blades.

Meanwhile the contraction of the field has led to a concentration of talent at Old Stillman. These days good feature-bout fighters, who were sure of ten thousand dollars a year not long ago, are glad to sell their tutorial services as sparring partners for five or ten dollars a session. This is particularly true of the colored boys who are not quite champions. Trainers who in the flush times accepted only stars or near-stars as students will now take on any kid with a solvent sponsor. The top trainers, whose charges appear frequently on televised shows, still make out pretty well.

Trainers, like the teachers in medieval universities, are paid by their pupils or their pupils' sponsors. A couple of trainers working as partners may have fifteen fighters, all pretty good, if they are good trainers. If they cannot teach, they get no pupils and go emeritus without salary. There are two televised boxing cards originating in New York clubs every week—the St. Nick's on Monday evening and the International Boxing Club show from the Garden on Friday. When the Garden is occupied by other events, the IBC runs its show from out of town, which is a blank margin around New York City, extending for several thousand miles in every direction but east. A team of trainers like Whitey Bimstein and Freddy Brown, or Nick and Dan Florio, or Chickie Ferrera and Johnny Sullo, figures to have at least one man in one of the three features every week, and a couple underneath. The trainer customarily gets ten per cent of his fighter's end of the purse. Because of their skill as seconds they are also sure to get calls to work in the corners of men they don't train. Noted Old Stillman trainers are called out of town for consultations almost as often as before television, because while there are many less fights, the out-of-town trainer as a species has for that very reason nearly vanished. In most places it is a part-time avocation.

Their reputation is international—last year, for example, Whitey Bimstein was retained to cram a Canadian giant named James J. Parker for a bout for the Canadian heavyweight championship at Toronto. Parker is not considered much of a fighter here—a good banger, but slow of intellection. In Canada, however, he is big stuff—he weighs over 210 pounds. The Canadian champion (now retired), whom Parker was to oppose, was Earl Walls, also a pretty good banger but a slow study.

Whitey took Parker up to Greenwood Lake, N.Y., where his troubles started when the Canadian insisted on doing his roadwork on the frozen surface of the lake. "He might fall through and roon the advance sale," Whitey said. Not wishing to increase the weight on the ice, Whitey declined to accompany him. He would watch him from a window of the inn where they were staying, prepared to cut loose with a shotgun if Parker slowed to a walk. Trainers blanch when they tell of the terrible things fighters will do to get out of roadwork. Nick Masuras, one of Whitey's friends, once had a fighter up at the Hotel Peter Stuyvesant, across the street from Central Park at Eighty-sixth, and every morning he would send him out to run a couple of times around the Central Park reservoir, which is right there practically. Masuras would then go back to sleep. By and by the fellow would come in panting and soaking wet, and it wasn't until three days before the fight that Nick learned he had just been sitting on park benches talking to nursemaids, after which he would come in and stand under a warm shower with his clothes on. After that Nick moved to a room on the eighth floor, with a park view. But it was too late. The guy's legs went back on him and he lost the fight. "He done it to himself, no one else," Nick says, mournfully, as he polishes beer glasses in his saloon, the Neutral Corner, which is the Deux Magots or Mermaid Tavern of the fighters' quarter. Instead of training fighters, Nick has taken to feeding them.

Parker, on the other hand, didn't skimp his training. He heeded everything Whitey told him. As a consequence, Whitey says, "He give this Walls a hell of a belting and in the sixth round cut his left eye open so bad that if you were a doctor you had to stop it." The Canadian doctor, however, didn't stop it. "He was pertecting Walls," Whitey says. "The guy could of lost his eyesight." Walls had in his corner another ambassador of culture from Stillman's, Nick Florio. Florio patched the eye up so well that Walls went the distance, twelve rounds. Whitey felt like calling Florio a carpetbagger. The announcer then collected the slips of the two judges and the referee, read them, and proclaimed James J. Parker, Whitey's candidate, "Winner and new champion"—of Canada, naturally. "But," Whitey says, "they take it very serious." Whitey posed for victory pictures, allowing Parker to get into the background, and then led him away to his dressing room. There, five minutes later, another man came in and said the announcer had made a mistake—it was really a draw, so Walls was still champion. "It was a outrage," Whitey says. "They pertected him." He came back from Canada with a bale of Toronto newspapers, which said Walls's cut eye had required sixteen stitches. "They were those wide Canadian stitches," Whitey said. "Here they took them kind of stitches to make him look better." The fight, which was not televised, drew thirty thousand dollars and the fighters whacked up eighteen thousand dollars. This was much better than they would have done at the Garden, where each would have received four thousand dollars from television and a purely nominal sum from the almost nonexistent gate.

For most fighters, however, pickings are lean between infrequent television appearances—so lean that they are beginning to recall the stories old-timers tell about the minuscular purses in the nineties. One of the best lightweights in the world, for example, went up to Holyoke, Mass., from the campus on Eighth Avenue not too long ago and fought on top of the gate against a tough local boy whom he knocked out in five rounds. He had signed for a percentage of the gate which turned out to be a hundred and fifteen dollars. After he had deducted railroad fare, the price of a Massachusetts boxer's license and a few dollars for a local helper in his corner, he wound up with seventy-four dollars. Freddy Brown, the trainer, wouldn't accept a fee, and the fighter's manager wouldn't cut the fighter because the guy was broke and he would have had to lend him the money back anyway. He had been out for several months with a broken rib sustained in another fight.

The club in Holyoke, one of the few stubborn survivors, functions Tuesday nights because of television boxing Monday, Wednesday and Friday.

All the great minds of the university have gone a few rounds with this problem, but none has come up with a thesis that his colleagues at the lunch counter couldn't flatten in the course of a couple of cups of tea. One school of savants holds that if the television companies are going to monopolize boxing they should set up a system of farm clubs to develop new talent. Another believes the situation will cure itself, but painfully. "Without the little clubs, nobody new will come up," a leader of this group argues. "The television fans will get tired of the same bums, the Hooper will drop, the sponsors will drop boxing, and then we can start all over again." Meanwhile a lot of fighters have had to go to work, a situation the horror of which was impressed upon me long ago by the great Sam Langford, in describing a period of his young manhood when he had licked everybody who would fight him. "I was *so* broke," he said, "that I didn't have *no* money. I had to go to work with my hands." Manual labor didn't break his spirit. He got a fight with Joe Gans, the great lightweight champion of the world, and whipped him in fifteen rounds in 1903, when Sam says he was seventeen years old. The record books make him twenty-three. (They were both over the weight, though, so he didn't get the title.) After the fight he was lying on the rubbing table in his dressing room feeling proud and a busted-down colored middleweight named George Byers walked in. "How did I look?" Langford asked him. "You strong," Byers said, "but you don't know nothing."

Langford wasn't offended. He had the humility of the great artist. He said, "How much you charge to teach me?" Byers said, "Ten dollars." Langford gave him ten dollars. It was a sizable share of the purse he had earned for beating Gans.

"And then what happened?" I asked Sam. He said, "He taught me. He was right. I didn't know nothing. I used to just chase and punch, hurt my hands on hard heads. After George taught me I made them come to me. I made them lead."

"How?" I asked.

"If they didn't lead I'd run them out of the ring. When they led I'd hit them in the body. Then on the point of the chin. Not the jaw, the point of the chin. That's why I got such pretty hands today." Sam by that time was nearly blind, he weighed 230 pounds and he couldn't always be sure that when he spat tobacco juice at the empty chitterling can in his hall room he would hit.

But he looked affectionately at his knees, where he knew those big hands rested. There wasn't a lump on a knuckle. "I'd belt them oat," he said. "Oh, I'd belt them oat."

When I told this story to Whitey he sucked in his breath reverently, like a lama informed of one of the transactions of Buddha.

"What a difference from the kids today," the schoolman said. "I have a kid in a bout last night and he can't even count. Every time he hook the guy is open for a right, and I tell him: 'Go twicet, go twicet!' But he would go oncet and lose the guy. I don't know what they teach them in school."

After Sam tutored with Professor Byers he grew as well as improved, but he improved a lot faster than he grew. He beat Gans, at approximately even weights, but when he fought Jack Johnson, one of the best heavyweights who ever lived, he spotted him twenty-seven pounds. Langford weighed 158, Johnson 185. Sam was twenty-six, according to Nat Fleischer, or twenty-five, according to Sam, and Johnson twenty-eight. Sam knocked Johnson down for an eight count, Johnson never rocked Sam, and there has been argument ever since over the decision for Johnson at the end of the fifteen rounds. Sam's effort was a *succès d'estime* for the scholastic approach to boxing, but Johnson, an anti-intellectual, would never give him another fight.

Johnson, by then older and slower, did fight another middleweight in 1909—Stanley Ketchel, the Michigan Assassin. Ketchel's biographers, for the most part exponents of the raw-nature, or blinded-with-blood-he-swung-again school of fight writing, turn literary handsprings when they tell how Ketchel, too, knocked Johnson down. But Johnson got up and took him with one punch. There was a direct line of comparison between Langford and Ketchel as middleweights. They boxed a six-round no-decision bout in Philadelphia which was followed by a newspaper scandal; the critics accused Langford of carrying Ketchel. Nobody accused Ketchel of carrying Langford. I asked Sam once if he *had* carried Ketchel, and he said, "He was a good man. I couldn't knock him out in six rounds."

Their artistic statures have been transposed in retrospect. The late, blessed Philadelphia Jack O'Brien fought both of them. He considered Ketchel "a bum distinguished only by the tumultuous but ill-directed ferocity of his assault." (That is the way Jack liked to talk.) Ketchel did knock Mr. O'Brien *non compos* his remarkable *mentis* in the last nine seconds of a ten-round bout (there was no decision, and O'Brien always contended he won on points). Jack attributed his belated mishap to negligence induced by contempt. He said Langford, though, had a "mystic quality."

"When he appeared upon the scene of combat you knew you were cooked," Jack said.

Mr. O'Brien was, in five.

December 5, 1955

II

One thing about the Sweet Science upon which all initiates are in agreement is that it used to be better. The exact period at which it was better, however, varies in direct ratio with the age of the fellow telling about it; if he was a fighter, it always turns out to be the time when he was fighting, and if a fight writer, the years before he began to get bored with what he was doing. Fight writers, since they last longer than boxers, are the most persistent howlers after antiquity; but Doctor Jack Kearns, the *doyen* of active fight managers who are doing all right, turned on them in 1952, when they were being particularly derisive of his current meal ticket, Joey Maxim, a light heavyweight who, Kearns said, was as good as Dempsey except he couldn't hit. Since Dempsey could do little else, this was a combination of big talk and veracity illustrative of the Doctor's genius. Back in 1919 and the subsequent years of universal inflation, Kearns had Dempsey, and the older fight writers of the time used to ask what good man he ever licked. "They said Corbett would of killed him," Dr. Kearns recalled.

The reason Kearns has more perspective than most old-timers is that he is still eating in expensive restaurants. "What right have the writers got to beef?" the good Doctor wanted to know. "In the old days they used to have good *fight writers*. That Damon Runyon, before he went on the wagon, could lay on the floor and write better than most of these guys."

Writers were always nostalgic. William E. Harding, the sporting editor of the *Police Gazette*, who was the undisputed leader of critical thought in the eighties when that publication was the tables of the law for the American milling world, held that Jem Mace, the English Gypsy, was "the most scientific pugilist that ever stood in a ring." Mace had retired in 1871. Harding, whose woodcut portrait shows a figure of superb dignity in a wing collar, stock and frock coat, with two feet of watch chain cascading down his stomach and his elbow on an Empire desk, rendered the opinion in 1881, when he reported the Sweet Science in a state of galloping decline. The heavyweight champion (bare knuckles) was Paddy Ryan, and the challenger a young fellow named John L. Sullivan, who, Harding said, was a mere boxer, a glove-fighter. Mace, according to Harding, would have confuted the two of them in a simultaneous disputation.

Yet 1851, when Mace was launching his career by knocking out Jack Pratt of Norwich in eight rounds that lasted a mere fifty-nine minutes—a round under London Prize Ring rules ended only with a knockdown—was a year made noteworthy in English literature by the publication of *Lavengro*, in which George Borrow lamented the downfall of the ring. Borrow said there hadn't been a true good bit of stuff since Tom Spring, who retired as champion in 1824, when Borrow was twenty-one. Tom Spring takes us back to the glorious days of Pierce Egan—the fighting son of Clio, the Muse of history—who covered the combats of heroes for some thirty years and published them in magazines of his own editing for nearly that long. Egan, a better fight writer than Runyon or Harding or William Hazlitt—who was a dilettante—was not a pitched-battle man himself. He believed in the division of labor. Egan recognized, as he wrote after the demolition of Dandy Williams, a highly touted gentleman boxer, by Josh Hudson, the "True Blue Bulldog" British pugilist, in 1820, that "Drummers and boxers, to acquire excellence, must begin young. There is a peculiar *nimbleness* of the *wrist* and exercise of the shoulder required that is only obtained from growth and practice."

From about 1800 on to the 1820s, the fighters, trainers, seconds, betting men, the idly curious and the swells who backed fighters for heavy sums—a fighter was smalltime until he found a patron—used to assemble daily at the Fives Court, a covered handball court in St. Martin's Street, near what is now Leicester Square, to spar and watch the sparring. It was the place where fighters learned from other fighters, where they could show their stuff, where they did part of their conditioning and where a lot of matches were made. The Fives Court was in short the Stillman's Gym of Lord Byron's England, and Byron would hang out there between cantos when his mistresses' husbands were all in town at the same time. He liked to spar, but not in public. John Jackson, a retired champion of England, would come to his lordship's rooms in the Albany and spar with him, sometimes for an hour at a time. Jackson conned his lordship into thinking he had a hell of a right hand; he advised him never to let it go at a husband or he might kill him and have to marry the widow. There are no swell backers around Stillman's now, but there is some Garment Center money, and some of the boys are hoping to interest Robert R. Young and a couple of Texas oilmen. Admission to the Fives Court was three shillings, or seventy-five cents at the old rate of exchange; Stillman's gets only fifty cents now, but there is no added attraction like Byron.

"Some are of the opinion that *Sparring* is of no great use," Egan wrote, "and that it takes from the natural powers of manhood, while it only teaches finesses, that cannot prove hurtful to a courageous adversary. This, however, is merely reviving an opinion maintained by the pupils of the Old School, in which strength generally prevailed over skill."

Whitey Bimstein, Freddy Brown and other lights of the faculty at the University of Eighth Avenue get a number of young fighters who have Old School opinions on this subject, but they generally iron them out by putting them in with some six-round kid who proves how hurtful a little finesse can be. Irving Cohen, the mildest-mannered of fight managers, a plump, fair little man with a wide baby-blue stare, says: "Fighting is like education. The four-round fights are elementary school. Six-rounders is high school. Feature bouts is college, but nowadays without the small clubs we got too many boys in college without sufficient preparation."

Ten years or so ago Cohen as manager and Bimstein as trainer had a boy who would have worn the Old School tie if he had ever worn a tie at all. He was a fellow named Rocky Graziano, who, like Jack Scroggins, one of Egan's heroes, relied purely on "*downright ferocity.*" "Nobody never learned him nothing," Professor Bimstein concedes. Graziano had, however, a precious asset in addition to a punch, which latter is not as rare as you might think. "If he hurt you, he wouldn't lose you," Professor Bimstein's associate, Professor Brown, descanted in one of a recent series of lectures on Mr. Graziano. "He would never let you go. If he had to he would grab you by the throat and knock your brains out and apologize after the fight." Fighters who do not warm up until stung are a dime a dozen, but the colleagues have a high esteem for a fighter who warms up when he stings the other guy. Graziano's scholastic deficiencies became apparent when he stopped fighting men lighter than he was. He met two good middleweights (he was a middleweight) in his life, Tony Zale and Ray Robinson, and they knocked him out three times in a total of twelve rounds. Against Robinson, Graziano was like Scroggins when the latter met the scientific Ned Turner, who could box *and* hit, at Sawbridgeworth in Hertfordshire, in 1817. "He was at sea without a rudder—no sight of land appeared in view." In between the Zale knockouts, though, Graziano knocked Zale out once, which remains as his only solid accomplishment in the record books. But as a drawing card he was, like Scroggins long ago, immense. "In point of attraction, what Kean has been to the boards of Drury Lane theatre, Scroggins has proved to the prize ring," Egan wrote in 1818.

Within an easy jaunt of the Fives Court there were numerous pubs that welcomed the trade of the milling coves and their knowing friends. The Castle, Holborn, which was kept in turn by three famous heroes—Bob Gregson, Tom Belcher and finally Tom Spring himself—was perhaps the best known. Gregson was a vast lump of a heavyweight who never quite won the championship, although he made several desperate bids for it. Tom Belcher—he had an even more famous older brother—was a cutie and a gentleman. In the Castle the critics would dissect the latest battles. The fighters would try to provoke turnups with more illustrious colleagues which might lead to official battles later on. The fighter who made a good showing in a rough-and-tumble in a well-frequented pub might attract a patron who would back him in a regular battle. If the fighter won, the patron took down the stakes, but he might give some to the fighter. When Tom Cribb beat Tom Molineaux in 1811, for example, Captain Barclay, a famous sport of the day, won ten thousand pounds over the match. Cribb got four hundred pounds—and all Boxiana thought it generous of the captain. Cribb had to fight only eleven rounds to win Barclay's bet, anyway—a breeze.

The fighters joined their admirers in lushing Blue Ruin, which was just another name for Daffy, or gin, and Heavy Wet, which was ale. There was a belief that a pint of Wet, taken after every gill of Daffy, would keep the drinker sober longer; the present notion is that a beer chaser, or boilermaker's helper, accelerates intoxication. So does medical theory swing full circle with the ages. The Blue Ruin was calculated to put the fighters in a proper mood for ad lib assaults upon their friends. The Wet was recommended to build up their constitutions. Water was considered debilitating. Some care had to be exercised, however, even in the use of nourishing intoxicants. An 1821 treatise on training is explicit: "Our man may avoid taking the beer of two different breweries in the same day; for the variety of proportions and kinds of ingredients used, (if nought worse), will kick up a combustion in his guts."

Dutch Sam, the greatest little man of his age—he weighed 131 pounds and beat good men of 160—trained on Blue Ruin, but his practice was not endorsed by the Bimsteins of his time. In fact when, in 1814, at the age of thirty-nine, Sam succumbed in only thirty-eight rounds to Bill Nosworthy, the Baker, they all said that if he had stuck to Heavy Wet he would not have had such a premature downfall.

The Neutral Corner, at Eighth Avenue and Fifty-fifth Street, is to Stillman's what the Castle Tavern was to the Fives Court. Managers and trainers adjourn there after Dr. Lou Stillman, the president of the University of Eighth Avenue, locks the iron grille across the portals of his Ivy-League sweatbox at three in the afternoon. The managers receive telephone calls at the Neutral, and the trainers exchange gripes, often about a hostile region known as out-of-town, which in their stories is the equivalent of west of the Missouri in the works of A. B.

Guthrie. Referees and judges out-of-town are notoriously treacherous, and the boxing commission physicians there are even worse. They will stop a fight if the New York boxer has an eyelash brushed back into his eye, but they will let the out-of-town fellow continue even if he looks like he had been hit by a Cadillac. Out-of-town it has gotten so you cannot even rely on an opponent. An opponent is supposed to offer a credible degree of opposition. That is why he is called an opponent. But a trainer who hangs out in the Corner came back from Washington, in the state of D.C., a week or two ago, spluttering with rage because the promoter had provided a cut-price opponent. "The opponent comes out in the first round and goes down three times without we had hit him yet," the trainer raved. The commission had accordingly declared the bout no contest, and held up the purse of the fighter the opponent had not waited to be hit by. "Can you imagine?" the trainer said. "A bum like that has the nerve to call himself an opponent."

Nick Masuras, behind the bar, said: "Out-of-town you're dead."

Nick, a restaurant man who used to be an armory middleweight, is one of the three proprietors of the Neutral. He thought of the name and founded the place, later taking in as partners Chickie Bogad, a former matchmaker, and Frankie Jacobs, better known as Frankie Jay, a former manager. That gives them quite a diversity of points of view on the Sweet Science, and a visit to the Neutral Corner has a didactic value for undergraduates of the University of Eighth Avenue, who go there to play shuffleboard, put slugs in the cigarette machine and listen to their elders if that is indispensable in persuading Nick to let their tabs run another week on account the six in Danbury fell through. Trainers do not mind their clean-cut American youths being in a saloon where they can watch them. Many features of the Neutral are qualified to instruct, for example the hundreds of photographs of old-time worthwhile fighters, men who have become classics, like the portraits of John Marshall and Coke and Blackstone in a law school.

Nick is a big man nowadays; he was a tall, rangy middleweight who broadened with the years. As senior proprietor he works the day shift, and as he knows all the day customers he can tell them where to get off.

"Don't be miserable," he will call out to an ex-pug who wants service when Nick wants to talk baseball at the other end of the bar, or "What makes you so miserable?" to a manager who wants change for a quarter so he can put in a call for out-of-town and ask if they will accept the charges. If Nick is looking up some important fact in Nat Fleischer's *Ring Record Book and Boxing Encyclopedia*, which is kept in the drawer of the cash register to settle bets, he will let the manager wait a long time. When Nick, who is forty-eight, was fighting, Whitey, who is fifty-nine, was already a trainer. (When Whitey was fighting, he would never train, but he does not emphasize that in his lectures.) Sometimes, when undergraduates are within earshot—they would have to go out the front door and run a block to get out of it—Nick tells about a time he was fighting a guy in the 102d Medical Regiment Armory and he was so arm-weary that he said to Whitey, between rounds, "Be careful with that sponge, Whitey, you're getting water on my gloves. It makes them heavy.

"And Whitey looks up at me," Nick says, "and he says, 'You little bum, if you done your roadwork right you wouldn't feel this way. I hope he kills you.'"

At this point an irreverent undergrad sometimes asks: "How many miles you run every morning in them days, Nick? A hunnerd, or a hunnerten?"

Nick goes on without honoring the interruption. "And the guy I was fighting was a bum," he says. "A nothing fighter. I done it to myself."

All the Neutral Corner wits consider it a misfortune that the period of technological unemployment in the Sweet Science caused by television should coincide with a time when the cost of feeding fighters has reached an unprecedented peak. It is an old, convention-ridden art, and none of the trainers has yet tried to feed Cheeri-wobbles, Pip-squeaks, or any other form of succedaneum for nourishment advertised by the sponsors of competing television programs, which might reduce feeding costs. Nick, who is a good restaurant man and has a good cook, Jimmy the Chef, says it costs at least three dollars and fifty cents a day to feed a fighter three meals, "and that's only giving him a steak every other night. If he has a fight coming up he's got to have a steak every day." Maybe he doesn't, but everybody connected with the Sweet Science believes he does, and there is a morale factor involved. A tear still wells to each eye when I remember a story by Jack London I read when I was twelve about a fighter in Australia, a has-been, whose family butcher refuses him credit for a bit of steak before his last stand. It is a real Jack London fight, like Marlon Brando versus Burt Lancaster on a carpet of eyeballs, and the veteran needs the strength for just one more appallingly terrific punch to pull it out—but he hasn't had the steak. His arm falls as limp as a vegetable dinner, and the sirloin-stuffed betting choice knocks him out. It would make a great brochure for the American Meat Institute. The managers, who usually okay the bills for fighters *en pension* at the Neutral, are lucky at that that they aren't living in the days of John L. Sullivan, who ate beefsteaks or mutton chops three times a day when he trained.

"Sullivan rises at seven A.M. and washes, brushes his teeth and rinses his mouth, and takes a swallow of pure spring water," it says in *The History of the Prize Ring* (1881), with lives of Paddy Ryan and John L. Sullivan, a work long wrongly attributed to William Dean Howells, "then removes his night clothes and is sponged with sea water [so his skin wouldn't cut], rubbed perfectly dry with coarse towels, dresses himself and takes a walk of a mile. It is then about eight A.M., at which time he breakfasts on beefsteak or mutton chops cooked to suit the taste, coarse bread, with butter, and a cup of weak tea. His appetite is always good, and there is no occasion for an appetizer. Half an hour after breakfast (he is dressed so as to be comfortable for the purpose) he takes a brisk walk of from eight to ten miles, the last two of which are with an increase of speed to bring on a good perspiration. Going direct to his room he is stripped and rubbed down with the coarse towels. When perfectly cool he is sponged with sea water and given another good rubbing. Then he dresses and remains quiet until dinner, which is at one o'clock P.M., and consists of beef or mutton, roasted or boiled, plenty of stale bread, with butter and one or two potatoes. [Being a heavyweight, he naturally wasn't worried about poundage.] He remains quiet after dinner for an hour, when he commences exercise in hitting a football suspended from the ceiling, or using dumbbells or club swinging, or short splint [sic] races, such as suits his fancy. He takes supper at six P.M., of cold roast beef or mutton or mutton chops, stale bread with butter, plain apple sauce and weak tea, and once or twice a week Irish or Scotch oatmeal, well cooked, with milk. After supper he takes a moderate walk of half an hour and retires at nine P.M., sleeping in none of the clothes worn during the day. He has sufficient cover on his bed to be comfortable and no more, as he says he never perspires excepting when exercising."

Sullivan, although it is scarcely likely that he had read Egan, held with the Old School of nonsparrers. He had a chopping left and a swinging right, and believed in bottling up his energy until he saw the other fellow in front of him, when he would simply rush. Anybody who read his daily menu could have predicted that he would outlast Ryan, who breakfasted on "mutton chops or beefsteak, medium cooked, with just enough salt upon it to make it palatable," dined on "roast beef and sometimes a leg of mutton," with a bottle of Bass or Scotch ale, but then weakened and took for supper "a couple of boiled eggs, some toast and a cup of tea." He obviously lacked stamina. Ryan had won his claim to the world championship by beating a man named Joe Goss in eighty-seven rounds, but Sullivan did him in in nine.

One of the results of high maintenance costs is that a good many kids go to work. This is a test of dedication. Ernie Roberts and Earl Dennis, two fine colored welterweights I know, do their roadwork in the streets at five o'clock in the morning, shower, change into business clothes, go into the center of Manhattan and work an eight-hour day, do their sparring after hours and then go home to their respective wives and families. The menace in this situation, from a cultural point of view, is that the fighter may get to like his job. Roberts is already betraying an alarming interest in the hardware business. Dennis appears to have a more definite vocation. "I have fighting all through me," he told me once. "Before I turned professional I used to walk down the street and hope somebody would give me a hard look. But then I decided if I get my head beat in I want to get it for money." Dennis won a voice contest at the Apollo Theatre in Harlem, however, and now every time he sings a cadenza in the shower, a shadow crosses his man-ager's face.

A visitor who brightens the Neutral Corner whenever he shows up is Charlie Goldman, Rocky Marciano's trainer, leading claimant of the American derby-hat-and-double-breasted-suit championship since the death of James Joy Johnston, the great manager known into his seventies as the Boy Bandit. The championship fell into Johnston's handkerchief pocket when Jimmy Walker skipped the herring pond in 1931, and when the Boy Bandit died, Goldman was left in a class by himself. Mr. Goldman, who is on sabbatical leave from the University of Eighth Avenue during Marciano's professional life expectancy, is a jockey-sized man with a mashed, intelligent face, who had four hun-dred fights as a bantamweight, sixty with the same adversary, a con-temporary named Georgie Kitson. They were as well known in their field as Van and Schenck, or Duffy and Sweeney. In the late thirties Goldman used to train a large stable of fighters for Al Weill, for whom he trains Marciano now. Weill kept the whole herd in a brownstone house on West Ninety-first Street, near the Central Park Reservoir, and Goldman had the front parlor bedroom so he could check on them. "In those days," Goldman said, joining one of the conversa-tions on commissary problems, "Al would give each fighter a five-dollar meal ticket good for five dollars and fifty cents in trade at the cof-fee pot on the corner of Columbus, and most of the kids made the week on one ticket. We were feeding four and a half fighters for what one costs today, and they were all feature fighters." It is a dismal statistic that a four-round fighter eats as much as a star.

Mr. Goldman, however, does not blame the present low level of ar-tistic competence upon either television or the high cost of living. "It is compulsory education," he says. "You take a kid has to stay in school until he is sixteen, he is under a disadvantage. All the things he should have learned to do when he was young he has to start at the beginning. How to move his feet, slip a punch, throw a hook—like finger exercises on the piano. [Here was Egan's old analogy with the drummer, proving that the Sweet Science is indeed a perpetuum, like the Manipuri dance or "My Darling Clementine." The tune of Clementine was old in sixteenth-century Spain.] A fighter shouldn't have to think about those things, he should think about how to use them. A kid learns them before he begins to think about girls, they are the most important thing in the world to him. Sixteen is too old, especially the way kids are today."

Professor Goldman himself, who is a modish sixty-seven if you accept the birth date in the record books, began to box professionally when he was nine years old, having been a mere street fighter before that. Goldman lived near Terrible Terry McGovern in South Brooklyn then—McGovern was a veteran still in his teens, with a string of knockouts as long as your arm. McGovern had a kid brother about Goldman's age, and Sam Harris, McGovern's manager, used to set them to fighting. Harris was George M. Cohan's partner in the theatre. He bought the boys boxing gloves and tights—real fighters wore tights that covered their legs then, a vestigial relic of the bare-knuckle days. Combining his flair for the ring and theatre, Harris used to present the boys in three-round bouts at smokers. Terry would work his kid brother's corner and another Brooklyn fighter named George Munroe would second Charlie. "We learned a lot that way," the savant says. "They always had a bet going, so we had to take it serious." By the time he was fourteen he was traveling around the country, arranging his own fights and collecting his purses when possible; and when he was sixteen he could place women in their proper perspective. "I never married," the Professor says. "I always live à la carte." Women are probably the most delicate pedagogical obstacle a trainer has to temporize with. "You can sweat oat beer," the great aphorist Sam Langford once said, "and you can sweat oat whiskey. But you can't sweat oat women." There is a theory among less profound exponents of the Science, though, that love, once legitimized, is no longer vitiating, and athletes with proper religious feelings who have been wary, moderate sinners sometimes become self-destructively uxorious after the church has solemnized the union. Professor Goldman sometimes has to function as a marriage counselor despite his inexperience, but he finds it a handicap. "One guy said to me his wife told him, 'What does Goldman know about it? He's never been married,'" the Professor says.

Marciano is the partial exception to all Goldman's rules. The heavyweight champion started late, but take him all in all, his preceptor says, he is a hell of a fighter. He always takes Charlie's advice. Also he is the hardest-working heavyweight who ever lived, training as if he purposed to make up all the lessons he missed before the age of twenty-three. (He is thirty-one now.) His great assets are stamina and leverage, but the Professor has taught him a lot about how to use them. "I don't like to be away from him long," Professor Goldman said. "He forgets. It isn't like he learned them things when he should. We got to have half an hour every day for review." Mr. Goldman was in the Corner not long ago when a resonant old gentleman—wiry, straight and white-haired—walked into the saloon and invited the proprietors to his ninetieth birthday party, in another saloon naturally. The shortly-to-be nonagenarian wore no glasses, his hands were shapely, his forearms hard, and every hair looked as if, in the cold waterfront metaphor, it had been drove in with a tenpenny nail. On the card of invitation he laid on the bar was printed:

BILLY RAY
LAST SURVIVING BARE KNUCKLE FIGHTER

and he wouldn't let anybody in the joint buy a drink. His purse-bearer, a large subservient Irishman who looked like a retired cop, put the money on the bar for him; the protocol recalled the days when every fighter had his retinue, with a first, second and third accredited toady.

I asked Mr. Ray how many fights he had had, and he said: "A hundert forty. The last one was with gloves. I thought the game was getting soft, so I retired." A minute later he was telling an affectionate but indelicate story about his seventh wife, now of course dead, and shortly after that complaining of the high cost of living for a male these days, citing with regret the consumer price index on Water Street, near the East River, in 1885. "Four bits then was as good as eight dollars and fifteen cents today," he said.

He said he had fought George Dixon, the immortal Little Chocolate whose yellowed photograph hangs among the immortals over the Neutral Corner bar, and I felt as if he had said that he once wrestled Abe Lincoln. "But the best I ever fought was Ike Weir, the Belfast Spider," he said. "He was the cleverest man ever lived, only his hands were so broke up he wouldn't hit you a hard one on the jaw. Jabs and body blows is how he done it." Weir fought between 1885 and 1894, Dixon from 1886 to 1906; my own father saw him lose the featherweight championship to the much younger Terry McGovern in 1900, and he held Dixon was the cleverest man ever lived. He had never seen Weir. The older you are, the further back your candidate is likely to be. Ray said he had fought Dixon before the latter won his first world's title as a bantam in 1890. They were thoroughly illegal fights, for trifling sidebets in the back rooms of saloons, and they do not appear in the record books, nor do hundreds of other fights the old-timers had.

Ray grew up in the gracious old Brooklyn of Henry Ward Beecher, in which prizefighting was as much against the law as cocking mains or dogfights, but less frowned upon, since there were no Humane Societies needling the police to stop the fist fighters. Left to their own devices the police were lenient. "A fellow named Hughie Bart ran a great place around 1882," Mr. Ray said. "It was right across the street from Calvary Cemetery and there would be dogfights in the basement, rooster fights on an upper floor, and we would be fighting on the ground floor, all at the same time. Mourners would stop in on their way back, to take their mind off their loss. The gravediggers were old tads with beards. They'd sit in Hughie's drinking between jobs, and when they were watching a fight you dassn't quit, because they would split your skull with a spade." Sometimes Mr. Ray and other Brooklyn fighters, like the original Jack Dempsey, the Nonpareil—"He was the *real* gentleman fighter," Mr. Ray said—would invade Henry James's New York and show at Owney Geoghegan's or Harry Hill's or the Bucket of Blood, all sporting establishments that ran variety shows and pickup fights. "You would fight on a stage against a house heavyweight," the old gentleman said. "And the idea was to go fifteen minutes without being knocked out. I weighed around 120. If you stayed you got three dollars. If you looked like making it, the game was to back you up against the stage curtain and a fellow would hit you on the back of the head with a hammer. If you knew it, though, you would try to work the house fighter up against the curtain. Then he had to come straight at you, so you could measure him for a counter. It was a nice easy touch, not like a finish fight. It took the place of sparring, and you got paid good for it."

Mr. Ray and his purse-bearer walked out to spread more invitations; Billy waltzed out as brisk as if he heard the gong for his ninety-first year. Mr. Goldman laughed happily. "It makes me feel young when an old guy like that comes in that was around when I just started boxing," he said. "I remember him when I was with McGovern, and he was already saying: 'You should have seen the Belfast Spider.'"

One thing you have to grant the Sweet Science, it is joined onto the past like a man's arm to his shoulder.

December 12, 1955

An Old
Thuburban Custom

On the floor of the Bardo Museum, in Tunis, there is a mosaic picture of a knockdown in a prizefight that took place about 200 A.D. Nat Fleischer's *Ring Record Book* does not go back that far, so it has been impossible for me to date the bout more exactly. The fighter who has been knocked down wears a beard, like Archie Moore, but it is improbable that even Moore was boxing that long ago. The mosaic came from the ruins of Thuburbo Majus, a Roman colony forty miles south of the Carthage-Tunis urban complex. The bearded fellow looks like a smart city fighter who was brought to Thuburbo for a soft touch and then encountered unexpected opposition. No Thuburban sport would have paid for a mosaic of a Thuburban boxer being jolted; the sport was going to look at that mosaic every time he lay down to eat, and he would want it to remind him of a happy occasion. I imagine he won a bundle of sesterces on the match and commissioned the mosaic to celebrate the coup.

The fellow on the receiving end has an experienced, disillusioned look, like that of a boy who has fought out of town before. The humiliation he has just undergone is the kind of thing that could happen to a visiting boxer in what Whitey Bimstein, a trainer friend of mine, refers to as the State of Cleveland, Ohio. He is older than his beardless opponent, who has nailed him with a right swing to the left temple. Blood is spurting from the point of impact in a long arc of separate drops, represented by red stones, and the swing has carried the local slugger part way around, so that he is looking over his left shoulder. The older fighter is squatting on his hunkers, neither knee quite touching the ground. The punch has not dazed him; he has his elbows pulled in tight to his body and his fists in front of him, ready to hit as soon as he can bounce up. There was no count in those days, and it was up to him to resume fighting as soon as possible. It must be difficult to give the effect of motion in mosaic; in any case, the fight scene has the implausibly static appearance of a picture taken with a high-speed camera.

The bout looks more modern than a print of a London prize-ring fight in the days of Pierce Egan, the favorite son of Clio, although the boxers in Thuburbo performed at least fifteen hundred years earlier than Egan's bare-knuckled Heroes. For one thing, the boxers in the mosaic wear the cestus. Their fists, clenched around bars of lead, are wrapped in thongs of hard leather, an arrangement that makes them look as though they were wearing boxing gloves. For another, the position of the vertical boxer is up-to-date. His left foot, slid flat along the ground, is in advance of his right, but not too far, and he is up on the ball of his right foot as he throws the punch, with all his body in it. The bare-knuckled Heroes leaned away from each other, bracing themselves as if against a push. They knew that the bare hand was a friable weapon, and that a man knocked down had thirty seconds in which to come to scratch. A one-punch knockout was almost impossible until the other fellow had been softened by a long preliminary mauling. In the meanwhile, the hands had to be employed with circumspection. Boxers wearing the cestus tried for a quick knockout, knowing that the hand was protected and that a punch almost anywhere could do the trick. A blow high on the side of the head, such as the one that dropped the bearded man, would not count for much with a bare fist or padded glove.

I was having a thin time in the Bardo until I caught this entrancing glimpse into an antiquity that apparently had its high spots. While I was extrapolating the progress of the fight, as the boys on the quarterlies would say, I was interrupted by my taxi-driver, who had accompanied me inside the museum to protect me from self-appointed guides. The driver, a middleweight wearing sunglasses, a sports shirt, and jeans, was a young Jew from Nefta, an oasis by the great dry salt lake known as the Chott el-Djerid, at the edge of the Sahara. He had come to Tunis to look for a job when he was thirteen years old, and he told me his life story on the way to the museum. Nefta has 382,900 palm trees and almost as many mosques, and its Jews have been there since the Dispersion, but the driver looked like a New York hackie in summertime.

"The referee will stop it," he said, in French. The Jews of Nefta speak Arabic by preference, but I don't. He was looking at the knockdown.

"Why?" I said argumentatively. "The guy's head is clear; he's going to get up."

"Look at that cut," the driver said. "What's the use? The kid will kill him if he gets up. The kid fights just like my Cousin Touniou in the amateurs. *Poum, poum!*" He started moving across the museum floor in a crouch, throwing hooks. "Touniou never grabs," he said. "He keeps on punching. This kid is the same kind of fighter."

I cite this excursion into archeology to show that the Tunisian passion for prizefighting has deep roots. It is true that there was a hiatus of about thirteen hundred years in the history of the Tunisian ring after the arrival of the Companions of the Prophet, who brought in crooked wrestling at the start of the seventh century. Right up through the eighteenth century, Turkish wrestlers operated on the Place of the Kasbah every Friday, "before a public always ready to applaud their prearranged prowesses," according to the memoirs of the Chevalier de St. Gervais, a French consul. Boxing, like other elements of classical civilization, was plowed under. But the soil had been prepared in the time of the Thuburbo Majus Sporting Club, and the seed of what Pierce Egan denominated the Sweet Science lay dormant, awaiting only the gentle rain of publicity. Publicity is what it now receives in torrents.

From the day I arrived in Tunis—which was on the fifth of April, 1956, by the Christian calendar; the twenty-third of Schaaban, 1375, by the Moslem; and the twenty-fourth of Nisan, 5716, by the Hebrew—I kept reading about the prestigious *réunion de boxe* contemplated for the evening of April 21st, which would be the tenth of Ramadan, the Mohammedans' holy month, and the tenth of the Jewish month of Iyar. The *clou*, or star bout, of the reunion would present the lightweight champion of Europe—Duilio Loi, of Italy—provided the promoters could get hold of an opponent sufficiently intrepid to face him. The sportswriters expressed grave doubts about the chances of this; the boxers of the Mediterranean littoral, I gathered, are a supersensitive lot, fearing public humiliation more than annihilation. "The organizers have *contacté* many men of the weight category of Loi, but all without exception, from fear of being mystified by the transalpine boxer, have declined the offer," the first fellow I read had written. He himself seemed slightly mystified, I thought, because Loi is transalpine only if you look at him from France. It was a mild example of what Tunisian nationalists call the colonial mentality.

Three of the four French-language dailies in Tunis print the date according to the Christian, Moslem, and Hebrew reckonings, in order not to hurt anybody's feelings, and matchmakers get up boxing cards on much the same principle, trying to attract cash-bearing fauna of the three chief Tunisois strains—Arab, Jewish, and Latin. A Tunisois is an inhabitant of the City of Tunis, and, as some people say of New York and the United States, Tunis is not Tunisia. Roughly half the population of the city is non-Moslem. Italians, if you count both Italian citizens and naturalized Tunisians, make up the largest segment of non-Moslem fight fans. The ideal Tunis match is one between an Italian or Corsican and a Moslem, but both factions have to think they have a chance. I sensed from the first that this was the promoters' difficulty in the present instance. The more miraculous they made Signor Loi appear in order to draw the Italian trade, the less plausible it would seem that any living human being could give him a rub. On the other hand, it was unlikely that Loi, a perspicacious fellow, would come to Tunis to fight anybody who could hurt him, even with a cestus.

In the next weeks, news about the impending, or non-impending, appearance of the great Duilio competed for my attention with stories about the birth pangs of the new Tunisian government and others about the war just across the border in Algeria, which, for Tunisians, is already "the sister state." Paris, but not Tunis, papers maintain that it is simply a part of France—"ALGERIA IS AS FRENCH AS THE LIMOUSIN," a Paris headline said a day or so before I came to North Africa.

The three French-language newspapers that employ triple dates have resident proprietors. The fourth, *La Dépêche*, which is the most conservative and sticks to one calendar, is owned by French corporations having heavy financial commitments in Tunisia. The readership of all four is composed in one large part of Moslems and in another large part of resident Europeans who hope the war won't spread to Tunisia, which it may if it goes on much longer. Consequently, the papers are full of hopeful rumors of negotiations in progress. The Algerian war you read about in Tunis has little to do with the one that the popular press in Paris wins, with gory details, every morning and evening. (The war always starts up again next day, in time to make new headlines.) The people of Tunis have been political skeptics ever since the fall of the Carthaginian Republic. They assess and dissect all public information with suspicion. The boxing writer for one of the papers wrote a debunking piece accusing the reunion organizers of never having had any serious intention of organizing anything. This was a necessary part of convincing the Tunisois that there would be a reunion, a friend told me, because the Tunisois never believe anything until it has been denied. The Moslem Tunisois is skeptical by inherited aptitude. This is because, on a site so historically stratifed, the Numidians most suspicious of the Carthaginians were the ones most likely to survive long enough to beget descendants. This was equally true of the Carthaginians most distrustful of the Romans, the Romans of the Vandals, the Vandals of the Byzantines, the Byzantines of the Berbers, and the Berbers of the Arabs. None of these groups exterminated its predecessor. In each case, the most autopreservative elements survived. The end product is the Moslem Tunisois. The European Tunisois is inclined to overrate importations, including prizefighters.

On the first of Ramadan, the promoters allowed the news to leak out that they had discovered a man brave enough to oppose the Italian. By a coincidence, he was a Moslem—not a Tunisian or Algerian but a native of Spanish Morocco, who had never before fought in Tunis. Since the promoters had been able to find no lightweight sufficiently temerarious to take up the challenge, the leak said, they had had recourse to a man of a superior category—a welterweight. "The choice," the story said, "has fallen upon the Hispano-Moroccan Ben Bucker, champion of Spain." The Spanish welterweight championship may mean a lot in bullfighting, but in boxing it is a minor title. "Loi will consequently box with a handicap of nearly three kilos [6.6 pounds]," the journalist continued. "But, over and above his resounding record of seventy-four combats (sixty-nine victories, four draws, and one defeat), Duilio Loi is a great stylist and a particularly attractive boxer. His body feints are those of a virtuoso, and more than one boxer has been mystified by him. Duilio Loi is the complete boxer par excellence, who is summoned to become a world champion."

Now that they had forced the promoters to divulge the identity of the complete boxer par excellence's opponent, the newspapers put aside their reserve. *Le Petit Matin*, a few days before the scheduled appearance, carried not only a throbbing biography of Signor Loi but an eyewitness story by a Tunis resident of Italian affiliation who had once gone to Milan to see him fight and, the paper said, had "consented to confide to us his objective impressions, tinted, perhaps, with enthusiasm." In the biography, Loi's father was identified as a Sardinian sailor who "heroically vanished in the Tunisian waters aboard a ship bombed by the English in 1943." The biographer went on to say, "Like his father before him, who chose the perilous adventure of the sea, Duilio undertook the hard and pitiless trade of boxer. Today he does not complain, because he occupies an enviable economic position." The returned pilgrim, a M. Italo Castanetto, had seen Loi win a decision in fifteen rounds over Séraphin Ferrer, the lightweight champion of France. (Ferrer, before that, had been knocked out by an American featherweight named Percy Bassett.) "What a devil of a *bonhomme* is that Loi!" M. Castanetto objectively reported. "All that he undertook he brought off, with an unheard-of *brio*. He calculated, he launched his blows with mathematical precision. A cold calculator, he was prodigious all down the line. He put Ferrer off by erudite evasions and retreats; he used, with disconcerting dexterity, ruses that just grazed illegality. . . . Loi for me is a champion—a very great champion."

Two days before the bout, which now, I was happy to see, was regarded as a certainty, *La Presse* announced, "Though he may not be furnished with a redoubtable punch, the Italian boxer constitutes a veritable attraction; he makes his adversaries suffer, and his great ring science permits him often to ridicule them." All it could find to say for Bucker was that "the boxer who will give him the reply can hardly be called *le premier venu*," which is boxing French for a nobody. The same day, *La Dépêche* catalogued a couple of Signor Loi's nonredoubtable punches—a left jab to the liver and a punch all his own that was a mélange of a jab and an uppercut.

Le Petit Matin, turning its attention to Bucker—and high time—announced that "in the plans of B. Bucker, Loi will have no walkover." Bucker was the kind of fighter who would think it beneath him to fight an ordinary lightweight, the story said, and he had consented to meet Loi only because Loi was a phoenix of the ring, the pride of sporting Italy. Bucker knew that he had all to gain and nothing to lose in confronting such a nonpareil. There, for him, resided the raison d'être of the match. "The obstinate boy may succeed in his task," *Le Petit Matin* concluded. This was the first suggestion of such a possibility I had read anywhere, but it was not quite the last. On the day of the fight, *Tunis-Soir* proclaimed, "The celebrated champion of Italy, Duilio Loi, will not have an easy game against the redoubtable Spanish boxer Ben Bucker."

The visiting boxers were in town by now, and *La Dépêche*, pulling a switch, said that Loi was not intimidated by the weight handicap. "He will not be the first boxer of a superior category I have encountered," the jab-uppercutter had reassured the reporter. But, *La Dépêche* warned, "the Hispano-Moroccan of Tetuán, Ben Bucker, is not ignorant of how profitable to him would be a good performance against a man of the class of Loi, so we can be sure of seeing him launch himself in the battle with the firm conviction of defending his chance to the limit of his possibilities."

La Presse echoed the new note of doubt. It also plucked at the heartstrings of its Moslem readers with a headline quoting Ben Bucker as saying, "IN SPITE OF RAMADAN, I WILL NOT BE DIMINISHED." All Moslems were abstaining from food and water between sunrise and sunset every day, and on the tenth day of the fast their hearts might be expected to go out to a co-religionist confronted by one whom *La Presse* itself described as "the champion of Europe— spectacular boxer, champion of grand class, and knowing to the bottom his profession." All boxers previously opposed to Loi, *La Presse* added, ignoring the four draws and one defeat, had been "beaten and arch-beaten," and none of them had been able to disquiet even slightly the champion of Europe, who made proof each time of a fulgurant superiority. A *Presse* reporter who had interviewed the undiminished Bucker, however, described him as "a soldier of twenty-five, who exudes good health." "I am not bothered by Ramadan, and I will compel myself to give a severe reply to Duilio Loi," Señor Bucker had informed the *Presse* representative. When the sunset gun sounds, unleashing the inhibited gastric juices, the Moslems are accustomed to put away a gigantic meal, and are in a good mood for an evening's entertainment afterward, but I wondered how this would work out for a fellow who had to box after dinner. Señor Bucker had my sympathy.

Le Petit Matin now held out no hope for the Ramadan Kid. "THE WEAPONS OF BEN BUCKER NOT SUFFICIENTLY EFFICACIOUS TO COUNTER THE IRRESISTIBLE ACTION OF DUILIO LOI," its boxing headline ruled. "Everybody knows Duilio Loi," its expert wrote. "Everybody follows intently his fertile activity in all the rings of the universe. From Milan to Melbourne he has been appreciated. With fervor the Italians turn out when he operates, and Loi, with elegance, with all the *brio* desirable, acquits himself of his task. During ten rounds, Ben Bucker, the Brown Boy, will try to checkmate the hability, the virtuosity of Duilio Loi. But with what weapons will he succeed? His determination and his robustiousness, his chief assets—can they break the *élan* of the Italian? We do not think so. To tell Ben Bucker to beat Loi is like asking him to swim the Atlantic Ocean."

When the boxing writer threw Bucker into the ocean, I rose from my table on the *terrasse* of the Au Vert Galant Milk Bar and American Coktail Salon, near where the European part of Tunis touches on the Medina, which is a section of the old Arab city. I was besieged by four small Bedouin children, who had been whimpering for money as I read the papers. This quartet greets me joyously every morning when I leave my hotel and pursues me all day with the persistence of a pack of hounds following a scent bag. They smile and dance when I present them with the little Tunisian five-franc pieces, which are worth slightly more than a cent and look as if they were designed for almsgiving, just as the silver dollars in Nevada seem to have been designed for slot machines. Every time I run out of five-franc pieces, the junior sheiks howl like fiends of hell and exercise a yogi-like talent for making their noses run. This lends a ghastly verisimilitude to their tears. They stay by my table sniffling and clucking while I nibble at my *chemia*, which is a Tunisian free lunch served with all drinks. A *chemia* usually includes pickled fennel, bits of dried octopus, and cooked beans served with a dish of coarse pepper, into which you dip them as you eat.

Whenever I want to make a break, I must pay tribute again, or the children will follow me down the street, making me look like an Arab cartoon of unfeeling colonialism. I ask the waiter for change in small coins, and place one in each of the pink, moist, upturned palms, which are exactly the size of poker chips. The quartet is convoyed by two louts about twelve years old, who operate at a distance just beyond adult kicking and cuffing range. They sit on the curb while the children beg, and their relation to them is that of a Chinese fisherman to his cormorant. When the boys see the children getting money, they rush up to take it from them, and while they are kicking the children in painful places, I make a temporary escape. I suppose that in the Medina, where the troupe returns every night, there is an older entrepreneur, who collects from the boys. The arrangement works out well for the children, for they are remarkably healthy, vigorous, and happy. Probably the boss allows some of the profits to trickle down to them. During Ramadan, when the life of the Medina is largely nocturnal, they stay up all night to work the Moslem trade and then turn out, bright-eyed, to hustle the European city in the morning. They confute the pediatricians who say that children need sleep. I can picture them, grown up, selling advertising for Henry Luce.

When I had shaken the tots on the afternoon of the fight, I walked to the house number on the Avenue Jules-Ferry that the newspapers had given as the address of the promoters. It turned out, by a weird co-incidence, to be a newspaper office. The Avenue Jules-Ferry, the main stem of Tunis, is named for the French Premier who, in 1881, placed Tunisia in French protective custody. It is a pleasant thoroughfare, with a wide, tree-shaded esplanade running down its middle. The trees are *figuiers*, which serve as business premises for the city's more substantial bootblacks. The customer leans against the tree, and there is no extra charge if he rubs his back against the bark. Bootblacks too junior to have trees of their own circulate on the café *terrasses*, grabbing feet from under tables; when they have daubed polish on one shoe, the victim has to yield to the other in order not to look silly. Just before sundown, the tops of the shoeshine trees fill up with birds that have been out all day hustling *chemia*, and they set up a continuous strident clamor, like katydids. It goes on late into the night, because the street lights keep them awake. The Tunisians are going to change the name of the street to the Avenue Bourguiba. Nothing, however, will change its French-provincial character.

The sidewalks on both sides of the avenue are lined with cafés, where the Moslem and non-Moslem customers are hard to tell apart, except for the minority of Moslems who top their European street clothes with a red *chechia*, the Tunisian fez. Most go bareheaded. The kind of Moslem who does not wear European clothes also does not, as a usual thing, have enough money to pay for a *consommation* at a main-stem café. During Ramadan, there is another clue. For eleven months of the Mohammedan year, the Moslem boulevardiers order fruit juices, *glaces*, soft drinks, or coffee. During Ramadan, they sit on the *terrasses* in greater numbers than ever, for fasting makes them languid and talkative, but their tables are bare. The proprietors know that if they give any indication of displeasure the customers won't come back when Ramadan is over.

At the promoters' office, I bought two fight tickets, fifth row ringside, for fifteen hundred francs, or a little over four dollars, apiece — a great price for Tunis, which has not been a money town since 1816, when Mahmoud Bey, under British pressure, abolished piracy on the high seas. A revolt followed this blow at free enterprise, but another Bey suppressed it and all the unemployed pirates at the same time.

I had already invited as my companion M. Roger Flageollet, a wartime friend whom I had met again in Tunis. M. Flageollet is a solid young businessman, an employee of the Bank of Algeria and Tunisia. He promised to be ideal company, I thought, because he had never attended a prizefight before, and so would not dispute my interpretations of whatever we were destined to see. Having been born and bred in a part of Tunisia where there are few Europeans, he speaks Arabic as fluently as French, and I hoped that if any particularly excruciating cracks were made in the language of the Prophet, he would translate them for me. Despite this background, M. Flageollet presents a most un-Tunisian appearance, because his parents came from the Département du Jura, a mountainous region of France near the Swiss border. He is blond, brachycephalic, square-jawed, and deep-chested, and he perspires obviously and wears purposefully quiet, citified, uncolonial bank-employee clothes, not well enough cut to arouse the envy or suspicion of his superiors. He would look at home in the front office of a bank in Racine, Wisconsin, or Darwen, Lancashire. In Tunis, he is exotic.

Like a good bank man, M. Flageollet called for me on time that evening; we were in our seats at the Palais de la Foire at the moment when the first amateur preliminary was scheduled to begin, which it didn't. The Fair Palace is a hangarlike building of the same architectural species as the War Memorial Auditorium in Syracuse and the Rhode Island Auditorium in Providence, and it was built a couple of years ago, my companion informed me, to house a colonial exposition. It is on a wide new four-lane boulevard, as far in time and mood from the Avenue Jules-Ferry as that good turn-of-the-century French street is from the *souks* of the Medina. The modern city has grown fast during the last fifty years; it will soon be as big as Punic or Roman Carthage. The parking lot outside the arena, where we left M. Flageollet's car, was jammed. Inside the building, there was precisely the same atmosphere as at the Sunnyside Gardens in Queens or the Central Sporting Club in the Faubourg Saint-Denis. Prizefighting everywhere, like carnal love in the old story, is just like in Cincinnati. The fight crowd in Thuburbo Majus could not have differed greatly. Tunis is now, as Thuburbo was then, "out-of-town"—on the periphery of the big time. It is, in fact, on the periphery of a periphery, because Signor Loi, who is a Mediterranean star, is only a St. Nick's attraction in New York. The Tunis crowd is knowing, up to a certain point, because it sees a great deal of local amateur boxing, and passionate because of its ancestral composition.

It was a hot night for Tunis in late April, which is like a hot night for New York in late June. The promoters had set up bleachers in the Fair Palace, with a ring and a relatively small level ringside section in the middle of the terraced ranks of shirtsleeved men. Roger Flageollet had seen a boxing ring only in newsreels, he said. He reported that he could now see the newsreels had been accurate. Two pairs of old boxing gloves were tied to the ropes in opposite corners of the ring. The program, as in France, was to begin with a series of amateur bouts, and the organizers obviously felt that not even a prestigious reunion justified new gloves for amateurs. The crowd, impatient, stamped in cadence and whistled for the first bout to begin, and Roger, embarrassed, asked if fight crowds behaved with similar informality in the great world. He appeared relieved when I said they did. "Tunis audiences are bad," he said. "At jazz recitals, they always get excited before the exciting moments, and then when they should be caught up by the music, they're talking about something else. It is an impossible country," he added, carried away by a vast nostalgia for an efficient, hep, blond universe he had never known.

Two brown-haired, fair-skinned lightweights got into the ring, and the referee, using a microphone, introduced them as Habib Hafnaoui and Haied ben Salah. (I got the spellings out of the next day's paper.) They flapped their arms with equal artlessness, except that all one boy's wild swings landed, while all the other's missed. One of the boys was knocked down, and a literal sponge came flying into the ring from his corner—something I hadn't seen in a long while. At home, only a referee can stop a fight. I had the impression that if the boys were to start over again, the bout might go exactly the opposite way; it was entirely a question of who landed the first swing. Habib was winner, Haied loser.

M. Flageollet made his first comment on boxing. "That must be fatiguing," he said.

By the second bout, he was in the groove. This one brought together a tall, light-skinned Berber and a tawny, hawk-nosed young Saracen type. The tall boy was a better puncher, but the Saracen was a gamester. He covered his face with his forearms and tried to get in close. When he succeeded in doing so, he sometimes landed a punch to the head, but not a hard one. He had a case of mistaken vocation. The tall boy, hitting the tawny one often but not discouraging him, became impatient. He began to bang the Saracen on the top of the head and in the back of the neck as he came in, but he had no cestus. "*Coup de lapin!* [Rabbit punch!]" shouted M. Flageollet. He must have read that somewhere. Then, as the tall boy did it again, Flageollet cried, "*Lâche!* [Coward!]" From then on, he sounded like any other fight fan. The referee stopped the bout in the third round, just as M. Flageollet's tireless favorite landed his best punch of the fight. The decision went to the tall boy. "It is an injustice!" my friend proclaimed. A couple of fellows near us agreed. Roger had become an expert just like me. It is this sensation of immanent injustice, official chicanery, *la condition humaine, quoi?*, sticking its thumb in mankind's eye while the referee looks the other way that distinguishes the fight follower. Horse racing makes a man sorry only for himself. I like horse racing, but it is on a low ethical level. (There is horse racing in Tunis on Sundays until the end of May, when what even the Tunisois concedes to be heat sets in.) The beaten boy protested, waving his bandaged hands at the referee, who smiled in a repulsively patronizing manner. "How much have you received?" M. Flageollet demanded. Then, as the young Saracen, who wore red trunks, descended from the ring, he shouted, "*Tu auras ta revanche, le rouge!*"

These boys, like the first pair, were Moslems—the fair one as well as the tawny. The hardest-up groups always produce the most boxers—in the United States it's the Negroes, with the Puerto Ricans and Mexicans not far behind them. In the third amateur bout, a young Italian, Caschetto, was boxing a fifth Mohammedan, Rezgui ben Mohammed, and there was a chance to measure the ethnic and cultural makeup of the audience. "Cas-chet-to! Cas-chet-to! Cas-chet-to!" the bleachers chorused. Ben Mohammed, a good boxer, spidery but a stinger, won easily. I learned afterward that Mohammed is the amateur lightweight champion of Tunisia. The bleachers shouted maledictions. "They do not understand boxing," M. Flageollet said of the bleacherites. "The decision was very equitable."

There was a pause after the third bout to mark the break between the amateur and the professional portions of the program. The worn gloves were removed from the ring, to be used in the next amateur show. The fashionables were now arriving, including a number of chic Moslems wearing tasselled *chechias* above their handsomely tailored European clothes. These were members of the government, however—not paying customers. One was accompanied by a spectacular pink-and-white blonde in a low décolletage, who held a minute black lace handkerchief in front of her nose as a symbolic substitute for a veil. Accustomed to the television-studio audiences at Madison Square Garden, I thought it was turning into a pretty fair house, although many of the expensive seats around M. Flageollet and me were occupied by young men whose knowing informality gave me the impression that they were in on skulls. The cheap seats, which are never complimentary, were half filled.

The first professional match was between welterweights—Ahmed ben Ali, a Negro Moslem described in some of the news stories I had read as Le Panthère Noir, and an Italo-Tunisois named Pino Azzaro.

The Black Panther was a southpaw—or *fausse garde*, as the French have it. Like most boxers who stand the wrong way around, he could use his right only as a child at table uses bread—for a pusher. He had a hard, lashing punch with his left, though, and was very aggressive. He boxed in the style the French call *à l'Américain*, his arms loose and his hands low, and he had a lot of confidence, which was justified in the present instance. His opponent was a game, stocky kid who had never given any thought to how to fight a southpaw. As a consequence, he got clouted unmercifully, and from the third round on, his right eye rose like a *soufflé au kirsch*. "Pee-no! Pee-no! Pee-no!" the Europeans crowed all the same, as if he were winning the fight. Between the rounds, Azzaro's seconds stood in front of him and pointed to their right eyes, to show him what was the matter. He shook his head impatiently. He knew. None of the seconds did anything about the eye, and it assumed the proportions of a *bombe glacée*, or Baked Alaska. The Panther applied himself cheerily to hitting this traumatic *entremet*. The fortitude of the Italian boy's seconds amazed me. They never winced. It was not until the end of the fifth round that one of them produced a one-drink piece of ice and held it delicately to the patient's eye, as if he had borrowed the ice from a bartender and had to return it before it melted. The referee, equally brave, refrained from stopping the bout, which went six rounds. When it was over, the bleacher chorus booed the decision in the Panther's favor. As *La Dépêche* had it next day, "his victory, although indisputable, was greeted by the whistles of the crowd." When the Black Panther came down from the ring, an old Moslem wearing a wraparound headdress with cheek panels, as in "The Sheik," grabbed him and kissed him full on the mouth.

"He beat him like Paddy beat the drum [*grosse caisse*]," I said to Roger, and he said, "Neatly. They should have arrested the combat. But who was Paddy?"

The treat of the evening was now on tap, and the chorus began a crashing chant of "Lo-ee! Lo-ee! Lo-ee!," like Silone's Roman crowd chanting "Ce-Du! Ce-Du! Ce-Du!" for Mussolini. Even the newspapermen around the ring, precisely resembling the newspapermen around the ring in a Hollywood fight picture (Hollywood fight pictures are popular in Tunis), stopped looking professionally bored. The fewer chances a newspaperman has to look bored in public, the more bored he is going to look when he has a chance. In Tunis nowadays, chances for a public display of boredom are widely spaced. In Punic Carthage, *la vie journalistique* was probably more animated. The town was in the big leagues then, and the Roman and Alexandrian trained seals came to town to interview Hannibal and write a feature on the baby-burning season. The press of Tunis includes four French, one Italian, and three Arabic dailies, besides several weeklies, and they were all putting on heavy coverage of Signor Loi.

The Signor, who has a barnstorming technique like Archie Moore's, stalked down the aisle wearing a garnet dressing gown of heavy Italian silk. He was a handsome, sleek little Italian with a proud but calculating expression, like a waiter captain's. Once in the ring, he revolved to survey the crowd that he was expected to electrify. I was sure he had in the back of his shiny head the scale of prices for various sections of the arena. His beautiful eyelashes fluttered with displeasure.

Loi had with him the customary flock of handlers, but Ben Bucker was accompanied only by one stout middle-aged man, his Spanish Svengali. The Brown Boy of Tetuán looked pretty frightened, and the Svengali rubbed the small of his back and crooned in his ear. When the boxers removed their robes, we could see that the Moroccan was a pretty thin welterweight—maybe he really had been observing Ramadan—while Loi was a pretty fat lightweight. A ham of an international, standardized variety now sprang lightly into the ring; in his long jacket and drainpipe trousers, he might have come straight from the Hammersmith Palais or Ridgewood Grove. He was a big blond with an Edwardian hairdo, through which he ran one hand while he grabbed the microphone with the other, pulling it across his chest in an intimate diagonal. When he had got the mike snuggled against his face, he burst into a stream of Arabic. Toward the end of the discourse, I twice caught the word "kilos," for which, apparently, there is no equivalent Arab weight measure.

M. Flageollet said, "He introduces the fighters and says Bucker weighs only nine hundred grams [two pounds] more than Loi. The man next to me says that the announcer is a prizefighter named Brahim Jeune." Brahim Jeune visited both fighters' corners in a tripping run, shook hands with them, and then lightly bounded from the ring, waving his right hand to the audience. A French-speaking announcer followed him and went through the same routine at a walk.

"Lo-ee! Lo-ee! Lo-ee! Lo-ee! Lo-ee!" the Italians in the bleachers howled. Loi had a chest like a pouter pigeon and a back that would have looked good in a ball gown. Bucker, taller and the color of old ivory—he had apparently faded since the Brown Boy story—rose from his stool with what appeared to be reluctance, gently impelled by Svengali's palm. Signor Loi gave him his version of what Moore calls The Look, designed to drain the marrow from a fellow's bones. Loi's Look is fiery and scornful, more of a stare than Moore's, which has elements of a squinch. When Loi began to box, the parallel with old Archie ended. The Signor is very run of the *moulin*. Poor Bucker, however, tottered forward to his doom. When the blow did not fall forthwith, he stood half unbelieving, like a shipwrecked sailor who finds himself unexpectedly within his depth. The lightning was poised, but the touring cobra did not strike; instead, he looked disdainfully at the Consul-General of Italy, who he was sure had not paid his way in.

Loi then cautiously approached his tense supporting cast and began what resembled a late-afternoon workout in a businessman's health club, when the combination rubber, locker boy, and boxing instructor, who has learned his third specialty by hearsay, takes on his last paying member of the day. The rubber is tired and wants to get the dirty sweatshirts to the laundry, take his own shower, and go off to meet his girl in front of a movie theatre on upper Broadway, but the customer is a good payer and it is important not to hurt him.

"*Combine*," a guest of the management with an ear like a clenched fist said in the row in front of me. "*Combine, cent pour cent*," which means a fix one hundred per cent.

"Bucker has the air of being overimpressed," M. Flageollet said politely, but the gallery cognoscenti, eager to show that they appreciated complete boxing par excellence, as distinguished from mere brutality, pretended to like it. "Lo-ee! Lo-ee! Lo-ee! Lo-ee!" they gushed thunderously. They reminded me of summer-resort people at a show of abstract paintings.

As the bout dragged on, Bucker began to cheer up. Like the tired businessman, he commenced to think that he was no worse than the opposition. Svengali no longer had to push him off the stool. In the beginning of the sixth round, the Signor, treacherous, or irritated by such signs of irreverence, struck him in what French boxing writers call the liver. The liver extends over the whole front of a Frenchman, from neck to navel, and is the source and cause of all his indispositions. I should refer to the part of the liver Bucker got hit in as his belly, but he sank to the mat grabbing at his groin—a mechanical reflex with many European boxers, who learn it before the left jab. (In the United States, for the last twenty years or so, referees have refused to award fights on fouls, and the gesture has disappeared.) As the boxing writer of *Tunis-Soir* subsequently put it, "Without the pressing encouragement of his manager, José Jover, he might have stayed down."

This was Svengali's feat of the evening. Rising at the ringside, his head on a level with that of his prostrate subject, he performed the great swooping, then soaring, motion of both hands with which a conductor draws the last decibel out of a mighty orchestra, at the same time fixing the Moroccan with a stare suggesting the Evil Eye, dreaded through all the Mediterranean. Bucker rose and, with the passion of a man whose confidence has been abused, rushed at Loi, seeming for the first time that evening to have an intention of doing him harm. It was then that I briefly cherished an unworthy wish that the outsider had a cestus. Signor Loi, either because he had a bad conscience or because he frightens easily, retreated. Then, annoyed in his turn, he launched a series of jab-uppercuts to the mutineer's ears and elbows. It looked for a moment as though they were going to start a fight, but the episode was a ripple on the millpond. Loi reverted to virtuosity and Bucker to humble gratitude for the last four rounds, and they finished at a wheezy pat-a-cake.

"Lo-ee! Lo-ee! Lo-ee! Lo-ee!" the gallery gods shouted when the

Arabic and French announcers gave out the judges' unanimous decision in favor of the devil of a *bonhomme*, but there was a puzzled note in their clamor.

"It is like a jazz concert," M. Flageollet said. "They applaud in the wrong places."

As for poor Bucker, he danced around the ring in glee, shaking hands with himself as if he had just stayed ten rounds with a famished Siberian tiger.

"Frankly, I expected better," M. Flageollet said. "I find him nothing extraordinary."

This was exactly the opinion of His Excellency Mohammed Masmoudi, Minister of State, when interviewed the next day by *Tunis-Soir*. His Excellency said, "The organization was impeccable. Tunis showed itself a worthy capital of international pugilism. I expected a much better fight."

As sometimes happens when the main bout is bad, a subsidiary fight saved the show. The promoters had resolved a secondary ethnic problem by signing Bill-Jo Cohen, a Tunisian Jewish middleweight, to meet a Portuguese middleweight named Emmanuel Martinheira in the chief supporting bout. Matching a Jew against an Iberian would provide another good Tunisois emotional attraction. Martinheira boxed out of Casablanca.

Bill-Jo, I had learned from the newspapers, was a local boy who had been rushed along too fast and, as a consequence, had been knocked out. Against Martinheira, a youngster, he hoped to begin a comeback. Bill-Jo proved to be a middleweight of settled, elderly appearance, with a retreating hairline and a well-defined *bidon*, or potbelly, which his manager had thoughtfully covered with a wide white elastic-satin ruffle to raise his foul line. He did not have the look of a particularly durable competitor. When I saw M. Cohen's opponent—a powerful, lantern-jawed lad, tall for a middleweight and in magnificent condition—I advised M. Flageollet to prepare for an early departure. But Bill-Jo, it turned out, was in just as good shape, for they fought ten of the maddest slugging rounds I ever saw.

The Portuguese from Casablanca used the conventional French

guard, leaning forward from the waist, feet wide apart, forearms and elbows in front of his face. The boxer so arranged is supposed to advance indefatigably within his cage of arms until he sees an opening or attains the *corps-à-corps*, which we call infighting. Once in a while, a fighter like the late Marcel Cerdan comes along who can make of this style an instrument of universal conquest. The trick lies in switching from the cage to the body attack. The device doesn't suit a tall man or a head-puncher (many of the best French trainers have now abandoned it), and an ordinary boy like Martinheira opens a bar in his cage every time he throws a punch. Bill-Jo just stood out there like a man lifting the sledge to ring the bell at an amusement park. Every time Martinheira threw a punch, he hit Bill-Jo, and every time that happened, Bill-Jo hit him. Neither of them ever aimed lower than the chin, and neither went back, except when knocked back. It was not complicated or beautiful, but with every exchange the wonder grew.

There was a more even split in the audience participation this time. A bloc of Latins on one side of the house took up their stylized chant for the Portuguese boxer, even though he was from Casablanca— "MART-in-heira, MART-in-heira, MART-in-heira!"—but it soon became audible that there were numerous Jews in the house, and they picked up the suffrage of the Moslems and also, I think, of a considerable number of European Tunisois who supported Cohen as a local product. "Beel-Zho! Beel-Zho! Beel-Zho!" the coalition shouted, and the competing noises, like the punches that never missed their targets, were continuous. In the early middle part of the fight I had a feeling that Martinheira was going to go, and then, in the middle middle, that it would be Beel-Zho who would succumb. In the last rounds, I felt Martinheira to be in danger again, but this was purely subjective. The visible, tangible gluttons just stood there and slugged each other. At the end of the tenth round, after the two heroes had staggered to their corners, the judges called it a draw. I find it difficult and unnecessary to refrain from quoting here part of the *compte rendu* in next day's *Petit Matin*: "Head against head, in the last round, the two boys fought each other with unheard-of violence. It was prodigious. An equitable draw sealed this captivating encounter." That just about summed up the situation.

A couple of days later, the Tunisian Boxing Commission, checking the cards of the judges, found that one judge who voted for a draw had made a mistake in adding up the points he awarded during the rounds. The mistake had been in Beel-Zho's favor, and so Martinheira became the official victor. The muddle made me feel at home. It is the sort of thing that happens in New York State.

M. Flageollet drove me back to my hotel after the fights and said, before we parted, "I enjoyed the evening thoroughly. The last combat was very moving."

The next morning, the room-service waiter brought the day's papers up with my beer glass of good Tunisian orange juice, and I noted that all the chroniclers began their stories by beefing about the slim attendance. "It is regrettable," wrote one of them, "that the Tunisois public, in particular the Moslems, did not respond in greater number last night on the occasion of the great international gala that unfolded itself at the Palais de la Foire."

I considered this a tribute to the intelligence of the Tunisois Moslems. They are the heirs of Carthage and Thuburbo.

June 9, 1956

They Must Tike
Me for a Proper Mugg

While reading my habitual London newspaper, the *Times*, not long ago, I strayed from the kind of story I prefer, such as "Getting Facts About the Elizabethan Playhouse" and "Chinese Writers Denounced for Deviations," to the portion of the paper that Englishmen refer to as "sporting news," which deals largely with cricket. I found little, at first glance, to set my pulses surging with emotion, an effect American sportswriters strive for even on a dull day, but in the investment, or racing, section, just under "Birmingham Selections," I came upon what I thought a promising headline:

BOXER MAY RIDE AT MANCHESTER
TWO MOUNTS OFFERED TO TERRY SPINKS

It is unusual for a professional athlete to engage in two such specialized activities concurrently, and I read the story that followed this announcement with some interest:

Terry Spinks, the 1956 Olympic flyweight champion, and now a professional boxer, has been invited to ride two horses at Manchester on Friday—Luing, a five-year-old, in the Cromwell Selling Handicap, and Dominion, a six-year-old, in the Loom Handicap. Both horses are owned by Mrs. E. Schmidt-Bodner and trained by E. Gifford at Skipton. Spinks, aged 19, a former stable lad and apprentice jockey, has accepted both mounts subject to permission from Mr. M. Marsh, the Newmarket trainer, who has him under apprenticeship. It will be Spinks's first public appearance as a jockey, though he has ridden training gallops on many occasions. He spends much of his time between fights at the Newmarket stables and hopes to be a full-time jockey when he retires from boxing. He will fly to Manchester on Friday morning after training for a fight at Shoreditch four days later. Mr. H. Grossmith, promoter of next Tuesday's fight at Shoreditch Town Hall, London, between Spinks and Ivan McCready (Belfast), said yesterday that he had objected verbally to the Boxing Board of Control against Spinks riding on Friday. "I can't take any chances against Spinks getting injured," he said. "This is to be his first fight over eight rounds."

My first reflection after reading this was that it was odd of an owner to offer two mounts in one day at a major race meeting to a boy who had never ridden a race. My second was that the story was not calculated to deter *Times* readers from attending Mr. Grossmith's show, if *Times* readers ever venture as far afield at night as Shoreditch, which is a fried-fish-and-jellied-eel-consuming autonomous borough about a mile inland from London Bridge and northeast of the Whitechapel district. Customarily, what a press agent seeks from the *Times* is consecration, rather than direct profit.

When I turned to Lord Beaverbrook's *Express*, one of the less serious London papers that serve as morning garnish to my *Times* reading, I saw that its boxing writer had gone for the story in an enthusiastic, Beaverbrookish way. The *Express* sports page carried a picture of Spinks, looking young and truthful, over the same data I had read in the *Times*, plus a bit of extrapolation: "What a row Spinks started when he let out this stable information." According to the *Express*, Spinks' manager of record, a recently retired boxer named Sammy McCarthy, wanted Spinks to ride, but the story did not make clear whether this indicated unlimited confidence in his boy's horsemanship or a heroic indifference to his fate. "I will offer Mr. Grossmith a three-figure sum as a guarantee for Terry's appearance at Shoreditch on Tuesday," the paper quoted McCarthy as saying. "It would well compensate him if anything did go wrong." But, the *Express* added, "Promoter Grossmith, heavily armed with a rulebook marked at clause 14, which refers to the right of promoters to restrain a boxer from endangering himself—and incidentally the box office—marched up to the offices of the Boxing Board of Control yesterday ready to do battle for his idea of a square deal. . . . And yesterday Spinks, the lad who wants to become a champion jockey as well as a champion fighter, was hoping that his racing licence would be granted before Friday." The author of the *Express* piece was Sydney Hulls, who is the son of a famous old-time boxing promoter and takes a kindly view of impresarial inventiveness.

The boxing expert of the Labour Party's *Herald*, which I generally read as a political counterweight to the *Express*, is Tom Phillips, whom I first met at the Helsinki Olympics in 1952. He took an Opposition line in his Spinks story, which was headed "HORSE LAUGH." Phillips, who has eight children, a couple of them considerably older than the galloping flyweight, also took a paternal line, advising young Spinks in a fatherly way not to lend himself to "silly publicity stunts" and ballyhoo. The story, he wrote, was "a dilly"—all "bunkum"—and in corroboration of this bit of intuition he reported that the husband of the owner of the two horses concerned had been a boxing promoter himself.

The *Times* had said that Spinks the horseman was currently apprenticed to trainer Marsh. But Phillips, who was a straight reporter before he became a sportswriter, had phoned Marsh, and the trainer had told him that he no longer had any hold on the boy—adding, however, that in his opinion Spinks had no more chance of riding at Manchester on Friday than he had himself. Spinks, Marsh said, couldn't ride unless he got himself indentured to another trainer, and that isn't the sort of thing one can arrange overnight in England. As for Grossmith, the promoter of the Shoreditch fight, Phillips wrote, "Somehow I don't think he need worry."

Phillips' story, I thought, was the best plug of all for the fight, because it pictured McCarthy, Grossmith, and the others as resourceful and charming characters, who would not be out of place in the Neutral Corner Bar & Grill, on Eighth Avenue—a cultural haven to which my thoughts fondly turn when I tire of getting the facts about the Elizabethan Playhouse.

I phoned Mr. Phillips to congratulate him on his exposé and found him still sputtering with honest North Country indignation over the situation he had unearthed. "Bloody Barnum could have doon no better!" he said. He pronounces all double "o"s as in "good." Phillips likes to remind his readers that he is a Geordie, or coal miner, from County Durham, north of Yorkshire. The Geordie devotes himself to British boxing with the selfless passion that Dr. Schweitzer lavishes on his African lepers. Many of Phillips' nights are spent riding on wretched sleeping trains bound for places like Swansea and West Hartlepool to make connections with buses that will carry him to still more peripheral pest spots, where promoters tout him on the local advent of a future British world champion, usually a coal miner. Phillips often arrives just in time to see the fellow being carried out of the ring, though occasionally, if he misses a connection or his bus is late, the phenomenon has already been revived and is back on the night shift in the mine by the time he gets there. This sort of thing never disheartens the idealist.

When Phillips' paper sends him to big bouts in the United States, he repeatedly corners his American colleagues to confide, "There's a lad in Llanelly"—or Newton Abbot or Eccleston—"who can bash like Jack Dempsey, but the question is can he take a punch?" The answer is invariably in the negative, but the next time Phillips shows up, he has another false Imam in South Leeds or Birkenhead. No great heavyweight has learned his trade in Britain within the memory of any living man under a hundred. Bob Fitzsimmons, who won the championship in 1897 and lost it in 1899, was born in Cornwall, but he did all his fighting in the Antipodes and in America. As late as the election of Warren Gamaliel Harding, though, there were a few top-notch men in the lighter classes. The last of these *illustrissimi*, Jimmy Wilde, was, like Spinks, a flyweight.

Over the phone, Phillips said that Spinks was a good boxer, of the standaway, quick-moving classic type adapted to amateur bouts, which are limited to three rounds, but that it had not yet been established whether he had professional toughness. He was tall for his weight, Phillips said, and, like all boxers built that way, he looked fragile, but there was no telling about him until he had been further tested.

What I had read and heard about Spinks made me want to see him box. I was happy, therefore, to learn from Friday's *Times* that he had been spared the perils of the turf; he had decided not to ride that day. (Of Mrs. E. Schmidt-Bodner's two runners at Manchester, I noted the next morning, Luing was scratched from the Cromwell Selling Handicap, while Dominion, carrying a weight of eight stone three, or a hundred and fifteen pounds, ran dead last in a field of ten in the Loom Handicap. This may have been due to the fact that he was ridden by A. J. Russell, one of the most accomplished jockeys in England but obviously an inadequate substitute for the boxer.) Grossmith must have been as relieved as I was at the fighter's decision, and on the following Tuesday afternoon, when I rang through to Shoreditch Town Hall, the telephonist there sounded as pleased as though she had a piece of Spinks. She said that the first bout would go on at seven-forty-five and that I had better come along early, because the house was nearly sold out.

London is made up of a galaxy of autonomous boroughs that operate within the framework of the London County Council and that—as any visitor who has strayed much beyond Mayfair and the Strand knows—have strong individualities. To pass, for example, from excitable Jewish Stepney—which includes Whitechapel—on the north bank of the Thames, to dour autochthonous Bermondsey, directly opposite it on the south bank, is nearly as striking a transition as crossing the Channel. (The populations of these two boroughs refer to each other as "the people across the water.") Shoreditch is a borderland where the rowdy old urban boroughs along the river shade into the faceless respectability of the boroughs that used to be suburbs. In Defoe's day, the breadth of London was reckoned to be "from the Haberdashers Alms Houses in Newington Butts," on the south, "to the Stone's End in Shoreditch." The stone's end was not half a block from Shoreditch Town Hall.

Forewarned by the cheerful woman on the switchboard, who had also kindly given me directions for reaching the scene of battle, I took the tube in time to get down to Old Street, in East Central London—the nearest stop—by seven. A bleak and silent thoroughfare, Old Street was made all the more discouraging by a filmy London rain that threw a protective glaze over the quarter's grime. From the tube station to the Town Hall is a fair walk, and as I plodded along, it seemed strange to me that anybody would think of putting on a prizefight in this metropolitan equivalent of a Yorkshire moor. But after ten minutes or so I saw an unmistakable municipal building—at once pretentious, inharmonious, and depressing—with vertical human figures covering the steps of a long stairway leading to it. The crowd spilled down across the pavement and over the curb, like people waiting in front of a church to rubber at a bridal party, its components as indifferent to the rain as the English always are. Inquiry revealed that instead of going into the hall, they were waiting for the arrival of Spinks—a small free part of the evening's entertainment, to be savored separately, like the pleasure of standing in a queue for an hour before entering a moving-picture theatre.

I made my way slowly up the steps, careful not to jostle any of the men, which would be "taking a liberty," and they slowly pulled out of my way, one by one, waiting until the last moment but not blocking me absolutely, because that also would be "taking a liberty." Among the common people of this freedom-loving country there is no social offense so heinous as the one they call "taking a liberty," or "making free." Trying to sneak into the middle of a bus queue, seeking to attract a barmaid's attention before she has finished serving another customer, and asking a man for more cigarettes in the course of a year than you proffer him in return are specimen crimes. Pushing in a crowd is an aggravated form. So is offering unsolicited advice, although in a crisis an altruist may dare it. At Sandown races one day, a small man who had been shadowing me so persistently that I thought he might be a pickpocket at length came within my speaking range and said, "Pardon me, sir, I hope you'll excuse me, but your shirt is hanging out, and I thought you'd rather I told you." Nobody else had taken the liberty, and if I hadn't chanced into the path of this bold eccentric, I don't suppose anybody ever would have. He scuttled away crabwise in the crowd, looking horribly ashamed of his inability to control his tongue.

Once, in a share-taxi returning to London from another track, I heard a man say to his companion, "You keep your eye on 'im. 'E's a liberty-tiker, and once you let a liberty-tiker tike liberties with you, 'e'll tread on you."

"Not much bloody fear," the other fellow said.

This cult of respect for the other bloke is diluted in the lower middle class, and at higher social levels it is as weak as Scotch whiskey bottled for home consumption. Britons trying not to seem common can be uncommonly rude.

Pushing open the glass doors of the Town Hall, I headed for the box office—in ordinary life, I suspected, the information booth at which taxpayers are directed to the borough officials they want to see—and there a bulky gentleman, obviously in good humor, told me that the only seat left in the house was one at two guineas ($5.88), in the first row ringside. I said that would suit me fine. "The plice is packed out," he said. "Never saw such a hinterest in a contest." At the moment, I thought this was a dodge to make me buy the two-guinea ticket instead of a cheaper one, but I later discovered that the ticket seller was truthful. The place was sold out.

Near the box office, I saw a number of fellows I had met at other fights. Among them was Phillips—a slender man with a pointed head, an iron-gray mustache, and wavy silvery hair. He introduced me formally to the ticket seller, who turned out to be Grossmith. I remarked that it was too bad Spinks hadn't ridden, since it would have made an unusual sports story, and Grossmith said, "The fellow oo 'ad the 'orse was very keen to 'ave 'im ride, but I couldn't chance it, what with 'aving already sold out the 'ouse."

"He couldn't bear to think of refoonding all that lolly," Phillips said. "Proper bloody Barnum!"

The glass doors now swung wide to admit Spinks and his faction. The fighter, a blond boy with cropped hair like the down on a duckling, had the face of a malevolent cherub. As Phillips had said, he was tall for his weight—perhaps five feet five inches. The members of his entourage had the air of men who surround a big fighter, although Phillips told me that the lad had had only seven bouts since turning professional. Still, he had won the Olympic title in his class at Melbourne. The English in the last twenty years or so have had such a thin time in international competition that a home boy who beats foreigners at anything is halfway to being a national hero. Spinks, who comes from West Ham, a Labour constituency a couple of miles east of Shoreditch, wore a cap, a long overcoat, and a suit that did not look out of place in the neighborhood. An English athlete who wishes to remain popular must avoid outward show of the Big Head—or 'Ead—which is a syndrome nearly as fatal locally as Liberty-Tiking, or Miking Free.

Spinks pressed along toward the dressing rooms, and the fellows who had been standing in front of the Town Hall pushed through the glass doors behind him. They did not wait to see McCready arrive—or maybe he was there already. I had not given much thought to Spinks' opponent, who had been barely mentioned in the thrilling yarn about the two dark horses at Manchester, but now I asked Phillips what sort of boy he was. Phillips said that he was reputed to be tough, and that he had had a good number of bouts as an amateur in Northern Ireland and, like Spinks, seven professional matches.

We all moved up a wide stairway leading to the scene of the evening's entertainment, a large chamber ordinarily devoted to balls, meetings of local associations, big wedding receptions, and amateur theatricals. It had green plaster walls and molded, gilt-painted decorative motifs, and a balcony and gallery—both full up, I noticed as I made my way to my seat, which was just under one of the two corners to be used by the boxers. There were vacant seats in my row, but they were soon filled with prosperously rounded citizens and their wives, who evidently had bought their tickets well in advance. The hall holds only nine hundred, and nine hundred spectators in a space designed to hold just that many set up a closed circuit of emotion that you don't get in a bigger cadre. (A cockfight in a fetid, crowded cellar benefits by the same *ambiance*; a cockfight in a high, well-lighted place like Madison Square Garden would be a bore.) The quality of British professional boxing is so rudimentary that it will not bear exposure to more than nine hundred and ninety-nine persons at a time.

I was flanked and backed by a number of chaps who appeared to know one another well. On my right, one of them was relating to a companion the disappointing course of a fight that he had witnessed at some other arena, unspecified.

" 'Work awye, Joge,' I told 'im," this fellow was saying. " 'Pound awye, Joge,' I says. '*Be* the guvnor.' But Joge wouldn't use that right 'and only in a clinch. 'E insisted on reservin' 'isself." Joge means George, just as a potable typewriter means a portable.

"What price was 'e?" asked the other fellow.

"Five to two on," said Joge's unheeded adviser, meaning that he was the favorite by a margin of two and a half to one.

"Cor," said the second man. "What was 'e reservin' 'isself for?"

"Cost me two fivers, and 'e wuhn't even 'ave a go," said the first. " 'E's a bit of a dodger, I fear—our Joge. Don't fancy 'avin' 'is 'andsome fice bashed."

The program I had just bought for sixpence informed me that the first bout would be a "6 (3 min.) Rounds Feather-weight Contest at 9–4," or nine stone four, or a hundred and thirty pounds. It listed the participants as "Terry Brown, West Ham, former A.B.A. champion, first pro fight," vs. "Billy Alport, Walsall." Brown proved to be one of those snub-nosed, good-looking, eupeptic, round-muscled boys who are so frequently adept at sports and so infrequently exceptional. Alport was spindle-limbed, flat-chested, and heron-necked. He looked unhappy—as if he had to live by writing book reviews at *NewStatesman* rates. The contrast, considered in conjunction with his modest billing and the international practice of giving an amateur champion an easy professional début, made it certain he would fall. For this reason, I was offended when the chap on my right, the chap who had been telling the story about Joge, said, in a loud voice, "Two to one Brown, two to one on!" I wondered if I looked so completely a Hick, as the term is defined in the New Canting Dictionary of 1725: "Any Person of whom any Prey can be made, or Booty taken from; also a silly Country Fellow; a Booby." It developed, however, that Joge's detractor was seeking to make no Prey of me. He was aiming his offer over my head, howitzer-fashion, at my neighbor on my left—a small, nervous, sharp-faced young man, who wore thick-lensed glasses and had a reddish Groucho

Marx mustache, and who was already under the stress of an excitement I did not at once identify. He twisted his hands.

"Three to one, Ginger," a man in the row behind us said to him.

"*Four* to one," the first fellow now bid.

"Mike it five," Ginger said, in the voice of a member of Alcoholics Anonymous backsliding.

"Five it is," the tempter behind Ginger said. " 'Ow many times?"

The boxers, who had been called to the center of the ring for the paternal spiel from the referee, now returned to their corners to await the bell.

"Wite!" Ginger pleaded. "I want eleven to two."

"Eleven it is for two nicker," the layer in back of us said quickly.

I found all this astonishing, since my program stated, in clear black letters, "Betting Strictly Prohibited."

For a couple of rounds, the ex-amateur pummelled the boy who looked like a book reviewer. The latter was hopeless. The referee stopped what the program misleadingly referred to as a contest before there was a knockdown. He was quite right. Ginger handed over two limp pound notes to the man in back of him, and I now recognized Ginger for what he was—an incurable short-end bettor. I wondered how he earned the money that I was sure he sacrificed, night after night, to a vice that can be more expensive than dope. The short-end addict is a man who can never resist a long price, even when he knows it isn't long enough. In the case of the short-endomaniac subjected to daily temptation, the disease takes a galloping, or geometrically progressive, form. When he has lost a hundred short-end bets, he needs a 100–1 shot to bring him even. He never lands the 100–1 shot.

On the motivation of the short-ender there have been many theories. One is that he is too fundamentally greedy to contemplate risking five dollars to win one under any circumstances. Another is that he has a craving for distinction that drives him to accept a thousand losing bets in the hope of being able to say in his old age that he made a killing on Jim Dandy or Harry Truman. A third is that he is an anti-social sadist, eager to rejoice in the discomfiture of the majority. I was, of course, unaware of the etiology of Ginger's case, but he had a peach.

His false friends knew it, and they went for him like piranhas for a swimmer with a nosebleed.

Before the next bout—"Johnny Kidd, Glasgow, KO'd Dick McTaggart in One Round, vs. Roy Hill, Hammersmith, a Tough Two-handed Fighter"—it was pitiful to watch Ginger struggle against his compulsion. Like Spinks, the Dick McTaggart whom Kidd had knocked out had been an Olympic champion. The blurb writer had been able to find nothing comparable to say for Hill; you would hardly expect a fighter to have only one hand. And in addition to the documentary evidence there was the ocular. Kidd looked like a fighter—impassive and confident, with sloping shoulders and loose-moving limbs.

"Five to two on!" the first tormentor cried. "I'll tike Kidd five to one!"

Ginger managed a weak smile and a feeble shrug.

"Six to one on," the fellow behind said as the fighters came out of their corners.

After the Hammersmith boy had remained upright for the first thirty seconds of the bout, Ginger accepted 7–1 against one pound. A moment later, the Glaswegian hit Hammersmith with a left hook to the body, and the two-handed fighter went down.

"Fifteen to two 'e don't finish the round," another of Ginger's undoers said, and the short-ender, leaping at the chance to pull out, cried, "Done!" The Hammersmith boy got up at "nine," and Ginger came to life as a rooter. "Box 'im, 'Ammersmith!" he shouted. "Don't tike no chances!" 'Ammersmith was still shaking his head when Kidd nailed him a second time and knocked him out. Ginger handed over a total of three pounds.

These first two matches were the votive sacrifices with which the games began. In the next one, at eight rounds, one of the contestants was listed as "Dennis Booty, Bethnal Green, Challenges the winner of Lazar & Downes," and the other as "Johnny Woolard, Glasgow, Gave Terry Downes a great fight here." The fighters were middleweights.

The borough of Bethnal Green adjoins Shoreditch on the east, and Booty had a strong faction of supporters in the house. He is a rarity in

contemporary boxing, being a new prospect from a Jewish neighborhood. One of the plangent laments of British promoters (as of their
colleagues in New York and Chicago) is that there are few Jewish fighters nowadays, even though the Jewish fight fan has been a mainstay of
the London ring since the days of Daniel Mendoza and Dutch Sam,
whose exploits filled the years between 1788 and 1814. Mendoza and
Dutch Sam proved that, pound for pound, they had the qualities their
age admired, and they did more to establish the Jew on the English
scene than any other two historical figures.

Booty, a muscular, balding young man of intellectual appearance,
looks more like a college physical-education teacher than a prizefighter. I had seen him fight once before, in another London arena,
and had noted that he is easily dazed by a fairly hard punch, although
he reacts with courage. In the other corner, Woolard, thick-necked
and heavy-muscled, had a well-worn, lustreless fighter's face that reflected more concussion than ambition.

When the sharpshooter on my right said "Four to one Booty, Ginger. 'Ow about it?," I thought that for once Ginger might have a
chance. But Ginger was cautious now, and held out for 9–2.

"All right, you can 'ave it," the other said magnanimously—and
hurriedly—as the bell rang. He sounded like a man buying a ticket for
a train that he will have to run for.

Booty, encouraged by his faction—"Let 'im 'ave it, Dennis. 'E's useless!"—stalked Woolard for ten seconds or so. He then hit him a one-
two—left to the face and right cross to the left ear—in proper
Amateur-Boxing-Association-Playing-Fields-of-Eton style. Woolard
retreated, and Booty hit him with an almost professional left hook to
the body, dropping his shoulder as he did so.

"I doubt whether Woolard styes a round," said the fellow who had
laid the odds.

"I doubt whether *Booty* styes a round!" Ginger cried loyally, although his man hadn't struck a blow.

So it went for the first round and the first two minutes of the second,
with Booty hitting and Woolard receiving or accidentally and narrowly averting. Booty was that uncomfortable object to contem-

plate—a visibly thinking boxer. After every punch, he paused to select the next one, and while he usually made the correct choice, each time he paused, he left Woolard an interval for recuperation. Then, toward the end of the second round, Woolard—although I would have laid 50–1 against the possibility—did some thinking on his own account. Just as the Bethnal Green Thinking Machine, after doing the one-two and, completing a run-through of what he knew about simple addition, was starting "three," Woolard said to himself, "Two and a half," and threw a right hand to the jaw inside the wide left hook.

Down went Booty, and up jumped Ginger, shouting, " 'E's 'ad it! Stop that fight, ref! 'E's lible to suffer a permnent injury!"

But Booty, who is game enough, got up on weak legs at the count of nine, and Woolard lost him in the few remaining seconds of the round. In the third, Booty—piqued and a bit out of his head—went in to slug, and so did Woolard. It was a good round, and Ginger, so solicitous of Booty's health a moment before, now shouted to the ref to "brike 'em" when he thought Booty was hanging on. By the end of the round, the original positions were reestablished. Woolard was again resigned to his fate.

At the end of the fourth round, Woolard's seconds summoned the referee to their corner to have him look at their man's left eye, which was apparently bloodshot. The master of ceremonies, who wore a dinner jacket, then entered the ring and announced, "Woolard retires, hon haccount hof han hinjured heye!"

Ginger, who by my unofficial, unsolicited count was now seven quid down, was painful for a tender bloke like me to regard. He had seen the near-realization of the short-ender's dream, which is all that most short-enders ever get to see. This is harder to bear than fiasco, because the short-ender pre-savors a delicious triumph over the forces of conformity, and when his horse fades out in the last fifty yards, he is overwhelmed by a sense that all organized society is against him.

Ginger was discouraged; for the first time that evening, as the main bout came on, he successfully resisted the predatory blandishments. "Terry Spinks," my program read, "West Ham. Former Amateur Fly-wt champion of Gt. Britain vs. Ivan McCready, Belfast, Ireland's best Fly-wt since Rinty Monaghan."

To cries of "Spinks, two to one on!" and even "Threes, Ginger! Come on, 'ave a go," Ginger replied only with a hurt smile. "They must tike me for a proper mugg," he said to me. "Spinks is terrific."

The jockey-prizefighter—long-legged, long-armed, and short-waisted, but with a wide chest and shoulders—stood a good four inches taller than his opponent, a short, dumpy figure hooded in towels and draped in an oversize maroon bathrobe that touched the floor. Before McCready's handlers peeled these wrappings off him, he suggested a bouncy little peasant woman. When they uncovered him, though, they displayed a big, powerful torso, short, strong arms, and short, thick legs, rounded like birch logs. Present-day Irish boxers, although not remarkable technically, have a tradition of hard physical workouts—running thousands of miles on the road and jumping rope millions of times—and they often win bouts on sheer condition. North and south of the border alike, Ireland is an ascetic country.

The two boys—both had the faces of pre-adolescents—were equal in weight, at eight stone two (114 pounds). Each had the advantages inherent in his particular construction. When the gamblers around me saw the grand shape McCready was in, they offered no more threes on Spinks, and some of them even began taking the odds. " 'E's trined up in grite shipe," one of them said. "Look at the legs on 'im." But Ginger, suspecting a lure, said scornfully, "They always pick 'im midgets"—by " 'im" meaning Spinks.

The Shoreditchers who had put their stakes on McCready immediately became Irish patriots.

"Up, Paddy!" one of them shouted. "You can do 'im!" McCready, who has a wide, flat Celtic face with small features, looked distrustful.

In the first round, McCready showed little to encourage the short-enders. He moved toward Spinks, as a man with arms like his must if he is to land at all, but the Cockney boy circled around him easily, flicking a long left jab in his face and immobilizing the short arms whenever the Ulsterman got near him. Once or twice, in these close encounters, Spinks utilized the leverage of his longer arms to shoot in uppercuts. There was nothing but confidence in his half-sulky, half-joking street boy's face. McCready went in for solemnity and concentration, and occasionally, growing impatient, he brandished his cocked right hand as if he held a stick in it.

At the end of the round, the gamblers were again chirping threes and fours, and Ginger was smiling proudly because he had not been had.

"The Paddy is 'opeless," the fellow on my right said. "The ref is entitled to stop this, yer know. It's no contest."

The second round was much the same, but the Ulster boy's tirelessness and composure made some impression, as did Spinks' evident eagerness to stay out of his way, except for stabbing him with lefts. " 'E respects 'im, you know," a fellow who had taken McCready on the short end of 5–2 said in a faintly hopeful tone, but he refused somebody's proposal that he take fours for another quid. McCready, when he came back to his corner, which was mine, was breathing as normally as if he'd been strolling through a park, and although long years of practice have proved me a complete failure in reading the Irish face, I thought I detected a confident and treacherous expression in his left eye.

Until what will go down in official history as nine seconds before the end of the third round, the match followed the same pattern. At that point, it is possible that the versatile Master Spinks let his thoughts wander to the picking of a long shot for the Autumn Double, which is a parlay on the Cesarewitch and Cambridgeshire Handicaps, the last of the season's important races. At any rate, he got into a position on the rail—as they call the ropes in his other trade—that was hard to back out of, and when McCready threw his ninety-sixth right hand of the evening over the young Arcaro's left, the jockey didn't pull his head back far enough. Down he went, dreamily rolling, so that the following horses would not step on him.

The referee, bending low over Spinks, shouted the numbers into his ear, but the boy was galloping two horses on Newmarket Downs, like the Roman Riders in the circus. Then a bell, inaudible to me, whispered, or so I was later informed, and Spinks' seconds were in the ring, carrying him to his corner, while McCready came dancing back to mine. "Nobody 'eard the bell!" the fellow who had bet on McCready shouted. But it seemed at that moment a quibble; I would have laid odds myself that if Spinks came to in time for the next round he wouldn't last it out. The fellow I felt sorry for was Ginger. "I could 'ave 'ad fours," he moaned miserably.

It is a grand thing to be nineteen years old. In the minute between the third and fourth rounds, Spinks recuperated sufficiently to come out boxing, and within a minute more he was fighting, which he found it necessary to do in order to live. McCready, sure now that he could hurt him, was in after him, Irish-wild, throwing strong lefts to the body as well as rights at the small, artistically swaying head behind the tormenting left hand. The referee gave Spinks a couple of precious seconds by stopping McCready to warn him about roughness, and the crowd howled. But Spinks did the rest himself. In close, he came down on a head-and-shoulder level with the little strong man, pulling his wasp waist back out of the way and pounding from underneath with uppercuts. When McCready smashed into the Cockney's body, he looked as though he might break it, but McCready was not the only boy in good condition. McCready won the round, by a shade, but Spinks survived.

The rest of the fight was a corker, even in the interludes when Spinks went into his jab-and-dance routine, because the crowd now had a sense of the danger he was warding off. I thought it an even thing at the end of the seventh, with McCready much stronger but Spinks doing at least as much damage. Spinks, although he may never be a great fighter, has many of the characteristics that go to make one, and among these is the ability to spurt for a limited period even when tired. The English have a racing term for it; they say that a horse can or cannot "accelerate." And in the last round, McCready, though better fitted to go on for another half hour, simply could not fight as fast as Spinks for three minutes, and Spinks won the decision. He had certainly been out for more than a second after the referee heard the inaudible bell. "'E 'ad plenty of 'elp," the man who had bet on McCready said. Looking at it another way, you might say that a boy who can fight five tough rounds and win after being knocked out is a prime bit of stuff, as the immortal Pierce Egan—the Ibn Khaldun of the London Prize Ring—would have had it.

After the master of ceremonies announced the result, a loud jingling noise began, and continued for a couple of minutes, as a great shower of half-crowns and florins—worth thirty-five cents and twenty-eight cents apiece, respectively—descended upon the ring, shied in from all corners of the hall by spectators appreciative of the battle. This is a custom surviving from a time when fighters met exclusively for side bets, and all the loser got for his work was the silver offering. Nowadays, I am informed, the fighters usually split the silver bonus, if any. On this occasion, though, after the seconds, the referee, the master of ceremonies, and other trustworthy persons had gathered the coins in towels, the m.c. announced that it was the wish of Spinks that all the silver be handed over to McCready. The papers next day called it a generous gesture, and it certainly was a gracious return for a punch in the jaw.

The happiest man in the hall, perhaps, was Ginger. He felt and articulated the inner satisfaction of an Anonymous Alcoholic who has just turned down a Christmas bottle of distinguished ninety-five per cent neutral spirits and five per cent aged bourbon whiskey. "Thought I was a muggins, did they?" he said. "Offerin' me fours on a dead cert like that!" Ginger could take it or leave it alone.

Unfortunately, there was still another fight on the card—"8 (3 min.) Rounds Feather-weight Contest at 9–2. George Carroll, Covent Garden, Has Won 21 out of 22 contests, vs. Johnny Howard, Holloway. KO'd Arthur Devlin." The two featherweights, muscular fellows of a hundred and twenty-eight pounds each, looked like heavies to eyes adjusted to the flyweights of the previous fight.

Covent Garden market porters have been considered good prizering material since 1746, when Richard Mills, known as the Onion Boy, beat a celebrated pugilist named Edward Hunt. I don't suppose that the Shoreditch punters knew about the Onion Boy, but they seemed to think that a fellow who had lost only one fight in twenty-two should do. "Two to one on!" the betting man to the right of me shouted. Somebody cried, "Done!" But Ginger was adamant, strong in his new power to say no.

The bell sounded, and the two toy huskies moved toward each other. There were more cries of "Two to one," and I, watching the fighters now, wondered if Ginger had held out.

I had not long to watch. Howard, the short-end fighter, who looked like a Charles Atlas correspondence-school strong man, hit the Covent Garden porter a single tremendous punch and knocked him stiff in one minute of the first round. It was the first time that evening that a boxer had upset the odds.

The man at my right was embarrassed. "I was bettin' two to one on '*im*—'Oward—that won it," he yelled to the man who had taken his offer. "It's a crossed bet. I didn't mention no boxers' nymes."

I turned to Ginger and asked, "Did you have the winner?" But Ginger had suffered the short-ender's ultimate disaster—to neglect a long shot and see him come in. "I didn't 'ave 'im," he said. "I was greedy. I was witing for five to two."

I bade Ginger good night, but he was too crushed to respond. The last thing I heard him say was "I could of won ite pounds."

October 12, 1957

An Artist
Seeks Himself

Not only rivers and the life cycle have a continuous quality that gives a fellow something to hold on to. The processes of art, too, are self-renewing. Leave a milieu devoted to a certain art form and bang about for a while in a world less single-minded, and when you return you will have a feeling that you have never been away. I had this comforting sensation one morning a week or so ago when I walked into the sitting-and-dining room of Ehsan's training camp for prizefighters, in Chatham Township, near Summit, New Jersey, and found two massive Negro men joyously asleep in front of a television set that was jabbering women's morning programs. Each was comfortably seated in a big armchair, and each had his square, hard hands folded on his hard belly, his right knee crooked over his left, and his left foot planted firmly and sensuously on the rug, like a tree rooted in reality. Outside, the sun lightly grilled a pastoral scene that was difficult to distinguish from others of the genre. Four sheep baaed from a steep hillside behind the Ehsan house, cars murmured along the state highway below, and the synchronized breath of the sleepers sighed like a wind in a grove of pines. They recalled three identical men I had seen sleeping on three identical chairs in a fight camp at Pompton Lakes, also in New Jersey, twenty-one years ago. These sleepers at Ehsan's were not two of that three, of course, but they looked the same, their positions were the same, and they sounded the same. The only major difference was the twenty-one years and the television set. The men at Pompton Lakes had been Joe Louis's sparring partners. The men at Ehsan's were the sparring partners of Floyd Patterson, the current heavyweight champion. All sparring partners have the same idea of a good time.

I turned off the television set, and the silence jarred the sparring partners awake. Still keeping time, they grabbed the arms of the chairs and uncrossed their legs, and when they opened their eyes I said, "Where's Patterson?"

"He asleep," they both said, and went to sleep again.

The sleep of a fighter in training is earned and necessary, and not to be interfered with, so I went outside and found an old wicker chair on the lawn, next to a cistern inhabited by goldfish, and sat down to wait. The fatigue induced by healthy exercise is communicable. The sun was warm, and I fell asleep, too.

By noon, when I awoke, Patterson had come down to the clapboard Ehsan house from his living quarters, behind a gymnasium halfway up the hill. For his age, which is twenty-four, he is an old acquaintance of mine; I first met him seven years ago at the Olympic Games in Helsinki, where, as an amateur of seventeen, he won the championship in the 165-pound class. He is also an anachronism—a good young fighter in an age when there are few. Television, with its giveaways of free boxing shows to sell razor blades, has put out of business the hundreds of small clubs that used to give work to apprentice and journeyman prizefighters, of whom, even at the best of times, few developed into masters. There are, consequently, almost no new adepts, and crafy oldtimers with pre-television educations hang on long past the age at which, in a happier era, they would have acknowledged obsolescence. Patterson at Helsinki, however, had been a *Wunderkind* not to be denied in any era. In the gymnasium there, I often watched him fighting against heavier teammates with a driving earnestness that transcended pugnacity. It was more like the rage of a literary stylist trying to get something down on paper, or of a painter who thinks he has seen a new color. The only thing he had in his head was boxing, and this is a vocation that cannot be altered by developments in the advertising business. The Patterson of the Olympics was a straight stick of a boy, exactly six feet tall, who had only the shoulders and arms of a truly big man. At Ehsan's, I could see that he had become a genuine heavyweight, which is, by definition, a man who can't get under 175 pounds, the upper limit for light heavyweights, without cutting off his right leg. (Technicians never say the left leg.) But, though his chest had widened and his rib cage deepened, he was still far from being a big heavyweight, like Louis, or a squatty Atlas, like Rocky Marciano, to mention two eminent predecessors. His long, dark face, with a long, straight nose turned up at the end, was diffident—half-humorously apologetic, as always. The expression befits the artist whose accomplishments have never measured up to his own opinion of his abilities. (This includes all artists worth a damn.) "I have never been more than seventy per cent of myself," he once said. "My ambition is to be a hundred per cent."

"How many per cent of yourself are you this morning?" I asked him now, and he answered, without hesitation, "About fifty-five, or maybe between fifty-five and sixty."

"That ought to be plenty," I said, because the fellow he was training to fight, a British heavyweight named Brian London, was not reputed to be much. The London fight, in fact, was to be merely the climax of his training for the fight after that—against a Swede named Ingemar Johansson, who was supposed to be tougher. Patterson would fight London in Indianapolis on May 1st, and then Johansson in New York on June 25th. It is not conventional for a manager to say before a fight that it is merely a job of piano-tuning for the real concert. The old promotional formula is to describe each new opponent as a man-eating menace. However, Constantine (Cus) D'Amato, Patterson's manager, not only had described the Indianapolis match as a tune-up but had arranged for London to come over and was guaranteeing his remuneration. Patterson was to get seventy-five thousand dollars and the television fee, which would amount to two hundred thousand dollars more. Out of this money, D'Amato would pay London sixty thousand dollars and expenses.

In most fighters, such a promise of a romp would have induced a mood of levity, but the champion said, "I never look more than one fight ahead. All I hope is that he helps me find my form."

I asked Patterson how much he weighed, and he said between 182 and 185. I asked him how low he could go without weakening himself, and he said 180. That made him the lightest heavyweight champion since Tommy Burns, who lost the title to Jack Johnson in 1908.

I recalled happily that the last time I had spoken to Patterson, in 1954, he had been at this same Ehsan's, where he was training for a little fight at a club in Brooklyn, now defunct. The star boarder at Ehsan's that year was Archie Moore, then and still the light-heavyweight champion, after an interim venture into the heavyweight division. Moore is an aging but buoyant virtuoso who in 1954 was thirty-seven years old but entering on a Late Silver Age. He was training for a defense of his championship. When Moore sparred, Patterson looked at him with the eye of a young ballerina watching Ulanova. Two years later, when Moore was thirty-nine and Patterson twenty-one, Patterson beat him for the heavyweight title, which in the meantime had been vacated by Rocky Marciano. Now I asked Patterson if he had learned how to beat Moore by studying him at Ehsan's.

"I wasn't watching him with any idea I could be good enough to fight him but with an idea to learn something," the champion said. "I admired him—he was my idol." But later, he said, after they were matched, Moore had offended him by speaking of him as a kid and saying that he would knock him out quickly. "I didn't like the way he talked about me before we fought in Chicago. I resented it, until he did it so much that the thought came to me: He isn't talking to me, and he isn't talking to the public. He's talking to himself, because he knows I can beat him. Then I wasn't angry any more."

In 1956, Moore was the last good pre-television heavyweight left in action. When Patterson's rising arc intersected Moore's descending one, Patterson was in the position of a Paderewski in a world short of pianos, or of a Delacroix who has run out of canvas. There was nobody left to fight whom he could prove anything by beating. Like any other artist in a sterile period, he had nobody to excel but himself, and he has been setting himself a hard pace ever since.

The champion and I settled into a prolonged silence, abetted by the two sparring partners, who had meanwhile introduced themselves as Ike Thomas, out of Indianapolis, the city where Patterson was going to meet London, and Julio Mederos, a Cuban. Both were much bigger men than Patterson, and Mederos had once knocked out Roland La Starza, a fading headliner. Thomas had been on the road with Patterson in the morning; they had run four and a half miles. Mederos, a beefy type, said that he had stayed in bed until ten. "I don't want to go overtrained," he said. He looked to be in no danger. After the run, all had slept, and now, as soon as Dan Florio, Patterson's trainer, returned from an errand in Summit, they were going to box. Patterson's silences are cordial. They are based not on any lack of ideas but on despair of being able to communicate them to a dilettante. They are all about boxing.

Florio, a small, cheerful white man from the west end of Greenwich Village, arrived and got the conversation going again. He has a gift for small talk that Patterson and I both lack, and a lot of it is about old-time fights. Florio is an expert at patching fighters' cuts and analyzing their errors between rounds; he has been with Patterson since the prodigy turned professional after the Olympic Games. Until then, Cus D'Amato, Patterson's discoverer, had trained him. When Patterson turned pro, D'Amato had to divert most of his own energies into getting his man matches with opponents he could learn from and at the same time beat. After Patterson became a star, D'Amato's managerial duties grew even more onerous, since he sees the world as a series of traps set for his champion by rivals in the boxing business. Florio therefore stays in camp with Patterson while D'Amato runs his counter-conspiracy agency from an office on West Fifty-third Street.

The trainer got me up some bacon and eggs, and asked Patterson if he wanted to eat, too. Patterson said no—he wanted to work early that afternoon, so he would have a chance to walk into Summit, about five miles, while the sun was still high. That meant that the sparring partners couldn't eat, either, until he had finished knocking them about. All this made everybody keen to get the work over with, and we adjourned to the gymnasium as soon as I had finished. Louis and Marciano usually trained at a roadhouse, or on the grounds of a summer hotel. They boxed at a regular, advertised hour, to draw as many paying customers as possible. Ehsan's is a quiet place, without a bar and without noncombatant lodgers. The ring and the gym are good, and a man has a chance to set his schedule by his moods. Three New York sportswriters arrived just as the champion was about to begin work. The four of us had virtually a private showing.

When I first saw Patterson at Helsinki, his basic style had appeared crude to me—almost as if he had thought it up for himself after a series of street fights. There was, however, a method in it. It was what his manager calls the D'Amato "system." Patterson came to D'Amato's grim little gym—over a dance hall on East Fourteenth Street—when he was fourteen, and learned his doctrine there. At Helsinki, Patterson would begin from a crouch, with a glove at each side of his head and elbows pulled in tight to his body, and then would start to wing punches, being as likely to lead with a right as with a left. He did not finish a man with a single punch, but all his blows hurt, and after throwing one he was usually in a position to throw a series. Sometimes, when he missed, he was badly off balance, but his reflexes were so fast that he recovered before the fellow he was boxing could take advantage of his opportunity. Since the system fighter has both hands equally advanced, he has to keep his feet on a nearly horizontal line, and there is no division of labor between the hands, as in the conventional standup stance. As boxing is usually taught, the left foot and hand are forward; the learner uses the left to annoy his opponent and the right to finish him. The system fighter can hit with equal speed and force from left and right, but he can't hit *as* fast with his left or *as* hard with his right as he could if he had them in the conventional positions. His footwork appears awkward, like that of a man going forward carrying a tray of dishes. What he has in compensation is the constant protection afforded by his "shell." The gloves protect his head from the hardest blows—the hooks and crosses—that move in lat-

erally; the forearms protect his body; and the tight elbows keep out uppercuts. All he has to worry about, theoretically, are the straight
punches, and he "slips" those by moving his head from side to side.
(This is not, however, an easy trick, or one to be attempted without
20-20 vision.) D'Amato thought up this system in his gym, where he
used to sleep in his pre-Patterson days. But while he is an original tactician, he nevertheless fell on something that had already occurred to
Daniel Mendoza, a London prize-ring champion and leading instructor of the late eighteenth century. These rediscoveries are common
among philosophers; the human mind moves in a circle around its
eternal problems.

Whether the system helps Patterson, as D'Amato believes, or
blocks his full artistic development, as his detractors maintain, it is his
basic style, a thing that neither a writer nor a boxer can change without risking everything. It is also a style peculiarly well adapted to a
boxer with fast reflexes who has to fight heavier men. He may have to
hit them a hundred times to win, instead of a beautiful once, but in
doing so he need not expose himself often. Patterson is no slave to the
system now—he boxes a lot "looser" than in the Olympic days, he
says, and improvises as he goes along—but it is still his idiom. What
usually wins fights is not so much style as content.

At Ehsan's that afternoon, Patterson worked three fast rounds
against the sparring partners—one with Mederos and two with
Thomas—and looked diabolically sharp. There are old-timers who
say that he has the fastest hands of any heavyweight ever. And although, as a heavyweight, he had no weight limit to make, he worked
in bulky, full-length sweat clothes, to get down even lighter. Each of
the sparring partners outweighed him by thirty pounds—as he knew
London would—so speed had to be his weapon in attack and defense.
When he had finished and showered, he drank two eggs beaten up in a
glass of orange juice, and went off for his walk.

The sportswriters offered me a ride back to town in their automobile, and on the way in we discussed the dynastic struggles that come
with the rise of every important new champion. The promoter who
controls a champion can set the terms on which he will allow chal-

lengers to meet him, binding them to contracts for return bouts if they win. The late Tex Rickard had a hegemony in New York boxing after the First World War because he had Dempsey, who lasted as champion for seven years. After Dempsey, who lost in 1926, and Rickard, who died in 1929, there was an interregnum of insignificant promoters, like the Anglo-Saxon kings, who tried to establish themselves on the backs of ephemeral champions. (There were five champions in eight years.) Then a ticket broker, the late Mike Jacobs, came along with Louis, whose reign spanned twelve years and founded the fortunes of the International Boxing Club. Since Patterson's rise, D'Amato has been trying to dislodge the I.B.C., and the subsequent involvements have been of Byzantine complexity, enlisting not only D'Amato and his foes but the television networks and *their* rival, closed-circuit television. All this interests sportswriters, but it should be on the financial page. It is extraneous to art.

That is D'Amato's view, too, when he speaks in his capacity as a teacher and admirer. (When he speaks as a captain of finance, it is another matter.) "They knock Patterson's brains out because they don't like me," he says, speaking of the sportswriters, who, he professes to believe, have all been set against him by his business foes. (His indictment includes some of the most honest fellows in the world.) "They are like somebody who looks at a work of art and don't notice it. Patterson beats a fellow, and they say whoever it may be is a bum. Maybe he is a bum, but they ought to say he is a bum that was ranked the leading contender until Patterson made him *look* like a bum." D'Amato is a middle-sized man of fifty or so, with a round head topped by white hair, which he wears close-cropped. He carries his head cocked argumentatively to one side, as if ready to slip a punch, and moves with brittle alacrity, like the straight man among the Fratellini clowns. His pale face and dark eyes add to the Fratellini effect. D'Amato talks as much as Patterson doesn't, and does all his protégé's boasting for him. His admiration is complete, and not confined to boxing. "Patterson is incorruptible," he once said to me. "I am incorruptible, too, but if I ever felt like it, I would think of him and then I couldn't consider it." Another time, talking about the Moore fight, he said, "I analyzed the situation, and Floyd agreed with everything I mentioned. Probably he had thought of it first, but he would not want me to feel I wasn't needed." At one stage of the negotiations for the London match, D'Amato told me, he feared that the National Broadcasting Company, balefully influenced, in his view, by the I.B.C., would withdraw the offer on which he had based his guarantee to the Englishman. (His fears are continual.) "Do you know what Patterson said to me?" he asked. "He said, 'Cus, can you get enough money together to pay London's end?' I said I thought I could get most of it out of the gate, and borrow the rest. Floyd said, 'If you can get that up, I'll fight for nothing.' I could have cried."

I called D'Amato on the telephone after I got back from Ehsan's, and asked him when he was going to take his work of art to Indianapolis. He said that they would depart in two days, and invited me to the information booth on the main concourse at Grand Central to see them off. When I arrived on the evening of the evacuation, D'Amato was already there, looking statesmanlike in a homburg and dark suit; over his arm he carried a gabardine topcoat with a red lining. He waved at me cheerily, like George Washington about to step into the rowboat. "There were a lot of people said this fight would never come off," he said. "But here we are."

With him was his public-relations officer, Sam Taub, a former fight reporter who has been writing about boxing for at least fifty years. In the days before television, Taub used to describe fights via radio, and with such excitement in his voice that listeners would frequently tune the fight out for a couple of rounds, to forestall thromboses. Taub still talks that way, and when he saw me, he urgently said, "You-may-think-I'm-getting-old-and-senilly-but-this-kid-will-be-the-greatest-champion-who-ever-lived-greater-than-Dempsey." A lot of the dullest boxers who ever lived are remembered as thrilling performers because of Taub's voice.

Ike Thomas, the sparring partner, was also at the station, with a slightly older colored man at least twice his weight, whom he introduced as his manager. The manager had just come to see him off. In camp, the Patterson sparring partners get twenty dollars a day and found, and it is a great load off a manager's mind not to have to feed a fighter while he seeks work for him. "If I would have a spirit of defeatism, I could get a match for this boy," the manager said, implying that there were matchmakers who would give Thomas a fight if he would consent to sacrifice his professional integrity. "But he is not the kind of boy who want that." A moment later, they began talking about a cop in Harlem they knew who had been arrested for taking a bribe, and I heard the manager say, "He was in a predicament that eighty per cent of people would be in the same predicament if they got caught."

Patterson was next to arrive—dark, discreet, and inconspicuous. Only one person in the station, apparently, recognized him—a young mulatto woman with a small boy by her side. She dropped the boy's hand and took a ball-point pen and an envelope from her handbag. "You Floyd Patterson?" she asked the champion. He nodded, and gave her his autograph. In the hurrying crowd, he looked even smaller than he did in the center of the ring; the expensive black suit he wore minimized the big shoulders.

When he saw that he had time to spare, he went off to a telephone booth to call his wife, who lives in Rockville Centre, and tell her that he had arrived safely at the station. Dan Florio, the trainer, looking like a tweeded Stamford commuter, was the next to get there, and a few minutes later an associate of D'Amato's—a manager named Charlie Black—and his wife, both smiling and middle-aged, joined the party. Patterson returned from the telephone booth. D'Amato, with a wave of his arm, summoned redcaps, who loaded the suitcases on dollies, and the expedition moved off, not a diamond ring or a cauliflower ear in the lot to mark their identity, and no newspaper photographer to advertise it. Times have changed since John L. Sullivan's was the best-known face in America.

Ten days after this affecting parting, I went out to Indianapolis myself. Five years ago, I wrote, apropos of one of Patterson's earlier professional bouts, "The purpose of going to a fight isn't always to see a close contest. A great many close fights are hardly worth looking at, while the development of an interesting performer is always an attraction; Native Dancer and Man o' War were drawing cards when they were 1–

100 to win." Joe Louis, when he was in form as champion, was in the habit of fighting bargain-basement pugilistic remnants all over the country—a practice labelled by the sportswriters "the Bum-of-the-Month Club." Nobody expected a bum to beat him, but profitable crowds turned out to see what Louis would do to the bum. I am fully cognizant of the decadence of the prize ring, and when I returned to this country a year or so ago after a long stay in the other hemisphere, I tried to drop it from my field of interests. But as I grow older, I am aware of a need for cultural continuity in my life, and in the train on the way out to Indianapolis, I felt the elation of a man who has said a lot of hard things about a woman and is now on his way to make up.

Indianapolis is a city of muted appeal, built around two large monuments to the wartime dead, which set the urban tone, but it is friendly and without side. It is in the catfish belt of American culture, a wide but varying longitudinal zone that wanders shiftlessly from the Gulf of Mexico to the Great Lakes, including places like Little Rock, Arkansas, and Springfield, Illinois, and then ducking Chicago to head east into Indiana. The people are marked by a friendliness I attribute to the historical circumstance that in the westward march of empire the most pushing emigrants either stopped in Ohio to found industries or pressed on to Chicago to found stockyards. Those who stayed in the middle to fish for cats left more amiable descendants.

When I had checked in at the Hotel Claypool, a glory of another age, I established contact with Taub and D'Amato by telephone. D'Amato said Patterson had finished his work for the fight and was out making a series of visits to schools, boosting sportsmanship and education. He invited me to have dinner with Patterson at the training camp that evening. The camp was in the Coliseum of the State Fairgrounds, D'Amato said, where Patterson and London were to fight two nights later. The Coliseum seats thirteen thousand five hundred spectators and is used at other times for cattle shows. The champion and his faction were sleeping and eating there while he trained. "There's a horse-trotting track out here, because it's the Fairgrounds," D'Amato went on, "and Floyd runs on it every morning."

I made the date and then went out into the special migratory society that gathers in every city where there is a championship fight—the out-of-town "promoters," some of whom haven't put on a boxing show since television struck; the managers looking for a good fighter to replace one they lost in 1923; the former fighters looking for a free ticket and a handout; the boxing writers from provincial newspapers, who seldom get an opportunity to leave home. The top caste among these nomads consists of the syndicated columnists, like Red Smith and Jimmy Cannon, whose fame exceeds local circulation limits. There are also, nowadays, a great many television characters, who don't look or talk like fight people at all but represent the chief source of money, like the swells who put up the stakes for the bare-knuckle Heroes long ago. They lend a new, Madison Avenue flavor to the old mixture. The Hoosier Boxing Club, which was promoting the fight, had hired a suite for the refreshment of the press on the same floor of the Claypool that the room clerk had chanced to assign me. I had only to walk to the bar to find out who was in town. Saddest of the visitors were ten British newspapermen, most of whom I knew. They were in Indianapolis because the newspaper business in the United Kingdom is still competitive. Not one of them gave London a chance to win, but if he did happen to pull it off—and nothing is impossible in the ring, since any heavyweight is theoretically capable of knocking out any other heavyweight if fist and jaw should make the right conjunction—none of the great national papers could afford not to have a detailed and personalized account of the unique event. The British, therefore, were present as insurance. In all probability, they would have the dismal duty of reporting only the annihilation of their compatriot. My London friends said they found Indianapolis on a par with Manchester on a Sunday. The boxer London would take a proper hiding, they all agreed; none of them were interested in London's role in Patterson's project of increasing the percentage of himself that he would get to be. This was a concern exclusive to Patterson.

At seven, I engaged a taxi for the trip out to the Coliseum. As a companion I had Jimmy Cannon, the Hearst sports columnist, who was an old depression-era colleague of mine in a newspaper sweatshop downtown. He is a vehement fellow, who worries over his writing the way

Patterson worries over his boxing; they have the same point of view. We arrived to find the Coliseum dark except at a single door. A watchman admitted us to the catacombs, where D'Amato, apprised of our approach by cries that echoed in the hollow corridors, came to greet us and lead us to the faction's living quarters—a string of casemates set in the Coliseum's outer wall, in back of the bleachers. The approach had an eerie suggestion of Visitors' Day at Sing Sing; the rooms, designed for the attendants of show cattle, each contained an iron bedstead and a chair. Sweat clothes, punching bags, skip ropes, and boxing gloves hung from pegs in the walls of tasteful concrete blocks. Only one room had a telephone—Patterson's, so he could talk to his wife whenever he wanted to. Amid this Trappist simplicity, the champion was as happy as Mozart with the beginnings of a new tune.

"How are you coming along?" Cannon asked him after an exchange of greetings.

"I'm a little bit off," Patterson said, "but I'm hopeful. If he gives me a good fight, I'll be sixty per cent of me. Then I'll take five days off, and before I drop under fifty-eight I'll go right back into hard training. The time to catch it is when you come right off a fight. Like when I started to train back in November—I was no more than forty per cent of me. Starting at fifty-eight, I might hit seventy-five or eighty for Johansson. Once I find my whole self, I'll be satisfied."

Last August, Patterson fought a challenger named Roy Harris, an inept fellow from Cut 'n' Shoot, Texas, who had to be publicized as a kind of Li'l Abner, because there was nothing in his record to suggest that he could whip the *Wunderkind*. Patterson dispatched him in twelve rounds—comfortably but without elegance. I saw the fight on theatre television, and ascribed most of the tedium to Harris, an awkward victim with few assets. After the fight, though, Patterson had a sense of inadequacy. "I had lost the feeling," he said. "I was so disappointed that I felt if I could give somebody else the championship just temporarily, I would—a champion hadn't ought to be so off. I thought, I'll just take it back whenever I find myself. But a champion can't give up like that. I couldn't put anything together. There he was, not hitting me, and he's a target, and I missed about a thousand punches. I could see his chest here and his belly there, and I think to hit him, but before I do, I have another target. But I miss that, too. Of course, when you think before you hit, you *know* you're going to miss, because you got to hit quicker than you can think. It must come from inside. Right then, I said to Cus he's got to get me more fights. That was August, and I went into training the first of November."

"Is is true that you said you'd take this fight for nothing?" I asked him.

"Well, I meant if I couldn't get anything out of it, I would," he said. "Fighting for nothing I could lose my championship and lose money, but by not fighting I'm losing myself."

Dan Florio suggested that we eat dinner before the cook burned the steaks. Trainers like their principals to eat at regular hours, and in achieving this they are aided by their own insides, which in the course of time become gastronomic chronometers. We all went down from the cell block to the Coliseum cafeteria, which serves the spectators at a cattle show. Only the members of the fight camp were using it now. A colored woman cook put the food on the cafeteria counter, and we served ourselves. This had some of the illicit charm of swiping cafeteria food and paying no check, even for seconds and thirds. Patterson, Florio, the big Cuban Mederos, and a couple of new additions to the faction—white men who acted as drivers, errand runners, and perhaps bodyguards—constituted the mess. D'Amato had left for a date to appear on a television program boosting the ticket sale. Ike Thomas, the other sparring partner, had gone out to look around his home town, which he hadn't seen for years. He had reknit old relationships quickly, though, and had telephoned in to say that he was on some street corner broke, and to ask instructions. Florio advised him to take a taxi, and borrow money to pay the driver after he got to the Coliseum.

Patterson ate a fair-sized steak—about a pound—and a baked potato and peas and two portions of a good salad with a dressing of oil and vinegar and onions. The menu was the same for everybody, but you could have as many steaks as you wanted, a privilege Mederos appreciated. When we had eaten, we got back to boxing, and Patterson said,

"The reason I need this fight now, before Johansson, is that outside— in the ring—is not the same as in the gym. Usually I am better outside than in the gym, so when I was training for Harris, even though I knew I was off in the gym, I thought it would be better when I got fighting outside. There is more incentive outside, because all the people have come to watch you, and you feel bad if you don't do good. But I did even worse against Harris than in the gym, so I knew I never can believe my gym form any more."

"Maybe you were sick," I said.

Patterson said hastily, "That's just excuses. Like fellows who say they have colds, or stiff legs, or they ate something. If I should lose with a cold sometime, it won't be because I have a cold."

It was hard to remember that he had knocked Harris out, and that Harris had barely hit him a punch. He sounded as if *he* had been knocked out.

"And when did you begin to feel you were getting your form back?" I asked.

"Not for two and a half months," Patterson said. "It seemed I was getting worse. Then one day I led a left jab at a fast man that had been getting away from them. I hit him so square that I said to myself, 'That hand is travelling fast.' From then on, I've been coming along." He sighed. "I used to feel so bad that I would dream about it," he said. "And in my dreams I would make a good move. I would wake up trying to remember it, and I'd run to the bathroom to try it out in front of the mirror—fix it in my mind. I'd try it out, and it didn't make any sense except in a dream."

"Floyd," I said, "you will never get to be a hundred per cent of your-self, because by the time you get to be what you now think is one hundred per cent, you'll think it's only eighty per cent, or seventy per cent. Only a bum ever thinks he is a hundred per cent."

Cannon said, "But then he's a hundred-per-cent bum."

With this intended consolation, we quit the champion.

The next afternoon—since a day and a night were to intervene be-fore Patterson's workout "outside"—I went over to a kind of suburban recreation center where Brian London was living and training. This time, I went with Tom Phillips, of the London *Daily Herald*, the Labour Party paper, which has a circulation of a million six hundred thousand—moderate for England but colossal over here. Phillips is a good gray prophet of the sports world, always making the most in print of being a plain fellow and a Geordie, or native of County Durham, in the extreme northeast of England, although he now lives in Guildford, an upper-class town in the effete south. I have known him, too, since Helsinki; he is an optimist, as a British boxing writer needs to be. The line that he has made his own in sporting journalism is "I'll bet my shirt," but he was keeping it on his back this time.

"Brian is a good lad," he said, "but not of international class. They made him favorite for his last fight at home, against a man who has the wrong style for him, and when he lost, most of the writers talked as if he were completely useless. He isn't that; he's a kind of Rocky Marciano without a punch. He'll stand up to a deal of punishment."

When we got to London's camp, he was sitting on the edge of a rubbing table and making a final pre-battle statement to those reporters who had thought it worth their while to attend. He was a beefy, pale young man with a long jaw and a tremendous chin—the most prominent I remember on any heavyweight since Fred Fulton, the Rochester (Minnesota) Plasterer.

"Frankly, do you think you have a chance of winning?" one of the Americans asked him.

"Well, I might have an exceptionally good night," London said. "You never know, do you?"

After the others had cleared away, Phillips approached him and said, in an impressive tone, "Brian, I want you to know that I have picked you—to go the whole fifteen rounds." A man less pale than London would have blanched.

London is the same age as Patterson. His wife, a rosy-cheeked girl, and his mother, a handsome woman in her forties, had flown in that morning for the fight. His father, a former British heavyweight champion, and his brother Jack had been with him all during his American stay, but his father was not there that day; an American friend had taken him fishing. Phillips invited the Londons and me to tea in a diner across the highway—the Chicken Shack—where the fighter and his faction had had their training table since their arrival. None of the talk there was about the fight. London appeared willing to forget about it, and the women talked about the heat, comparing it to what they had left in Blackpool, on the coast on Lancashire; about the tea, which the London men had taught the Chicken Shack cook to brew shocking strong; and about their plane journey. Nothing was said, either, about London's guaranteed sixty thousand dollars, of which twenty-seven thousand would go in American income tax, but they must all have been thinking of it with some satisfaction. It was the biggest purse Brian had ever earned—more than he had made in twenty-six fights over there. Nick Baffi, London's American trainer, confided that he had not attempted to teach him a new style—there wasn't time—but had simply tried to get him into physical condition and keep him cheerful. Baffi, a thin Brooklynite, said, "The problem was to adjust his mentality."

The fight next night was not much of a contest, but it was, after all, for the heavyweight championship of the world—the first championship fight ever held in Indiana—and it was more protracted than most of the audience had expected. London weighed 208 pounds to Patterson's 182¼. The Swede Johansson, who had flown out from New York, was introduced from the ring, and shook hands with both men. Then he took pictures of them. The Coliseum was more than two-thirds full; the Indiana promoter announced after the bout that 10,088 persons had attended. The Governor of Indiana was there, but not one former heavyweight champion put in an appearance to be introduced from the ring—a mark of the inconsequence of the occasion. Patterson, concentrating, had the air of a surgeon who has paid for a cadaver and is determined to get his money's worth dissecting it.

When the bell rang for the first round, London moved forward in what looked like a burlesque of Patterson's guard—his great chin buried on his breastbone, and his hands high in front of his face to protect it. His plan of battle, however, apparently included no offensive measures, for as he advanced he did not hit. On his face there was the expression of a man walking into the water at Blackpool to see if it is tolerable or too cold to bear. His great white rib cage was exposed behind his cramped elbows. Patterson hit him a couple of swinging blows, one on each side, and the outline of the ribs began to glow red through the skin; a few more, and London pulled his elbows back to protect them. Patterson then hit him a short right to the jaw, and I saw a surprised look on London's face, as on that of a man who finds the water nearly ice. He was used to being hit, but not that hard. I think that punch ended any dream he might have had of winning, but he was game, in a fatalistic way. Patterson went at him so briskly in the first round that I was surprised when the Englishman not only was on his feet at its end but waved his right arm at Patterson in dismissal—a sort of truncated bon voyage.

In the second, Patterson, either recalling for himself or reminded by D'Amato that he wanted a long workout rather than a quick finish, took things easier, and in the third London showed a bit of enterprise, as though he would have liked to knock Patterson about if he could only get the hang of it. After that, Patterson switched his attack almost wholly to the body, banging ribs and belly until London's arms came down helplessly. After about the fifth round, the Englishman couldn't have punched effectively even if he had known how. The snap was out of his arms. By punching mostly for the body, instead of the Englishman's big, bony head, Patterson, incidentally, was guarding his own hands from any injury that might have forced him to call off the more important fight in June. It was also an interesting tactical exercise, because Johansson is a fighter who stands straight, with what is supposed to be a thunderous right fist cocked under his chin. That kind of body-punching can disable any right hand in a few rounds.

After a while, I thought Patterson began to show distaste for what he was doing. He had solved all there was to solve about London and had illustrated the safe way to beat him; now he was bored. He couldn't let him stay, though, or the papers would cry "Fake!" But London, determined to obliterate past taunts about British heavyweights' courage, stayed on his feet and continued to move in—but on feet so awkwardly placed that he couldn't have caught anybody. Patterson—now moving away from him, now letting him come close—banged the white body at will. The crowd cheered for London, because he was the underdog and because he was so game. Some people may even have thought that he occasionally hit Patterson; when you are close to the ring, as I was, it is hard to interpret the crowd's yells, because you don't know what they think they're seeing. A few seconds before the end of the tenth round, London, his arms hanging heavy, lurched and half turned from the executant, helpless. Patterson hit him with a left and a right to the head, and when London dropped to one knee, Patterson put an open hand on his head in a strange gesture of mercy. The referee waved him aside, and had counted to five when the bell rang, ending the round.

That London should come out for the eleventh was more than anybody had the right to ask, but he did. Fifty-one seconds after it opened, Patterson, with a flurry of blows, drove him across the ring toward the side where I sat. The last punch sent London staggering back toward me and Arthur Daley, of the *Times*, my neighbor. From the way London landed—on left hip and shoulder—it was plain that a left had sent him down, and the crash of the fall, knocking the wind out of his body, finished him. He lay with his left cheek against the canvas. I thought he might be seriously injured, and so did Patterson, who came bounding over to him as soon as the referee had finished counting. That kind of beating takes more out of a man than a one-punch knockout or a spectacular cut. But in a few seconds London could stand, and by the time he had had his shower after the fight, he was fit. The thirty-three thousand dollars should come in handy in Blackpool.

I shared a taxi back to town with a couple of native sons, who said they thought their fellow-citizens had been well satisfied with their first championship fight. Later that night, I was in the coffee shop of the Claypool (the bar closes at twelve) when Dan Florio, who had been in Patterson's corner, came in. I asked him if the artist had hurt a hand, and he said no, thank God. He added that Patterson had looked to him about sixty-six and two-thirds per cent.

May 23, 1959

A Reproach
to Skeptics

Ibn Khaldun, the immortal Tunisian historian, says that events often
contradict the universal idea to which one would like them to conform, that analogies are inexact, and that experience is deceptive.
This is particularly true of events of the prize ring, but, like a boxer deaf
to sound advice from his corner, I sometimes fail to heed the precepts
of the most astute of pedagogues. Because of this failure, I arrived at
the press gate of the Yankee Stadium at approximately half past eight
on the evening of June 26th with an annoying feeling that I had been
a fool to come at all. A warm rain, falling harder every minute, made
it seem certain that the fight for the world heavyweight championship
between Floyd Patterson, the champion, and Ingemar Johansson, of
Sweden, would be postponed for the second night running. The rain,
a mere mizzle when I left a restaurant in midtown, had got heavier at
each red light on my taxi's course north, and by the time I got to the
Stadium, it looked a good bet to pour all night. Boxing audiences in
this country traditionally refuse to be drenched, and promoters coddle
them; English fans, a hardier breed, simply set out equipped with um-
brellas. Nevertheless, since the fight had not been called, I stayed.

The rain was about the temperature of a wet tea bag at the bottom of a cup, and so fine that Father Divine might have called it tangibilized humidity. My raincoat repelled it but increased the precipitation of sweat inside. After alternately putting on and discarding the garment a few times, I was soaked through, and the origin of the moisture made no difference; the sensation everywhere was of total immersion in spilled soup that smelled of wet wool. It was like a night in Paramaribo. Under the bleacher stands, where all of us early arrivals huddled, there was less rain but more heat; out in the open there was less heat but more rain. More basic to my feeling of being a fool, however, was my conviction that the fight itself would not be worth the present discomfort. I considered Patterson the only good heavyweight in active practice, although a small one. (He had weighed in at only 182 pounds.) The Swede, I thought, would be not even *smörgåsbord* for him but *ost och sill*, or cheese and herring, the limited preprandial selection you get at a Scandinavian restaurant for less than the full *smörgåsbord* price. This was my conviction even though I knew Johansson to be considerably bigger than Patterson—fourteen pounds heavier, to be exact. There is an old saw that a good big man can always beat a good little man, but I did not think Johansson was good.

All the acquaintances I met under the stands—newspapermen and boxing types—were of the same opinion, although not all of them admired Patterson equally. Some thought, as I did, that he was a good fighter in an age of mediocrities; others considered him a mediocrity in an age of incompetents. All were impatient for Mr. William Rosensohn, the promoter, to declare the evening's entertainment on or off, so they could go about their business, but I heard none say that he expected to witness a memorable contest. In this we were like the crowds who went down to the shires from London long ago in full confidence that they would see Hickman the Gasman beat Neat the Butcher, or see Dutch Sam the Jew annihilate Nosworthy the Baker—or like the sports who went down to New Orleans from New York in 1892 to see John L. Sullivan pulverize Jim Corbett. Hickman was butchered and Sam well baked, and if American history is properly taught in the schools, everybody knows what happened to Sullivan. We were like that wise money of old in another respect, too: we were destined to be wrong. The only uninvolved observer I can truthfully say I heard pick Johansson before the fight was a physician totally unacquainted with boxing, who remarked after reading the newspaper account of the fighters' pre-match medical examinations that he preferred Johansson's pulse rate. He asked me where he could get down a small hunch bet at the odds quoted in the newspapers, 6–1 against, but I dissuaded him from throwing his money away.

This expert unanimity persisted despite Johansson's repeated assurances that he would knock the champion out. Such mass incredulity demands some explanation, and I think Ibn Khaldun hit upon it. I had begun to form my own idea about the two men on a summer night in Helsinki in 1952, when I first saw both perform publicly, in the finals of the Olympic boxing championships. In the 165-pound class, Patterson (who could then make that weight with ease) knocked out a Rumanian boxer with such dispatch that he could not, as of last month, remember what the fellow looked like. My estimate of Patterson's promise, though, was based not on his public showing but on his workouts with heavier members of the United States team. In practice, he had held his own, and a bit better, with the American heavyweight entry, Ed Sanders, an Apollo who weighed 220 pounds. Sanders, six feet four inches tall, was a well-made man, but he was a dilettante boxer. He played football, baseball, and basketball at a Western college, threw the javelin, and ran anchor on the mile-relay team, and he was more interested in all of them than in boxing. In the heavyweight final, Johansson, then nineteen, was his opponent. It was an extraordinary show. Sanders would move forward and Johansson back, Sanders forward and Johansson back again, circling clockwise as he retreated. The Finnish crowd, with a neighborly hostility toward Swedes, began to hoot, and Johansson's withdrawal became a flight. The judges stopped the bout in the second round and disqualified him for lack of combativity. From that evening I retained an impression that he could not fight, although all I had seen, reflection tells me now, was that he would not. The Olympic judges refused to give Johansson even the silver medal for second place that he had earned by reaching the final. Conceivably, such a failure could leave a boxer with a memory of panic that might recur, or it might fortify him with a need to redeem himself. In the moving pictures, the second answer would be inevitable; the ex-coward would slug his way up from the preliminaries and finally fight the champion under the eyes of his best girl. From the Hollywood point of view, the odds would then be 100-1 on him to win. Since I reject everything connected with the movies, I considered this result impossible. The clincher for me was that Johansson's best girl, Birgit Lundgren, had accompanied him to this country and would be at the fight.

What I had seen at Helsinki also made me disbelieve reports that Johansson was a great hitter. A boxer with faith in his punch can only with difficulty restrain himself from throwing it at least once; it could turn a sure loss into victory, and a hitter is necessarily a bit of a gambler by nature. Each time a boxer throws a full punch, he commits himself to a risk—first of a counterpunch and then of being momentarily off balance if he misses. At Helsinki, Patterson, then only seventeen, was an Olympic *Wunderkind*, with three years of boxing already behind him. His moves and reflexes were astonishingly quick, and he lived for boxing. In the seven years since, I had seen him improve enormously, and he had put on twenty solid pounds. Moreover, I liked his attitude toward his art. He wanted to be "a hundred per cent of himself"—a noble ambition, which he pursued, unsatisfied, through months of lonely training. Once, and only once, he said, he had made seventy.

I think this first impression of the two men betrayed me into trying to make subsequent evidence conform. For example, when I was informed last spring by an old friend, Whitey Bimstein, that the regenerated Viking's courage was now beyond cavil, I discounted the statement, because Whitey had been hired as Johansson's American trainer. "Some of these amateurs that run like thieves get brave when they see a dollar," Whitey said. "This fellow is a businessman. He sweats ice. For a million dollars in sight, he will have a heart like a line." The lesson here is that even an interested statement may be valid. I rejected still more decisively Whitey's encomiums on his new pupil's punching power. In 1958, before becoming associated with Johansson, Whitey had taken a harmless colored heavyweight named Archie McBride to Stockholm to oppose the Swede on his home ground. Returning, he had said that Johansson couldn't fight a lick, even though he had won on points. "Every time McBride hit him in the body, the referee warned us," Whitey said. "To win there, you got to knock a guy out hitting him on top of the head." Now he talked about the McBride-Johansson match as if it had been some other fight. "Johansson hit Archie one shot, and I seen if he hit him again he like to kilt him," the new Whitey said. "I told McBride to go into his shell and just try to stay the ten rounds. McBride was lucky, at that." I could imagine a fighter's improving, but not retroactively. "Johansson's a big, strong guy," Whitey said, "and he's a banger. He could knock Patterson's brains out." After the McBride bout, Johansson had, in fact, knocked out a pretty good American Negro heavyweight—as heavyweights go these days—named Eddie Machen in one round, but a one-round knockout can be an accident. I should have reminded myself that it can also be not an accident, and I should have considered the possibility that Whitey's second account of the McBride expedition was more veracious than the first.

The eye itself can be influenced by a universal idea. Ten days before the fight, I had joined a number of newspaper correspondents in a visit to Grossinger's, a resort that is to the Catskill Mountains what the King Ranch is to Texas, to see the by now famous Swede in training. Johansson's mysterious right hand—his hammer of Thor, as some news writer had labelled it—had already become a syndicated gag, good for a laugh on any sports page. He indeed had a right hand— you could see it hanging from his arm—but he had not used it once in sparring. "When I need it, it comes," he had been quoted as saying. Somebody in our party suggested that his success against Machen had stimulated this childish automyth. I recalled that I had once allowed a four-year-old boy to knock me down, picking a thick, soft rug to fall on. Subsequently, the kid, thinking he had really flattened a portly adult, went right-hand crazy at kindergarten and suffered a bloody nose. This was an instance of the inexact analogy that Ibn Khaldun would have warned me against. So was another fellow's recollection that when Georges Carpentier was training for Jack Dempsey in 1921, he held his workouts *in camera*, on the pretext that he was developing a mystery punch. Carpentier's purpose was twofold—to needle public curiosity and to conceal his fragility. He succumbed in four rounds. The Johansson we saw spar that afternoon, without using the right, operated slowly and without heat, moving almost as cautiously against routine sparring partners as I remembered him moving against Sanders at Helsinki. A large, woolly-chested young fellow, he kept retreating, pumping his left arm gently in front of him, like a man raking a lawn. When he advanced, he pumped the same arm, as if warning the partners to get out of the way before he hit them. He did a great deal of this slow work, followed by interminable calisthenics, and looked in good condition—but for a marathon race or a tug of war. According to American theory, a fighter coming up to an important bout should be working fast, simulating actual battle conditions as closely as possible to sharpen his reflexes and timing.

When the reporters talked to Johansson in his dressing room after the workout, he was as calm as a plumber who says he thinks he can fix a leak. One chap asked him when he would throw the right against Patterson—when he saw an opening?

"When I see an opening, it's too late," Johansson said. "The right sees the opening. Then—*poum!* I dream about it often." It sounded silly.

Johansson's secretary-fiancée, Miss Lundgren, was a center of sympathetic attention. None of us liked to think of how she would feel when Patterson went to work on her dreamer. She is a slender, pretty girl, and was wearing a well-cut red suit—jacket and pants. No American manager would allow a fighter to have a girl like that with him in a training camp. Our training methods are not only a conditioning process but a form of torture, designed to put iron in the soul and to spoil the temper.

I felt sorry for Bill Rosensohn, the promoter of the match, when I talked to him a day or so later in his office in the Hotel Manhattan, which used to be the Lincoln. Rosensohn, a drawn, youngish man with a long, cadaverous, El Greco face, had made the match but had somehow been maneuvered out of "ancillary rights"—closed-circuit-television, radio, and moving-picture—by Patterson's manager, Cus D'Amato. These were the only rights that were likely to show a profit. The fight itself was not drawing, principally because the public agreed with the seers that it would be one-sided. Rosensohn, who had to bear all the expenses of promotion, would therefore be lucky to break even, though he had worked himself near to nervous collapse. (That was before the rains came and condemned him to a loss.) He had quarrelled with D'Amato, and it was a cinch that after Patterson disposed of Johansson, he would get no chance to recoup. The champion's manager, who dictates the conditions under which his man will fight, would find another promoter, and Rosensohn would have only his unsalable experience to show for six months' work. His sole future asset was a contract with Johansson, which guaranteed a return bout with Patterson if Johansson won the championship. Rosensohn, with his air of rapt martyrdom, said, "I think Johansson will knock him out." I shook my head pityingly; he had a clear case of wishful thinking.

A few days later, I rode down with another carload of newspapermen to Patterson's camp at Chatham Township, New Jersey, to confirm my preconceptions. I found what I expected. In an austerely male environment—a white clapboard gymnasium on a hill, with sleeping quarters behind it—the champion was training, as he had been ever since last winter, with only a five-day break after his winning fight in Indianapolis against Brian London, of England. He had fought London simply as a tune-up for the Johansson bout, and had nursed him along for eleven rounds to get a better workout. Patterson, boxing in his gymnasium, looked lightning fast. There was a battered, professional air about his camp and faction, commanded by the white-haired D'Amato, who tied Patterson's first boxing gloves on when Patterson was fourteen, and has had him ever since. Patterson went after his sparring partners without a letup, throwing the combinations—sequences of punches—that mark what we think of as modern boxing, in contrast to the one, one, one, and every now and then one-two of the classical Y.M.C.A. style. Johansson, by comparison, had looked like a fellow just learning to box. When Patterson's work was over, he gave audience from a white iron cot in his narrow bedroom. With a regal gesture, he motioned to a close-cropped, tailored Swedish newspaperwoman—the only female present—to share his throne. D'Amato then made a speech about what a tough fight it was going to be. "The challenger's training methods have aroused some criticism," he said, "but they await a closer evaluation. You can't fault success. They have brought him success in relation to other heavyweights. They have not been tried in relation to Patterson." Everybody smiled. D'Amato was obviously trying to stir up business for the box office.

Riding back to New York with the others in a Cadillac provided by Rosensohn, I felt that I had properly evaluated the situation. It was why I viewed that rainy evening's prospect with so glazed an eye.

When I was so wet that there was nothing to be gained by remaining under cover, I sauntered out onto the baseball diamond, converted for the night to a nobler purpose, and made my way along a path of duckboards to the press section, passing the rows of ringside seats, priced at a hundred dollars each and at that moment totally unoccupied. It was then about nine. The floodlights used for night baseball games cast a wavering light through the rain, creating an effect of yellow steam. There was a roof directly over the ring, and the ring canvas was shielded from the wet by a tarpaulin. A number of groundskeeper's workmen and several boxing officials assigned to the first preliminary bout were in the ring, all wearing transparent-plastic raincoats, which venders were selling at the gate for two dollars apiece. Increasing numbers of newspaper and radio or television men, driven into the open by the heat, straggled toward their places around the ring apron. As the management put off announcing the postponement, a feeling spread that the fight would go on, come hell or hot water.

The British correspondents reporting the fight, an amphibious breed, were among the first to gather about the ring, dressed in rainwear appropriate to mid-winter soccer. One, a fellow named Frank Butler, told me it looked like a jolly fine night. A Swede was already broadcasting—telling the folks at home about the weather, I suppose. The rain stopped, but there was so much moisture in the air that the transition to vapor was hard to detect. One of the fellows in the ring, discarding his mackintosh, got hold of the public-address microphone and announced that the first preliminary bout would go on at nine-thirty. The championship bout, then, would presumably begin at ten-thirty, as scheduled.

I got myself into my undertaker's chair, of a width specially manufactured for fights and midgets' funerals, so that it couldn't be pre-empted by a practitioner of one of the ancillary journalisms. Often these radio and television fellows move in like a school of mackerel, spreading over the places allotted to newsmen, some of whom always arrive late. First you see one chap, like the first fish of the school—in some cases he may actually have a ticket—and then, before you know it, they are all over the place, breaking water across your bows and on both sides at once, and invariably asking you to move into somebody else's seat, so that they can deposit some ominous piece of factitious apparatus on the narrow writing shelf in front of yours, where it will be most obstructive. When the latecomer who has a legitimate claim to your new seat arrives, he finds you in it, and meanwhile the ancillary fellow who has your old one pretends to be talking into his bogus mechanism.

Once seated, with my arms pinioned by equally constricted neighbors, I had little to do until ten-thirty except review my reasons for not anticipating much of a fight. The three preliminaries offered small distraction. In the first, two imposing Negro heavyweights—one a Patterson sparring partner and the other a sparring-partner type—posed and snorted impressively through four inoffensive rounds. There is an unwritten universal pact among sparring partners, who get hit so much by their principals, not to hit each other, even when paid to do so. I declined to recognize an omen in the decision, which went against Patterson's man. Ticket holders who had been waiting downtown until they learned the fight was on were now beginning to arrive, but the big ballpark was still lightly populated.

The second bout provided a unilateral interest; it presented D'Amato's new potential star, the Puerto Rican middleweight José Torres, against Al Andrews, who had once been considered promising but had now declined to the rank of "an opponent." Torres, a hard puncher, is one of the few fighters around who can fill a small arena with dollar-and-a-half and three-dollar customers even in competition with free fights on television. This was his first appearance before a big-fight crowd, and he owed his place on the program to his affiliation with D'Amato. There was little chance that the champion's manager would appoint an intractable opponent for such a première. Torres, compact, thick of neck, beige, and confident, used the D'Amato boxing system; he carried his hands high, one at each side of his head, with his elbows tight to his body. He bent his knees, and swayed from side to side to slip straight punches, advancing on his victim like a Bronx Zoo cobra about to devour a mouse. It is difficult for a novice to hit hard from this position, or to keep his balance; the technique has to be learned, like dancing on the toes. Theoretically, however, the system offers considerable safety, and it disconcerts a boxer accustomed to conventional adversaries. It also involves a considerable amount of waste motion; Torres, with a redundance of energy, appeared to be enjoying it. Andrews, pale and apprehensive, had long since lost the confidence that comes from winning. He still had pride, though. When Torres knocked him down in the first round, he got up. For four rounds after that, he carried on, sometimes making Torres miss awkwardly but never seriously inconveniencing him. In the sixth round, just as I was getting used to this *divertimento*, Torres hit his opponent a couple of oblique, chopping blows and definitively knocked him out. The system is the first and only style that D'Amato ever taught Patterson, but Patterson has loosened it up and added mobility. It provides protection against swings and hooks, but the system boxer must rely on the speed of his reflexes, like a dodger at a county fair, to keep out of the way of straight punches. I failed to relate this to Patterson's opponent of the evening, because I had never seen Johansson throw a punch.

There was another preliminary—a four-rounder without educational value—and then the chief business of the night was at hand. Because of the postponement from the night before, the fight was running in conflict with the regular Friday-evening show at Madison Square Garden, which is televised, and thus immovable. (It was the first time in a decade or so that New York had two boxing shows on one evening.) The Garden has an agreement with Johnny Addie, who serves as announcer at most New York bouts, and so Sam Taub, an old friend of D'Amato's, entered the ring at the Yankee Stadium as master of ceremonies. Taub, a bustling, rhetorical little man, has been around the game for fifty years as a writer, radio narrator of bouts, and press agent, and he has more style than most of the newcomers. "And now the zero hour has arrived," he began, "but allow me to pause to introduce . . ." He presented Mr. Rosensohn, the promoter, to the crowd. Rosensohn climbed the ladder to the ring and flung a hand up in salute to the crowd. It may have been the fulfillment of a boyhood daydream, but the members of the audience, viewing the empty spaces around them, knew it was costing him a lot of money and applauded him only as a game loser. Ruby Goldstein, an old fighter and a merciful man, was to referee, and the crowd applauded him, too. I remembered that I had seen Goldstein stop the middleweight championship bout between Ray Robinson and Randy Turpin in 1951 to save Turpin from further punishment, and it was a satisfaction to me that he would be there to protect Johansson from permanent injury.

Now Johansson and his faction entered the ring, taking the corner at my left and across from where I sat. The fighter had the air of a man bound for a massage and a nap before dinner. With him were three other unexcited Swedes—Nils Blomberg, his Swedish trainer; Edwin Ahlquist, a Stockholm promoter who has no power to sign contracts for Johansson; and Dr. Gösta Karlsson, his personal physician, a blond and portly M.D. who looks like a Wagnerian singer. With him, too, was Whitey Bimstein, a Scandinavian only in coloration, gambolling excitedly, like a Border collie in the wake of four giant sheep. Whitey, I knew, was there to act as a short-order plastic surgeon, or cut man, between rounds, Dr. Karlsson having specialized in other fields of medicine. Dr. Karlsson would intervene only in case his patient's long-term health appeared to him to be in danger. Blomberg and Ahlquist, I guessed, would translate Whitey's tactical counsels into Swedish, since he talks too fast for one interpreter to handle. Whitey would also protect the party from native treachery, such as short counts or any effort to put a roll of nickels inside the champion's glove.

Patterson and his seconds took the corner to my right and on my side of the ring. They were as calm as Swedes themselves, the way an experienced, well-organized corner should be. Patterson has worked with the same people since he turned professional, and until that evening he had won thirty-five fights out of thirty-six, his one loss being a disputed decision when he was on the way up. That is the kind of history that creates confidence in a corner. The champion looked out on the crowd impassively, grappling, I was sure, with his constant preoccupation—how to prove, in an age of nothing fighters, that he is a something fighter, seventy-five per cent or higher, if measured against great champions of the past. In the light of what has happened since, he may have been insufficiently intent upon merely winning. He is a serious young man, proud without swagger. If he thought at all of the half-million dollars coming his and D'Amato's way as a result of the evening, it was only as a poet might think of an endowment that would enable him to practice his art without fear of want in the future. He had said, after his last workout, that he had no set battle plan. "If he starts to unload, I will unload with him, but otherwise I will just have to see" was the way he put it. D'Amato looked like a parent who has come to see his boy graduate *summa cum laude*. The others in the corner were Dan Florio, an old-time trainer from the lower West Side, and his brother Nick, both eminent cut men, and Buster, a young Negro contemporary of Patterson's who is the training-camp factotum.

While both men were in their corners, going through the championship ritual of having their gloves put on under the eye of an agent from the other camp, Taub introduced Rocky Marciano, the heavyweight champion who retired undefeated in 1956, leaving the way open for Patterson and old Archie Moore to fight for the title. Marciano, a training-camp Spartan for eight years, has given rein to his splendid appetite since retiring, and the results are monumental. The crowd cheered him, remembering his battles; he had never taken a step back. Marciano shook hands with both men and returned to the crowd, his worries over, a spectator at last.

When the bell rang, Patterson came out to prove himself—an odd psychological fix for a champion. Usually it is the challenger who carries the burden of proof, but Patterson, ever since he won the title, had been accused of picking on cripples and not obliterating them as quickly or as completely as his critics thought Marciano would have done. Johansson, with nobody except his own corner and his countrymen expecting anything of him, was in an easier position. He began as he had at Grossinger's—jabbing with the old lawn-raking motion and moving away—but I noticed that he moved faster, and that the jabbing left fist reached out more briskly. There was a new authority in his manner, as if he might indeed be a professional. The champion followed, but at arm's length, studying. The jabs being thrown at him were harmless, but they kept him off. And the mysterious right had him puzzled. Johansson still held it in reserve. Patterson tried to draw him with feints, but he wouldn't be drawn. The *idea* of the right titillated the crowd, but in fact the round was without damage or incident. My sole note on it is a large "o," for "Nothing." (One judge, it was revealed next day, scored it for Johansson, and the referee and the other judge for Patterson, but this was on the theory that *somebody* has to win every round.) It was the sort of round that seems to presage a long, cautious fight, and the second round did little to change that feeling. Patterson now was beginning to work a bit closer and to throw a few well-meant punches. I remember a stiff straight left that reddened Johansson's open mouth, and a blow to the ribs, followed by one to the chest, that must have stung. Johansson, however, confined himself to the left and to retreat. It was clearly Patterson's round—what there was in it—and the champion may have come around to thinking that the self-directed right was a myth. I myself had now seen Johansson "fight" four rounds—two at Helsinki and two in New York—and spar half a dozen at Grossinger's without hitting a solid blow. I was impressed, though, because the Swede didn't fluster, and everybody in the park, I think, was astonished that Patterson hadn't done more with him. He was as calmly exasperating as a strange poker player with a pair of tens showing who goes on betting into a pair of jacks; either he is silly or he has the third ten in the hole, and unless you have played with him before, you can't tell which.

Patterson at that point may have made the wrong guess. At the beginning of the third round, he came out "very gay," as the old London Prize Ring oracle Pierce Egan would have said, and moved in closer than before. I had scarcely settled into watching the round, it seemed, when he came crashing down a yard or so in front of me, with a face as blank as that of a hypnotist's stooge. The instant before, he had had his back to me, and I had seen him pull away from a left hook. His trajectory indicated that he had pulled into a right that was no more of a myth than a horse's ability to kick. I did not think that he would get up—or that he even knew he was down—but at the third or fourth count something seemed to be dimly stirring behind his eyes, and his legs began to grope, as if independently, for where the floor was. I remembered once hearing him say that he had never been in real trouble "outside"—by which he meant outside the gymnasium—and that when people asked whether he could take it, he had to answer that he simply didn't know. "I hope I never have to prove I can," he had said. Now legs and reflex pulled him up at the count of nine—it could not have been pride or courage, because he promptly proved that he didn't know where he was. With hands dangling by his sides, he began to walk in the wrong direction, as if he had been saved by a bell and was going to his corner. Johansson followed, as he had a right to do, and went around the champion to hit him with a left to the face and then with a clubbing right on the back of the head as he pitched forward. The mild Johansson is a good finisher. But these blows, landed on a sagging target, did not have the same efficacy as that first punch. The champion, young and in magnificent condition, was patently in better shape the second time he went down than he had been the first. This time I was sure he would get up; he started struggling sooner. But he hadn't yet begun to think; he bounced up, and again Johansson knocked him down, and again, but each time it took more blows to do it. After the fourth knockdown, Patterson, with a half glimmer of where he was, clambered up and began swinging, like a man in a dream whose arms feel like strands of spaghetti. He hit Johansson two or three times, and Johansson must have hit him fifteen. Patterson should have tried to hold on or get away, but he couldn't think that clearly, and his legs wouldn't have carried him anyway. Johansson did not appear to be enjoying the role that Patterson's body was now forcing on him. The hair on his chest was matted with blood from Patterson's mouth, and blood dappled his shoulders, too. But he battered the champion down a fifth and a sixth time. Patterson was on the floor yet again, and rising, when Goldstein stepped in front of him, as he had stepped in front of Turpin, to save him from further punishment. I had lost count of the knockdowns, but a methodical neighbor assured me that it was the seventh.

The punch that sent Patterson down the first time, I thought, must have been a marvel, because he was in worse condition the first time down, after twenty-seven seconds of the round, than he was when Goldstein stopped the fight, ninety-six seconds later, during which time Patterson had received dozens of hard blows. I was even more impressed two days later, when I saw the moving pictures of the fight. The right that hit Patterson as he moved to his own left, away from the left hook, was not a long punch, with body and back thrown into it—Patterson is too fast to be caught by that sort—but a straight, short punch at half-arm range. It was as good, in its way, as the right with which Marciano knocked out Jersey Joe Walcott in their fight for the championship in Philadelphia in 1952. That kind of punching is not lucky but a combination of a rare talent and an acquired knack.

After the fight was over and Sam Taub had announced the time of the knockout—two minutes and three seconds of the third round— and a jubilant Johansson and a revived Patterson, now aware of what had hit him, were saying their pieces into the microphone, I saw Whitey hanging over the ropes and waving both hands, as if he had never told me what McBride done to the bum. A practitioner of the ancillary arts, a British Broadcasting Company operative, was standing in front of me describing the scene to his early-morning auditors in the United Kingdom, and before I knew it, he had said into his microphone, "I shall now ask a spectator to give you his impressions," and had put the object in my hands. I was on the point of saying "It was the goddamnedest thing I ever saw in my life," but then I recollected my audience and said, "It was a *shocking* surprise."

I did not remember Ibn Khaldun until later that evening.

July 11, 1959

A Blow
for Austerity

When Ingemar Johansson, a heavyweight Swede, arrived here in April, 1959, he brought with him the seed of the dissipation of authority and the germ of the disintegration of discipline. From the beginnings of the London prize ring, professors of prizefighting have taught that unremitting exercise, austere surroundings, and general abstinence to the point of ill temper constitute the indispensable preparation for combat. The presence of women, chaperoned or not, is contra-indicated in a training camp; Sir Gordon Richards, a great trainer in an allied art, will not even suffer girl grooms around his stables, although whether because of their effect upon jockeys or upon horses he does not state. Mr. Floyd Patterson, the heavyweight champion at the time of Johansson's arrival, was a pattern of orthodoxy in his training methods, and all the educators who hang out in the Neutral Corner Bar and Restaurant between seminars in the Eighth Avenue Gymnasium (formerly Stillman's) held him up to their pupils as an example of the rewards of self-denial. Although a loving husband, Patterson lived far from his young wife for months on end, in quarters appropriate to a nearly indigent agriculturist, where he concentrated with intensity upon the cultivation of endurance. Daily, he ran hard upon the hills, sometimes paced by a friendly jack rabbit until the rabbit pooped out. He whaled sparring partners chosen for their absorptive capacity; he refrained from reading mystery stories, lest they intrude upon the hours of sleep required to fill his reservoirs of energy. Only Patterson's art interrupted his rest; once, he awoke, full of a sudden inspiration, to rehearse before the bathroom mirror a punch he had dreamed, like a Romantic poet rousing to scribble a dream verse on his nightgown. (The exit of the male nightgown coincided with a decline in the output of lyric poetry.)

Johansson, an autodidact, scorned the precepts of the scholastics. He brought with him a retinue that included his parents, his sister, his brother and his brother's fiancée, and—most reprehensible of all, in professional opinion—his own fiancée, a very pretty girl named Birgit Lundgren. Their arrival was like that of the Magician and his entourage in Ingmar Bergman's Swedish film of that name. The prizefighter installed them at Grossinger's, in the Catskills, in a pavilion usually reserved for the royalty of the garment industry, on the periphery of a golf course where mink sweaters are de rigueur among women players. Worse, from the orthodox point of view, he played golf personally, as if he contemplated entering politics instead of the ring. Golf, like swimming, nurtures all the wrong reflexes, boxing savants say. Pinochle is the safest game between workouts. Johansson handled his sparring partners with a forbearance bordering on affection, on the public pretext that he was afraid of killing them. He ordered from the Grossinger menu, a long and rich one, instead of sticking to raw eggs, orange juice, and underdone steaks, and he went dancing and drank ice-cream sodas with Birgit at midnight. Johansson's right hand would tell him what to do when necessary, he informed observers, whom he offended by his levity. It was, according to him, a self-directed artillery, leaping to the target. The distrust that his hedonism inspired in academic circles was buttressed by the ineptitude he displayed when he sparred. He stuck out his left hand and backed away, like a fellow raking a lawn, and cared not what his right hand did. He left it perched on the side of his chin like a pigeon on a cornice, depending on it to take flight when its moment came. As a consequence, no competent critic hesitated to select him to be annihilated. On the night of June 26th, at Yankee Stadium, Johansson knocked out Patterson in three rounds. Patterson, approaching the stranger with caution, like a cat pawing at an unfamiliar object, was incredulous, then delighted, at what he thought he had found. He felt no need to hurry. In the third, Patterson moved a bit closer. Johansson, ice cool, hooked a left without force; Patterson mechanically pulled his head to his own left, away from it and into the path of the Swede's right, thrown with geometrical economy and every bit as good as advertised by its owner. Patterson did not recover. He was knocked down seven times and got up only six.

The climax showed that Johansson was crafty as well as confident, and that he could hit hard and fast with his right hand. It proved nothing more; it was like a poker pot that a player takes down with two aces, throwing away his three other cards without showing them. The result, however, shook the moral foundation of American sport—the coach's speech that goes, "You get out of a game exactly what you put into it." Here was a fellow who did not punish himself and who won anyway. If he continued to win, other athletes might get the idea that sport was fun, and coaches would cease to rank as character builders.

This year, I myself went over to Johansson's insidious system. I decided that last year I had overtrained; I had visited both camps, had observed the men's form when they sparred, and had compared it with what I remembered of them as young amateurs at the Helsinki Olympics in 1952. My effort to arrive at truth produced error; I figured Patterson to take it. This time, when Johansson, now the champion, and Patterson, now the challenger, were rematched, I made up my mind simply to go to the Polo Grounds on the night of June 20th and look at the fight, leaving all the arduous work of divination to others. In arriving at this decision, I was influenced by reading Ibn Khaldun, the immortal Tunisian contemporary of Chaucer, on the subject of the fallibility of soothsayers. "They concentrate their thinking upon the matter in which they are interested, and apply guesses and hypotheses to it," he wrote. "They base themselves upon an unfounded assumption as to what basically constitutes contact with, and perception of, the supernatural." (Hunch players.) Khaldun does not mention, specifically, boxing experts, but he records that in pre-Islamic times there was a famous soothsayer named Satih, of the tribe of Mazin ben Ghassan, who "used to fold up like a garment, as he had no bones save for his skull." I have known boxing writers who behaved like that on the floor of a speakeasy called the Sliding Pond, which existed on the south side of Forty-ninth Street, across from the Garden, in pre-repeal times. The prescription that the immortal Khaldun came nearest to endorsing went this way: "When a human being is placed in a barrel of sesame oil and kept in it for forty days, is fed with figs and nuts until his flesh is gone and only the arteries and sutures of the skull remain, and is then taken out of the oil and exposed to the drying action of the air, he will answer all special and general questions regarding the future that may be asked." Even here Ibn, never a man to go out on a limb, did not say whether the man would come up with the right answers.

A few days before the fight, I walked over to the lobby of the Hotel Astor, where Feature Sports, Inc., the promoter, maintained a box office, and for thirty dollars purchased a seat in the fourth row of the lower stand, between home plate and third base, from which I knew I could view the combat better than from any hundred-dollar seat on the field, especially if I remembered to take with me a pair of small field glasses. From the Astor, I sauntered west and north to the Neutral Corner, at Eighth Avenue and Fifty-fifth Street. It was the interim period between the day and evening sessions at the gymnasium, when the academicians repair to the Neutral, as to a faculty club. The fact that there is an evening session at the gym does not denote a boom in professional boxing, but the contrary. So few fighters nowadays are able to maintain themselves entirely by their métier that many boys cannot afford to train between noon and three o'clock, the hours hallowed by tradition; the ambitious must support themselves by jobs, and come to the gymnasium as to a night law school. This is because there has never been a period when the gap between the earnings of the leaders of the ring and the journeymen has been so wide. A fighter is either on television and earning considerable sums of money, or off and earning nothing at all. The neophyte, if he can support himself by outside work, has one consolation: the gap in ability between the top class and the beginner has never been so narrow. In pre-television boxing, a professional had to fight his way through many strata, gaining in skill and toughness at each rise, until, after seventy-five to a hundred fights, he began to attract attention. Now ten fights, or a dozen, constitute "experience," and a youngster without form may hope soon to confront a champion hardly more seasoned than himself. This had been Patterson's sorrow; he believed himself a good fighter, born into an age when he might never be able to prove it, because of the insignificance of the opposition. In an era more normally endowed with heavyweight heroes, he might have been content to remain a light-heavyweight, contending at a class limit of a hundred and seventy-five pounds, because he is narrow for his not extraordinary height. In the present order of things, however, he had beaten men bigger than himself with such ease that he thought of himself in heavyweight terms. Johansson's right-hand punch reminded him that there is a difference between big-framed six-footers and slenderer men of the same height. Johansson weighed 196 pounds for that fight and Patterson 182. Moreover, each had looked to be at his normal fighting weight.

In the Neutral, its walls hidden by photographs of heroes and near-heroes, I encountered Charlie Goldman, once the gnarled Aristotle to Rocky Marciano's Alexander, and Whitey Bimstein, a tactician and lay surgeon who had been the only American in the Swede's corner in 1959, and would be again. Whitey's specialty is repairing cuts, but in the first Johansson-Patterson bout he had had no opportunity to display it.

I asked the learned Goldman how he thought the return match would go, and he replied, without feeding on a fig or a nut, "The Swede will take him again. Patterson isn't big enough. A good light-heavy can lick a bad heavy, but a fair heavyweight will take him. Look at the trouble great light-heavies like Paul Berlenbach and Jack Delaney used to have with ordinary heavies like Jim Maloney and Johnny Risko that you hardly hear of today. The Swede figures to be at least fair. He licked twenty-one guys in Europe, and they couldn't *all* be terrible. You got to go with a winner."

I was astonished that Mr. Goldman, a stickler for rigorous living by his own students, did not allude to the Swede's sybaritic training procedures, but he didn't. He believes that wives are, on balance, more damaging to fighters than any number of fiancées.

Whitey, a family man himself, felt called on to minimize his principal's singularities. "Ingemar works harder than any fighter I ever seen, including Rocky," he said. "In secret." His position obliged him to predict victory for the champion, so I did not ask him his opinion. Having no time for the sesame-oil test, I let my consultation of the oracles end there.

On the afternoon preceding the international contest, I fell in with a man I know who had acquired a complimentary ticket for a seat in the twenty-third row ringside, and we decided to make the journey to the fight together, each paying half the taxi. We made the entire progress by daylight, observing the people on the sidewalks along the Harlem reaches of Eighth Avenue. They gave no evidence of a celebration building up, as they used to on the evenings leading up to Joe Louis's fights and, later, Sugar Ray Robinson's; they simply stood and looked at the long, dragging procession of taxis and buses and private cars as if they wondered what was bringing all the strangers up through Harlem. Only once we heard a little tan boy yell, "Vote for Floyd Patterson!"— meaning, we supposed, "Root." He was soliciting public support for a man who led an American life.

My friend and I parted a couple of blocks from the old ballpark, leaving our cab hopelessly mired in traffic, although it was still an hour and a half before the scheduled time of the big fight. (How the elegant latecomers at every fight make it is always a mystery to me; as the fateful minute approaches, traffic on all streets leading to the Polo Grounds is always packed as tight as a glacier.) Now, suddenly, as we debarked, there came the feeling of a really big one. The crowd around the gates was tremendous. The match, hardly talked of a few days before, had caught on. Immediately after the first Patterson-Johansson encounter, interest in the return had been intense, but the long squabbles over the business organization of the fight through winter and spring had drawn attention away from the sporting issues and made the Fancy doubt whether it would ever come off. And now, when the last dollar of anticipated "ancillary" profit—from peepshow, or closed-circuit television, performances in theatres no closer than Asbury Park, from films, and from the radio advertising rights—had been cut as fine as coleslaw, it became clear that no time had remained for the promoters to make any arrangements for the comfort or safety of the customers. It was as if the promoters themselves had not really believed they would bring it off.

I moved into a kind of chute called the Speedway, which slopes down from the Eighth Avenue sidewalk to the gates under the lower stand of the old baseball park, and found myself caught in a struggling mass of braced bodies, moving, against their will, toward an immovable barrier. The gates were closed, and more people hurrying into the chute from subway exits created a constant forward drive. By the time each sought to disengage, he was pinioned by the forward press of the newcomers behind him. All the people in the chute were holders of twenty- or thirty-dollar tickets. These are denominations that are never complimentary—your free-rider goes ringside or not at all—and the people in the chute included many out-of-towners and their women, caught in a perilous trap of a kind they had not expected when they left Memphis and Akron for a holiday in New York. We were all prisoners together, pushing without hate, until, after a long interval, the pressure began to ease slightly—a few ticket takers' turnstiles were working again. I learned afterward from the morning papers that the gates had been closed because, earlier in the evening, a mob of roughs, mostly young, had taken the turnstile men by surprise and crashed their way in. The first remedy that occurred to the promoters, a new lot, was to lock the people who *had* tickets out. (This was nothing, of course, compared to what roughs sometimes used to do in bare-knuckle days, when they would tear down the ring to prevent their favorite from losing. Apparently, we are coming full circle.)

Once inside the field, however, and still unaware of why I had come near having my ribs cracked, I made my way to my seat, guided by the excellent directions painted on the walls by the departed New York National League Baseball Club, like the cave paintings of a vanished race. No usher offered to interfere with my advance, nor did any usher offer to assist me; they all maintained a contemptuous neutrality between ticket holders and non-ticket holders, and allowed priority of arrival, or else predominance of force, to decide tenure. I was lucky enough to find nobody on the seat called for by my ticket, and sat down. I was thirsty, but none of the customary butchers of beer or pop or ice cream or coffee appeared. The stand swarmed with venders, but they were without exception selling either one-dollar souvenir programs that did not tell you who was fighting in the preliminaries, or else genuine high-power field glasses at one or two dollars the pair. The field-glasses salesmen had them draped over them, like bandoleers; occupants of aisle seats were constantly being lassoed in the passing straps or banged on the side of the head by swinging binoculars.

The two preliminaries I saw were of the squalor now habitual. Promoters since the great Tex Rickard have never been generous in the matter of preliminary cards, but it must be owned that their excuse is easy now—there are few boxers worth watching even in main events. The extinction of the small clubs by giveaway boxing on television began to have this effect in the early fifties, but there were then still some hundreds of pre-television fighters in various stages of development. Now the best of these are superannuated. Those who were merely promising have quit for lack of matches. Nineteen-fifty was no Golden Age of boxing, but, compared to 1960, it was at least gold-plated.

I put away all these melancholy reflections when the principals in the second maladroit scramble left the ring, at about five minutes past ten. One of them, a Swede brought along by the Johansson party, had two badly cut eyelids; the referee, therefore, had stopped the bout, on doctor's orders, after four rounds, instead of the planned six. This left extra minutes to fill before the scheduled start of the big fight, at tenthirty. I spent part of the time looking down at the crowd on the field to see if I could spot the chap who had shared my taxi, but I failed. (The next day, when I did find him, he said, "No one in Row 23 looked as though he'd paid for his ticket, and I became certain of this when the promoter, Humbert Fugazy [executive director of Feature Sports, Inc.], was introduced from the ring and received a standing ovation by

my neighbors while the rest of the crowd sat on its hands.") The announcer, a small one in a tuxedo, now took to calling up boxers from
the audience and asking them to take a bow. This was against protocol,
for the principals were not in the ring. Traditionally, the old boxer or
the future contender comes into the ring to shake hands with the principals and wish them good luck. A number of the old-timers solicited
didn't respond. Next, a tall announcer in tails—a carefully thought-
out touch of class, this—took the place of the little one in a tuxedo.
Eddie Fisher, a popular baritone, sang the national anthem, off key all
the way. A stocky Swede with a thick neck sang the Swedish anthem,
but whether well or not none of us was in a position to say. Patterson
came into the ring, and the new announcer, shilling for coming at-
tractions, continued his spiel without looking at him. Patterson wore
a white robe and a white towel over head and neck like an Arab kaffi-
yeh. I trained my glasses on his face, which can be mischievous and
boyish. This time, it was blank as well as sombre. I couldn't tell
whether he was planning a murder or was sorry he was there. Cus
D'Amato, the white-haired, round-headed manager who had presided over Patterson's corner in all his earlier fights, was not there this
time. The New York State Athletic Commission had barred him for
technical "irregularities" that I never took the time to read about. Dan
Florio, the boy's trainer—a small, merry man from the lower West
Side—was in charge. I had a feeling that this might free Floyd from the
weight of the manager's anxiety; D'Amato is a good boxing man, but
he identifies too closely with his *Wunderkind*. Patterson may feel as if
he had his father in his corner when Cus is there, and this is a disturbing situation for a fighter. It is good for a mature fighter to have a second
whose advice he can disregard without qualms of guilt.

After a psychological delay, designed to give the challenger time to
think about what happened to him last time, Johansson and his faction entered the ring and occupied the corner diagonally across from
Patterson. He was accompanied by two Swedish seconds, to me indis-
tinguishable, and by my friend Whitey Bimstein. Whitey has the coloration of a Swede but is only about one-quarter of median Swedish
size. His face was compressed into its normal expression at the begin-

ning of a big fight—the look of a man carrying the pistols for the duel between Aaron Burr and Alexander Hamilton. Johansson wore *his* habitual pre-fight expression—that of a large, apple-headed boy who is preparing to shout "Boo!" to frighten his sister. He did not look dangerous, and I had to remind myself that he was—that he could hit like the devil with his right hand, and that I had seen him do it. He impressed me as being fatter than last year, although the official scales found him a pound or so lighter—a hundred and ninety-four and a fraction pounds. Patterson, who had deliberately tried to come in heavy, was up to a hundred and ninety pounds. And still, bearing out the distinction between the frames of fighters, the bout looked definitely like one between a big man, Johansson, and a man a good deal smaller.

Patterson had been much disparaged since the first fight. The soothsayers of the sports pages, who had made him such an overwhelming favorite, and the readers who believed the soothsayers, were let down when the Swede knocked him over. But when the Grover Whalen in tails introduced the two fighters—Patterson first, as challenger—the greater cheer by far was for the Negro. After Johansson's name, there came another mighty roar, but it assayed forty per cent boos. (Most of the money was on him—he was the betting favorite, 8–5—so the disapproval had no venal motive.) At the moment, I felt a warm glow of gratification—we were a solid *patrie*, where American citizenship meant more than race or color—and it was not until later that I further analyzed the motivation of the cheer for Patterson. It was, I am now sure, moralistic—the crowd was cheering for Benjamin Franklin, who rose early; for Abraham Lincoln, who worked hard; for Horatio Alger, who lauded the boy who put the highest shine on the shoes.

But right then I thought only of the fight. For Patterson, coming out of his corner, it was the moment of decision. A fighter's left hand, held in the normal boxing position, is nearer the target than the right. Patterson was boxing normally now, instead of in the odd stance he had once affected, with elbows on a line and feet close together. The old, heterodox stance had brought him within range of the Johansson right. The new—for him—and conventional style made it easier to keep away from the right. But survival would not be enough to regain his championship. Sometime—probably many times—he would have to get within half-arm length to hurt Johansson, and when he did he would be within the orbit of the champion's good hand. The first problem, then, was to discombobulate Johansson—to pull him out of the safety of his rather stiff, conventional boxing-school guard, with the left poked forward and the right cocked to strike. Johansson is a fighter who moves on a straight line, forward or back, as if he had never quite learned to trust his feet.

Patterson circled counterclockwise, away from the right hand, and then reversed—but never far enough to get clipped. He took targets of opportunity, hitting to the left ribs to bring down that pawing, hayraking left, knocking aside leads to hit to the body, hitting glancing blows when he could not get a clean shot. Johansson made the game easier, because in this fight he came forward. In the first fight, he had constantly backed away, like a girl trying to get away from her date at the front door. (His retreat had been tactical, of course, designed to draw Patterson into the right, but he knew that this time he could not rely on the same booby trap. This time, Johansson may have thought, his chief asset would be Patterson's fear, just as last time it had been overconfidence. He was wrong.) Patterson is unusually fast with his hands, even for a light-heavy. He is fast, too, on his feet, in a hopping, bounding way that frequently looks awkward and often leaves him off balance. It is not wise for a slower, heavier man to try to keep up with such speed; Johansson would have done better to go back into his shell to think things over. But he was the overconfident one this time. It was a fast, sloppy first round for heavies. The crowd, sensing what was happening, howled happily. The great fear of all of us, I think, had been that Patterson would fight timid, like Jersey Joe Walcott and Ezzard Charles in their return fights with Rocky Marciano. When he showed game, he captured the crowd. Any fight in which one man can punch and the other must disarm him is exciting, like watching an attempt by a bomb squad to remove a fuse.

In the second round, with about a minute to go, Johansson landed the right, high on the side of the face. The men were not in close. All

the crowd saw the punch—it was a fight without mysteries. Patterson
went back fast. He did not stagger, but the speed of his departure from
the immediate neighborhood acknowledged the force of the punch.
The crowd yelled. Three young colored boys in front of me shrieked
with fear. This is how the tide of war can turn—you can never figure a
puncher beaten until he has been counted out. Johansson followed,
but he could not connect again. Patterson boxed coolly, and the effect
of the right wore off, visibly, before the end of the round. That was the
only moment of the fight when it looked as if Johansson might win.

In the third and fourth rounds, Patterson, full of energy, continued
to hustle and cuff, pushing his man and spinning him. As Johansson
tired, or grew discouraged, the challenger could afford to get set and
punch more solidly. He was hurting Johansson with body punches in
the fourth round, and although Whitey, whom I have since seen several times, insists that Johansson wasn't exhausted then, I thought he
was. In the fifth, Patterson, very gay, as Pierce Egan, the Cholly Knick-
erbocker of the London Prize Ring, would have said, went about his
man and nobbed him merrily. With the Swede, it was a case of bellows
to mend, in Pierce's idiom. He was gasping. I saw him pull the right
back for a punch; he was moving it so slowly that I could watch it from
the lower stands. There was no snap left in his muscles, and he probably wished he had never seen an ice-cream soda. Patterson had no time
to think about the rewards of virtue—he was too busy reaping them.
He hit the hedonist with a left hook to the body and then switched it
to the head. The Swede was in the same place when the punch landed
as when it started. He went down like a double portion of Swedish pancakes with lingonberries and sour cream. He got up, though. There
was no quit in him; he was still, in spirit, disputatious. Patterson swung
his left again, like a man with a brush hook clearing briars. It hit the
champion's chin, his head went back on a loose neck, and he struck
the mat with a crash that I swear I heard at a distance of at least three
hundred yards.

Patterson knew it was over without listening to the count. He
jumped with joy, as if he were a fan watching Floyd Patterson recover
the heavyweight championship of the world. Johansson disappeared

from my sight as first the handlers and officials, and then the State Athletic Commission doctors, gathered around his flattened form. I had my glasses on Whitey Bimstein's face as he looked down at his client, and I could see how badly Johansson was hurt; Whitey, for all his insouciant exterior, has a tender heart. Later, he told me that Patterson hit Johansson only a "fair punch" but that the champion hurt his head on the floor. When a fighter goes down that hard from only a "fair punch," he is exhausted, which supports my theory.

The ring now filled with roughs, mostly in their teens, who had nothing at all to do with the official proceedings. They were driven, I thought, by a thirst for distinction, but they were, although they did not look it, moralists—defenders of the doctrine that you get nothing in life without working for it. It's O.K. to be a millionaire, for example, as long as you have ulcers to show you came by it honestly, and to be a great actress you should have Suffered. Johansson hadn't suffered enough.

My friend with the free ticket ran forward to get close to the ring, like half the people on the field, and he told me next day, "They were all yelling at Johansson, who was still spread out like a wall-to-wall carpet. 'Too much Grossinger's, Ingo!' they shouted, and 'Go on back to Sweden, you bum!'" They wanted him to leave before he got up. Johansson looked bewildered and badly beaten. When he at last left the ring, the crowd thinned out, and the teen-agers disappeared as mysteriously as they had come. There were almost no reporters left in the press section. One old reporter, though—a white-haired man who must have been in his seventies—was typing out his story on a battered Royal portable. He typed with a jerky, one-finger, overhand motion. I looked over his shoulder at his lead. "Floyd Patterson rose tonight like a Phoenix bird from the ashes," his story began.

July 9, 1960

A Space
Filled In

While in training for a fight, Mr. Floyd Patterson, the heavyweight champion of the world, spends most of his time sleeping. He sleeps regularly from nine in the evening until six next morning, rises, runs, eats four or five eggs or a few chops, and sleeps from eight to ten. Then he sometimes takes a nap until noon, when he does his gym work and boxes, and after that, if he is not worried, he takes a long walk and, on his return, sleeps until suppertime. If he has anything on his mind, he sleeps instead of taking the walk. "Fighters have different ways of reacting to tension," he has been quoted as saying, although the choice of words is not characteristic. "Some get nervous and jumpy and can't eat. Others eat a lot and do practical jokes. Others just sleep. That's me."

Sleeping has made Patterson's success possible. In the years since he won the Olympic 167-pound boxing title at Helsinki in 1952, he has had to put on more and more solid weight to become an authentic heavyweight. (In 1956, when he fought Archie Moore for the championship that Marciano's retirement left vacant, he weighed about 180; in his 1959 bout with Johansson, which he lost, he weighed 182;

in the 1960 Johansson fight, which he won, regaining the championship, he weighed 190.) The only effectual way to "build" a fighter is to
feed him quite a lot and make him work hard enough to turn part of the
fodder into muscle. There is no way to induce his bones to grow, and
simple stuffing will do more harm than good; nothing is worse for a
fighter than surplus weight. Patterson picked up eight solid pounds between the 1959 defeat and the 1960 win, but he trained for ten of the
twelve months that intervened between the two fights. A fighter who
sleeps poorly or who frolics about during his waking hours will either
fret or burn away the hard-won gain in fighting weight. Patterson
sleeps and holds it. Dan Florio, his trainer, told a London interviewer,
"If we put him on a diet, we'd soon have a middleweight on our hands."
This confirms my own inexpert opinion completely; I see Patterson
not as a light-heavy in a padding of fat but as a tall middleweight in a
carapace of smoothly flowing muscle. He has to keep after the muscles
to hold his weight and their fluidity. (A muscle-bound boxer is in as
bad a state as a fat one.)

Patterson's sleep performs more than a physiological function. He
thinks a lot, subliminally, while sleeping. Once he dreamed of a new
blow that nobody could block, and, waking, leaped from his bed and
ran to a mirror to try it out, like a poet carrying a couplet to the escri-
toire. "It wasn't any good," he admitted afterward, which put him one
up on most poets. Because of the essential part that sleep plays in his
career, he has carefully refrained from building up any hobbies that
might keep him awake. He shies away from paperbacks, for example,
as if they contained gin—he has observed others lying awake nights
reading them. His only outside interests—aside from the civic good,
which does not interfere with his rest—are his wife and children,
whom he can reach by telephone from his bed.

I was therefore not astonished at being told, when I called him at his
quarters in Miami Beach the day before his third match with Johansson, "Floyd's upstairs, sleeping." I sent my name up by Buster Watson,
the champion's Figaro, handyman, counsellor, and supernumerary
second, hoping that Floyd might remember me or, if not, think I was
somebody he did remember. I looked around the place while Buster

was gone. The house was a large white villa on a good residential road. A big dining room and living room, without a wall between them, occupied all the visible first floor. There was wall-to-wall carpeting; a fireplace; a department-store kind of furniture, neither beautiful nor cheap; and a long sideboard covered with Class C Members' golf cups and Junior Girls' swimming trophies, left by the family from whom Patterson's faction had rented the house. It was more pretentious than the small, crowded dining room of the farmhouse near Summit, New Jersey, where I had visited Patterson before other fights, but the set was essentially the same. There were two weighing scales and a Valpak overflowing with soiled boxing clothes near the front door, and, grouped around a television set, two sparring partners—long, the color of a good Havana wrapper, and sprawled back in lounge chairs at an angle of twenty degrees, with the soles of their gigantic shoes pointed at the machine. They, too, had bouts scheduled for the following evening—"underneath," or on the supporting card of preliminary bouts—but they had little to worry about. Their opponents would also be sparring partners, and sparring partners are the least bellicose of prizefighters.

The noise of the television rose above the hum of the air-conditioner. I said "Beautiful day, isn't it?," and one of the partners, waking politely, said "Yes, sir," and then reclosed the eye with which he had sighted in on me. A third, intermittent hum sounded between the two other noises, like a flight of bumblebees flying under a flock of macaws and above a washing machine.

Patterson, polite beyond the call of courtesy, came down to see me. He was reproachful, just the same. There were only thirty-three hours left before fight time, and, according to his lights, he *needed* his sleep. "The other writers been down here four, five days already, and you just come in at the tail end," he said. "No time for talking now." He was wearing a silk Oriental dressing robe—orange and black, like a butterfly wing—and under it his back made a blocky rectangle, no longer an inverted triangle as in the Helsinki days. There were ropes of muscle at the base of his throat—he was a full-scale heavyweight now. He is a dark man, about the color of semi-sweet chocolate, and has a long uptilted nose and little sleepy eyes, which give him the look of having a small joke with himself.

He was a favorite at four or five or six to one to beat Johansson this time, but he was sleeping as conscientiously as ever. Perhaps being so hot a favorite reminded him unpleasantly of the weeks before their first fight, when all the sportswriters had touted him to win easily and he had got knocked out for the only time in his life. He had been surprised on that occasion; the Swede—his claims unbelieved, like those of all boastful foreign athletes who come to America—had landed on him early and never let him recover. Then, in the second fight, Patterson had done what we had all predicted for the first one. But by that time most of the writers had hurt his feelings by questioning his vocation; he would never take an opponent—or a friend—for granted again.

Unexpectedly, he said to me, "It's lucky I'm not superstitious. If I was, I wouldn't go through with this fight."

I said, offhand, "There's nothing the matter with fighting on the thirteenth. The bad luck will split even."

The champion said, "It's worse than that. I had a dream."

I asked, naturally, what it was, and he said, "It was so bad I couldn't tell you."

"Dreams go by opposites," I told him, and added, "I know a lot about dreams. If you told me, maybe I could advise you." (I wondered if they had a copy of Erich Fromm's "Forgotten Language" or of "The Old Gypsy Dream Book and Fortune Teller" in the Miami Beach Public Library.)

The champ wouldn't go for that feint, but he promised, "If things come out right for me, I'll tell you what it was." And then, as if defying dreams in general, he said, "A dream is just an empty space waiting for somewhere to fill in."

I wished him success in his contest, and he left me to puzzle over that one. "I got to catch up on sleep," he said.

I decided that this wound up my own roadwork for a fight that looked so easy to cover. I took the Swede less seriously than Patterson did. (I did not have to fight him, of course.) In the second fight, when Johansson was champion, he had not acted like a champion, and I could not believe that now, after having been knocked out of time for a quarter of an hour in that bout, he would have much zest for the fray. The only weapon he had revealed in either fight was a fast, dangerous right hand, and Patterson, warned by his experience in the first bout, had had little trouble keeping away from it in the second. Moreover, Johansson, who had scandalized American trainers by his hedonism before the first two fights, was now, from reports, out-hedonizing himself. He not only had his father, mother, brother, sister-in-law, and secretary-fiancée living near him in his training quarters, a hotel in Palm Beach, but he was, I had heard, on an eating jag—creamed chicken, strawberry shortcake, cherry cheesecake. There was no limit to his reported transgressions. It sounded compulsive to me—the prisoner stuffing before the execution. Whitey Bimstein, Johansson's American trainer, copes with a gluttonous client, if he can get him out on some lonely farm, by eating half the food on the fellow's plate at every meal, as well as a double portion of his own. But Florida, crammed with restaurants, slippery with borsch, soggy with lime pie, offers too many opportunities for evasion. Besides, according to my sources, Johansson had the other Swedes smuggling for him. His reported conduct reminded me of that of the Sultan Muhammad of Khorazm, in the thirteenth century, who was engaged in war with the invincible Genghis Khan. It is related in the famous book of Juvaini, the Persian historian, that the Sultan, when he knew the jig was up, "strayed from the path of seriousness in compliance with his desires, and set foot in the wilderness of merriment, and for some days tasted the pleasures of riotous living."

I accordingly returned to my own training headquarters in a hotel called the Fontainebleau ("Fourteen Acres of Oceanfront Luxury")— a rococo interior of bibelots and buhl encased in a structure like twin United Nations Buildings. The Fontainebleau has six places where you can eat: the Fleur de Lis Room; the Poodle Lounge; the Boom Boom Room; Chez Bon Bon, which is a subterranean blintzerie, open twenty-four hours a day; La Ronde, the supper club (Frankie Sinatra that week); and the Pavillon Dining Room (in the Cabana Club area). There is also room service, but it is slow, since the distances to be traversed are so vast. Among the private dining rooms are the Voltaire Room and the Louis Philippe Room. I meant, before I left, to investigate the hotel's link with the *grandeur* beloved of General de Gaulle, but I never got around to it. Natives call the hotel the Fountainblue, and it has one thousand rooms. The fellows who hang out in the lobby of the Garden on fight nights were not in evidence at the Fontaine-bleau. If I had not just seen Patterson, I would have feared that I was in the wrong town. The bellboy who took my bag to my room, however, said that a lot of other guests had come down for the fight. Seats were scaled at twenty, fifty, and a hundred dollars. I had a fifty, since I had not wished to be ostentatious, but I felt that if this became known at the Fontainebleau I would be asked to leave.

When I attended the weighing of the fighters at the Miami Beach Convention Hall, where the fight was to be held, at eleven o'clock the next morning, the fight boys were there. Miami Beach is a bit off their regular beat, but, as Pierce Egan, the Juvaini of the London Prize Ring, has observed, "the pleasures of a mill, to the heroes of the sporting world, rise superior to all difficulties that may present themselves." Since there is no regular rendezvous of the Fancy in the city of burnished torsos, I assumed that the kids had found roosting places, as Egan would put it, here and there among the Deauville, the Dakar, the Eden Roc, the Americana, the Versailles, the Carillon, the Barcelona, the Marseilles, the Algiers, and the hundreds of other soberly named hostelries, each crouching over a subterranean bazaar with an outlet on a narrow strip of beach. In the Convention Hall—a great, clean hangar that Billy Graham, the evangelist, had vacated for the night—the kids rediscovered one another, like castaways from the same wreck reunited on a coral isle. It was reassuring. Mr. Al Weill, manager of Rocky Marciano, the last champion before Patterson, stood just within the turnstile leading to the hall, a monument to glory's evanescence. In other years, he would have been a center of attention, but now the crowd hurried by—a bitter reminder that a Frankenstein, no matter how profound, has got to have a monster or he's dead. I waved to Weill and rushed up to Cus D'Amato, Patterson's manager except in New York State, where he cannot get a license. D'Amato, who looks like a Roman senator with a snow-white crew cut, is said to be having a spot of trouble with his own monster, but he attributes the talk to the wishful thinking of sportswriters who do not like him. I asked him whether Patterson was going to finish Johansson off early—a question of the kind intended solely to start a conversation.

D'Amato, who speaks in parables, became indignant. "What we got here is a military situation, which is a puzzle to explain how anybody could get it so wrong," he said. "There are two countries, each represented by an army, say. Each army has the best of equipment, plenty of ammunition, good generals, and high morale. But Country Number One hears persistently the report that the ammunition in the guns of Country Number Two consists exclusively of duds, right?" His eyes grew wide, and he punched me under the heart with his right index finger.

"In other words," I said, to let him know I was on, "they say the Swede is stiff."

"It is the most preposterous thing in the world," D'Amato-Clausewitz said. "They make us an out favorite over a guy that knocked us dead in the first fight. But let us resume our campaign. Is Country Number One going to be conned into an attitude of overconfidence? No. It will follow all the usual procedures in order to win. They know that."

"Who know it?" I asked.

"Patterson's critics," Cus said. "The newspaper guys. Now, if we knock him out good," he went on, leaping lightly into the ring to help his man, "they will say he was out of condition and incompetent, so Patterson's due is withheld. But if he knocks Patterson out"—I noticed that Cus leaped out of the ring before the blow landed—"then Patterson is a bum because he got knocked out by a bum that wasn't even in condition."

D'Amato has had a conviction since he first tied boxing gloves on Patterson, then fourteen years old, that all the world is in a devious conspiracy to bring about the ruin of both of them. It is indeed true that few small managers—like D'Amato, who runs a one-room gymnasium over a dance hall near Lüchow's—find a prospective champion as young as that and hold on to him. Pierce Egan's "pugilistic hemisphere" is still liberally populated with wolves. D'Amato tries conscientiously to conspire more deviously than the putative conspirators, who include a lot of fellows who aren't conspiring at all. "Take the atom bomb," he went on unexpectedly. "In order to get it across, a country must not only possess the bomb but the means of delivering it. Now, this fellow we are fighting not only *has* what you might call an atom bomb but he has *proved* he can deliver it, by some mysterious, unpredictable method impossible to figure out. They say he is scary, but what difference does that make? What is more dangerous than a scary guy who has a weapon?"

This convinced me that D'Amato expected Floyd to win easily, and that he wanted the newspapermen to write about it as if he had knocked out Sam Langford on a good day.

On the scales, Patterson, without a surplus ounce on him, weighed 194¾—the heaviest fighting weight of his life. The four and three-quarters additional pounds of muscle were a tribute to sleep, hard work, lamb chops, and Dan Florio's magic vitamins. Johansson looked lardy, as well as anxious. His weight—206½ pounds—was also the highest in *his* life, but it had an ill-earned look, rolling around his waist like recently converted cherry cheesecake. He had gained twelve and a half pounds between fights. Mr. Al Weill remarked of the challenger's facial expression that he "looked like he was going to be electrocuted." Mr. Whitey Bimstein, my friend in the Swede's entourage, appeared to be as unhappy as his principal, and since I do not like to intrude on a chum's sorrow, I made no attempt to interrogate him. I just waved, as to a friend seen across a wide expanse of graves at a funeral. Whitey looked ashamed, as if I had caught him in a hock shop with his wife's wedding ring.

The fight was set for ten-thirty that evening, to suit the closed-television people, whose showing of the fight in theatres the country over was expected to bring in five times as much money as the flesh-and-blood conflict. (When Marciano and Walcott fought eight years ago in Chicago, the open-television people made us all show up to watch them at eight o'clock. Men are becoming the slaves of their shadows.) It was an open secret that the fight had not sold out. Antic-ipation was low, and the long evening to kill before the men got into the ring seemed an added insult. The early-hour fight in Chicago had ended in the first round, when Marciano knocked Walcott down and the latter—an ex-champion, like Johansson—rose one second after the referee counted ten. This had at least allowed the spectators to go home early. It seemed hard that we would have to wait so long if Jo-hansson felt in a Walcott mood.

I must confess that I have always resented Johansson's attitude to an art that engrossed Lord Byron and me. He is like that Dutch master, whose name I am glad I have forgotten, who had a knack of painting cows, so cows were all he put in his pictures. He had no ambition to en-large his repertory. Cows sold like hot cakes, or hot hamburgers. He sold them to everybody in Holland who had the price and a wall to hang them on. "What's the good of learning any more?" he must have said to himself. That is the way Johansson is with his right hand—"a man with one punch in his head," as the immortal Professor Mike Donovan once said of John L. Sullivan. He is not artless; he is a com-mercial artist. Patterson, by contrast, is always trying to improve. He is his own severest critic. Training for this fight, for example, he had tried to develop a left jab—a punch not previously included in his ar-mory for reasons connected with the style that was first taught him by D'Amato. He was a hooking, uppercutting, overhanding kind of fighter, with the kind of style that looks improvised. Having beaten Jo-hansson decisively without a left jab, he had no need of one now, but he likes to expand his scope.

When I went back to the Convention Hall that evening, having had a swim and a Pattersonian snooze, the crowd was already surging around the doors. Feature Sports, Inc., the New York firm promoting the match, had, I heard, cut the prices of all unsold hundred-dollar tickets to twenty dollars. In consequence, business had picked up. I went in with my fifty-dollar ticket, which I had secured via the United States mails, regretting that I hadn't waited and bought a hundred-dollar ticket for thirty dollars less. Feature Sports, which is principally owned by Roy Cohn (late with Schine) and Bill Fugazy, a travel agent, had promoted the second Patterson-Johansson fight in New York with such dazzling ineptitude that I was agreeably surprised by the cheery courtesy of the Miami Beach ushers. Instead of wandering in to find my own seat, as in the previous Cohn-Fugazy promotion, I followed a swift and efficient young man who made for the right spot like a homing pigeon. It was behind a wide steel post. The usher saluted and left me wondering whether Cohn had found my name on some F.B.I. blacklist. If I could have had my spot wired for closed television, I would have been all right, but it was too late, so I steamed out to the lobby, where I saw a line already looped on itself like a rattlesnake's tail—and rattling with fury, at that—in front of a single ticket window marked "Exchange." I was relieved to discover that the insult was not personal; the management had sold seats behind every post in the house. Feature Sports had doubtless indulged in the innocent hope of a clean sellout, in which case we would have been stuck. The line looked hopeless, but a riot-averting gentleman in a slouch hat took peremptory charge and led the steel-posted patrons back into the hall and put us, by platoons, under the leadership of head ushers, who found vacant unposted seats for us.

Mine was far away, but visibility was good. The chase had helped kill the evening. Nothing else happened of the slightest interest until just before the fighters entered the ring, when a young friend of Patterson's and D'Amato's named Mickey Alan sang "The Star-Spangled Banner." It was the high point of his public career, and he socked it out, awakening the squirming crowd that had sat with mounting boredom through the introductions of local notables and old fighters. At about ten-thirty-five, the Johansson faction appeared in one corner of the stadium floor. From my position far above, I could watch its progress toward the ring—dismounted motorcycle cops in white helmets running interference, then foot cops, and then Whitey and his two Swedish corner colleagues, whom I cannot tell apart, though I was seeing them for the third time. The organist played a rollicking version of the Swedish anthem. Johansson, in a white terry-cloth robe, followed in the wake of his attendants, like a sacrificial ox on the way up the Acropolis. When he reached the ring, he climbed in and began to shadowbox, as if trying to awaken the immanent demon who had not manifested himself since the first fight, when he had stretched Patterson on the floor. A couple of minutes later, the Patterson faction came in, with Floyd, in a black robe, walking like a toreador amid his attendant pin-stickers. He would have four in his corner this time, I noted: Dan Florio, small and merry; Dan's big brother Nick, who is an equally experienced trainer; Buster Watson; and D'Amato. D'Amato, Floyd's chief second in every bout before 1960, had not been permitted in the ring in the second New York fight, when Floyd regained his title. Mean tongues hinted that his absence contributed to Floyd's victory. My own feeling is that D'Amato makes Patterson nervous; it must be like having your old man in your corner.

I have never viewed the beginning of a fight with more apathy. Last year, at the Polo Grounds, the Swede had looked heavy with danger. In 1959, I had seen how hard he could hit with his right, but his other abilities, if any, had gone untested. In the second fight, it developed that the other abilities were slight, and that Patterson, leery of the right hand, could avoid it comfortably. All he had to do now was to keep Johansson off balance, work in close—but to Johansson's left—and bang him a bit about the body. In the third or fourth round, Johansson, in no condition to go the route, would come apart again. His arms would go limp, and Floyd would knock him cold.

It might have gone that way if Patterson, ever the would-be virtuoso, had not begun the bout by trying out the new jab. He landed it, got away, and landed it again—and about that time Johansson, the opportunist, must have had an idea. The jab and the right cross form the kindergarten curriculum of conventional boxing; they are as sound as can be, like the four-times table, but through familiarity they have lost the power to startle. Patterson is a highly conscious boxer, but he had an unorthodox teacher. He is therefore like a boy who skipped arithmetic and began schooling with algebra. The Swede never got as far as algebra, but he has a solid first-grade education. Again Patterson jabbed, like a kid with a new toy, and this time he failed to step away. Johansson, still fresh and strong, crossed his right over Patterson's left, and down the champion went. At that moment I remembered the dream, too bad to tell, and so, maybe, did Patterson. He looked disgusted but not stunned, and he got up at the count of two. The referee then restrained him until the knockdown timekeeper counted eight. This is not the rule in championship fights in most states, but it is in Florida, where they have very few of them. It is designed to save a fighter who bounces up, from pride or reflex, before he is in shape to defend himself. This, however, is part of a fighter's trade, and a champion should be capable of using his own judgment. By "eight," Patterson was fresh, but I wondered how many times he would make the same mistake. A few seconds later, Johansson hit him again and he was down again.

Whatever the challenger's mood had been on entering the ring, he was merry enough now. He is a gambler, like all right-handed hitters, and, like all gamblers, believes in luck; there is certainly truth in his tale that his right hand "sees" the opening and throws itself. It is his fetish. The second time Patterson went down, I thought of a senior I heard of at Harvard last year who had A's in all the courses in his specialty and was a cinch for a good fellowship if he continued on his scholarly way. But, like Patterson, he was a victim of intellectual curiosity. He took elementary Latin (like Patterson's left jab), flunked it, and went out unlauded. (Naturally, I can think a thought like that very fast.) But now Patterson got up and hit the challenger a good left hook after a right to the head, and Johansson, in turn, went down, reflecting, possibly, that arithmetic is not enough. He got up, too, rather to my disappointment. But some of the steam had gone out of him. All Patterson had to do was to keep on hitting him in the body, I thought hopefully.

In the second round, though, they fought like kids on a schoolground, Johansson banging away with his right toward the head, which was sensible, because he had little else and had to win before he ran out of puff. What troubled me was that Floyd, too, as if ashamed of himself, was throwing rights at Johansson's head—an unnecessary risk. He hit him a few painful right-hand shots in the ribs, under the left arm, and a couple of good belts to the body, which were all to the good and would tire Johansson faster than missing his chin. In the third, Johansson still had more steam than I would have expected, but he was now beginning to bring the right a long way around. Part of the snap was gone.

Negro and white groups were interspersed throughout the audience, and there was no overt ugliness, but behind me I had a Snopes, who now began to ride Patterson. The odd part of it was that he wore a Patterson badge with toy boxing gloves on it and, before the fight, had generously offered to bet me even money that Floyd would win. I was happy when somebody farther back began to yell to Patterson, "He's tahd! He's tahd! You can tell from his ahms he's tahd!"

"Who's tahd?" shrieked Snopes.

"Johansson, you fool," the other fellow yelled. I don't suppose that Snopes had ever seen a fight before.

In the fourth and fifth rounds, they scuffled away, and Patterson, although ahead on points, couldn't steady down to anything coherent. But merely keeping Johansson moving was enough, if sufficiently protracted. There were bellows to mend in his corner after each round, as Egan would have put it. When they came out for the sixth, Johansson made his last charge, and Patterson backed away, as if to gauge the force left in the harpooned, dying porpoise. Next, Patterson went on the bicycle, skipping back and then circling around Johansson in a comic imitation of fear. His idea was to draw Johansson on, but the Swede hardly had strength enough to respond, even if he had wanted to. Then the conscientious sleeper stepped in and hit him a left hook to the body, followed by a chopping right to the jaw and, as Johansson fell, a downward-arching right that hit the side of his head before the head hit the mat. The challenger landed on his forehead and face. The first right was not the sort of punch that would have downed a fresh or well-conditioned fighter, and the second couldn't have happened without the first. Johansson squirmed about, and at "seven" made a good effort to get up. It seemed to me that he got both knees and both hands off the floor, but he fell down again. Should the referee then have started a new count? Or wasn't he all the way up? A few seconds later, he heaved himself upright, but, like Walcott at Chicago, he was a second late. The referee, a local fireman named Regan, stepped in front of him—and he was right, because Johansson was through.

Half the crowd booed as if Patterson had been kicking a baby, and most of the sportswriters said the next day that he had fought like an amateur, although there has never been an amateur who could whip one side of a big, experienced professional heavyweight with a right hand like Johansson's. It is improbable that Patterson will ever be remembered with Jack Johnson and Joe Louis, who were truly big heavyweights as well as great talents, or with Marciano, who was a crude phenomenon, or with Sam Langford, who should have been Chairman of the Joint Chiefs of Staff, because he was a tactical genius. "Whatever that other fellow want to do, don't let him do it," Sam used to say, and he would never have stood there trading rights with a one-punch fighter. But Patterson is a conscientious, hard-striving artist—the kind who, if he were a writer, would win the National Book Award and the Pulitzer Prize and get an obituary in the *Times* three-quarters of a column long. He gets up when he is knocked down, and keeps on knocking the other fellow down until he doesn't get up. This is the pugilistic equivalent of one little word after another, and bears out the apothegm of Jack McAuliffe's mother, in Cork. McAuliffe was an old bare-knuckle lightweight champion, and his mother's words, which he passed along to all the friends of his old age, were "Once down is no battle." To a world that demands nothing less than genius, the only answer is "Why don't you go and be one?"

Next morning, I slept late and then took a taxi over to the Deauville, a hotel only a half-size smaller and one width narrower than the Fontainebleau, to attend a Patterson press conference and victory lunch. Patterson, a patch crisscrossed with sticking plaster on his left temple, stood under the converging beams of mysterious lights—television, photographic, and X-ray, I suppose—and shook hands with his well-wishers.

I approached him and, having engaged his attention, said, "Floyd, now that everything has turned out all right, will you tell me your dream?"

He smiled happily and said, "Oh, sure. I dreamed he put me down."

"Did you get up, in your dream?" I asked, and he shook his head.

"What hand did he hit you with, Floyd?" I asked.

"The right hand, of course," Patterson answered. "If he'd a hit me with the hook, I would have got up."

March 25, 1961

Ad Lib

The Shreveport, Louisiana, *Times*, a paper I sometimes see in the course of my researches, carried on June 5th an editorial quoting "four eminent scientists," whose names it did not furnish, to the effect that "the Negro I.Q. becomes *progressively lower* as he ages." "The Negro," the editorial said, "is brightest as a child, and from adolescence on gains and loses fitness fitfully, with a final rapid enfeeblement of the intellect." A Negro sesquicentenarian of my acquaintance, the boxer Archie Moore, puts the editorial thesis in doubt by growing smarter as he goes along. Moore is conscious of no disrespect in doing this, for he has not read the paper. I term him a sesquicentenarian because a generous professional life expectancy for a boxer is ten years, compared to, say, a doctor's or lawyer's fifty; Moore, who has boxed for money for twenty-five years, is thus of the same professional age as an attorney who has practiced for a hundred and twenty-five, and if you tack on to the front end of his public career the nineteen or twenty-two years he spent studying for it (his chronological age is slightly uncertain), he is, at forty-four or forty-seven, the equivalent of a cardiologist or a bone-setter who is a century and a half old, give or take a couple of years. It is equally easy to demonstrate that Moore is getting smarter as he ages, because in 1939 or 1942, when he was twenty-six, he had difficulty in outsmarting both Negroes *and* whites who were approximately his own chronological age; he lost two fights out of six in 1939, and was held to a draw in 1942 by one Eddie Booker, an opponent who has left no footprints on the sands of time. On this past June 10th, in Madison Square Garden, however, he made a twenty-six-year-old control subject look as foolish as any anonymous eminent scientist ever looked. Moore's guinea pig in this demonstration was a handsome white Italian of apparently average intelligence named Giulio Rinaldi. He was Moore's two-hundred-and-thirteenth recorded professional dialogist, and there must have been a few—especially early in Moore's vocation—that the record book missed.

In 1954, after I had written about Moore's first appearance in Madison Square Garden, achieved when he was chronologically thirty-seven or forty and professionally ninety, I received a plaintive note from him, signed "the most unappreciated fighter in the world." I had called him "a virtuoso of anachronistic perfection in an age when boxers in general are hurried along like artificially ripened tomatoes, and with similarly unsatisfactory results," and this had done him not a whit more than justice. My chronicle of this initial metropolitan recital was headed "Début of a Seasoned Artist." He had knocked out a challenger named Harold Johnson—twenty-six years old, like Rinaldi—in the fourteenth round, but the public, instead of acclaiming him, had by its apathy tacitly accused him of undue deliberation. In those days, as now, Moore would patiently, with pleasurable application, befuddle and disarticulate an opponent before letting him have it, just as Clytemnestra threw the web over Agamemnon before Aegisthus hit him with the axe. The axe was part of Moore's equipment, but the web of guile economized his energies and saved him from the hurts that come to more receptive fighters. (He can take a good punch, but he considers it a reflection on his workmanship.) Refusing to cheapen his art to please the public, he waited for the public to rise to his level. The public didn't do so, but in maintaining his standards he has protracted his career. Now he is at long last popular, but for a reason that he rather

scorns: he is so old that the fight fans come to see whether he can survive one more adventure. They watch him as they would a rodeo
clown without a barrel.

Because I am even older than Moore by simple chronology and because I admire his skills, I attend his public performances when I can.
Each time, I wonder how much (except for the I.Q.) he has left for the
skills to work with. He keeps this a mystery; the public would be less
curious about the next show if it could guess. Rinaldi was the ninth
challenger that Moore has beaten off for the light-heavyweight (175-
pound) boxing championship of the world, which Moore picked up
when he was thirty-six or thirty-nine, in 1952—a circumstance in itself as astonishing as for a lawyer to earn his first big retainer after
eighty years at the bar. The progressive *rise* in Moore's I.Q. as he ages
should all the more disconcert the Shreveport savants, because he was
pretty smart to begin with. Archie's rise to popularity was long delayed
by his intellectual approach to his art. He was a boxer's boxer, as Stendhal was for a long time a writer's writer. Archie was caviar to the general public, which prefers sluggers or, in their default, prancers, like
Sugar Ray Robinson in his early period, when he was a study in grace-
fully wasted motion. The kind of fighter the uninitiate relish is the fellow who will "take one to give one," rushing in to occupy the other fellow's gloves with his face while he slugs away at the face in front of him.
This is a type technically known as a "club fighter," because such fighters provided the bread and butter of the small neighborhood fight clubs
that flourished before television put them out of business. Artists like
Moore worked their way up by practicing on the bodies of these specimens. Moore's vocabulary contains no term more pejorative than
"club fighter"; it impugns culture and I.Q. together. It is the club
fighter, white or Negro, who frequently suffers a rapid enfeeblement of
the intellect. I once climbed into a taxi late at night on the Place Pi-
galle and soon discovered that the driver was Yves Laffineur, a former
welterweight champion of France, who had had a brave manager in
the late twenties and early thirties. The manager had put Laffineur in
with all the good ones, including middles and light heavies. Laffineur's
intelligence, Laffineur affirmed, had survived this festival of percus-

sion—but *tout juste*. "It escaped like the sole survivor of a shipwreck," he said.

Nothing like that will ever happen to Moore, whose head, though covered with gray astrakhan, is sound outside and inside, as I reobserved with pleasure when I encountered him and his Minister of Foreign Affairs, Dr. Jack Kearns, in a hotel suite a couple of weeks before his scheduled Rinaldi concerto. Kearns is called "Doctor" because he looks like a Ph.D. Moore despises the word "manager," and he hasn't one. He and Kearns are employees of Archie Moore Enterprises, Inc., a California corporation set up to mitigate the tax impact of too many dollars' arriving in one calendar or fiscal year. Kearns does the conspiring outside the ring, and Moore is the inside man. "I like Jack," is the way the virtuoso puts it. "There is nothing but a handshake between us. He gets a share of the money, but he is not my manager." His highest praise of Dr. Kearns is "He always got the most for his fighters." Kearns' fighters included Jack Dempsey and Mickey Walker, two bonanzas of genius, and Joey Maxim, Moore's predecessor as light-heavyweight champion and a fellow with a thin vein of talent that Kearns exploited almost as auriferously as he did the others. This is the real test of a fight manager's I.Q. Kearns, who is rising eighty, is not a Negro, but his intelligence is not enfeebled, either. He is professionally not as old as Moore, because he gave up boxing in about 1908, after being beaten by a couple of immortals who died poor, which he never will.

The chief change in Moore since I had last seen him—in 1956 in a dressing room in London after his rendition of a Trinidadian named Yolande Pompey—was that he had stopped dyeing his hair. It was now short and frankly gray, instead of long and brown with menacing flashes of chestnut red, like lightning among the thunderclouds. This, I saw, marked a change in emphasis in the presentation of the act; instead of inspiring opponents with terror, he now wanted to appeal to their inhibitions against striking an old man. While they struggled with their inhibitions, he would be in there jabbing the compassion off their beaming countenances. Moore and Kearns are world travellers. There was a period in Archie's life when he had to go as far as Australia to get fights, and he formed a taste for moving around. Last year, the associates discovered Rinaldi in Rome, and Moore boxed ten rounds against him there on October 29th, losing the decision. The title had not been at stake, because the bout had been at a liberal weight—185 pounds—and Moore had not even made that, coming in at 190 and losing a weight forfeit of a thousand dollars, which he regretted. Accounts of the event were cloudy, like all travellers' tales, but Moore did not appear to have suffered marked damage. Seizing on his recitalist's defeat as a selling point, Kearns had succeeded in booking the return match into the Garden, at a whacking fee of a hundred thousand dollars, with twelve thousand more for expenses; Rinaldi was to have twenty-five thousand and his expenses, plus the alluring chance to lift the sesquicentenarian's title. All of this would come out of a hundred and fifty thousand dollars paid by a television sponsor; the Garden would keep the box-office money. This arrangement guaranteed that the two elder statesmen would do well out of their trip to Rome.

Kearns is a slender man now, and his face, in contracting, has summarized itself into a high forehead, honest blue eyes, and a generous display of store teeth, all bracketed between two great, soaring ears, which occasionally make his head look as if it were going to fly right off his neck. Ten years ago, when he had Maxim, he used to talk all his attraction's fights in the first person singular. "I'll fight anybody in the world," he would say, meaning that he would let Maxim do it. Now the Doctor, aware that he represents a more autonomous personality, speaks of Moore in the third person, thus recognizing Moore's right to an independent existence. He even lets Moore talk—a privilege Archie appreciates.

Moore is of an agreeably ordinary appearance, being neither very tall nor very short—five feet eleven—and of a light but unmistakably non-white shade. His silhouette has no exaggerated tapers, and he has no obtrusively overdeveloped muscles; his body looks as if it would consider them vulgar. Phrenologically, he is an egghead with the large end up, and his pencil mustache and imperial beard accentuate this ovoid quality. When his face is in repose, they seem to have been drawn on a tan Easter egg, but when he talks he employs a plausible undershot smile that breaks the egg into friendly wrinkles. It is as if he were making advances to a cat that he wanted to lure back within grabbing range. On the occasion of my visit to his hotel room, a sportswriter in attendance asked him what he honestly thought of Rinaldi as a fighter, and Moore said that he was young and strong and a great drawing card in Italy. (This limited praise reminded me of a time when I heard Artur Rubinstein say of a rival pianist, "He plays with all his fingers.") "Rinaldi beat me, didn't he?" Archie asked, and his smile cracked the egg all over its surface. "I should characterize him as a glamorized club fighter," he then added, revealing to me the true direction of his thoughts. Moore said that he was already within easy reach of the class weight limit, and his appearance confirmed him. He was as trim as a clothing-store dummy. Before one of Moore's 175-pound fights, there is always a lot of factitious excitement over whether he will make the weight, but he always does, and there is no reason he shouldn't, since he is not extraordinarily tall or wide. Because he finds eating agreeable, he often puts on twenty or thirty pounds between fights at weight, but they are easy pounds to get off, since he does not give them a chance to stay on long. He said he had been training hard in Southern California—he lives in San Diego—not because of the weight but because he needed to be in form. "When I was young," he said, talking like a speed chart, "I used to rate myself 100 and those other fellows 92 or 94, so I could afford not to be in the best shape—I still had a margin. Now in my *best* shape I'm only about 97, so if I let myself go I might slump to where one of them might beat me." (Floyd Patterson, the heavyweight champion, also has an arithmetical system of rating his own efforts, but a more modest one: he never rates himself above 75.)

When I left the old men at their hotel, they were getting ready to board an automobile that would carry them away to a resort called Kutsher's, in the Catskill Mountains, where Moore was to finish his training. A week or so later, and about five days before the fight, I went up to Kutsher's myself, to see how Moore was getting along. I was not worried about him, but I wanted to see him again. Sharing my transportation was John McClain, the drama critic of the *Journal-*

American. These are lean nights for the theatre, and McClain had decided to attempt a column on Moore the actor, since you can get Archie to say something on almost any subject and he likes to dramatize himself. He is, in fact, a one-man repertory company with a large number of bits: "Moore, the Unappreciated Genius"; "Moore, the Yogi, Starving Himself to Death"; "Moore—How Old Is He?"; and "Moore, the Pitcher Going to the Well." He has even been, on one occasion, a paid actor, playing the role of Jim, the escaping slave, in a moving picture based on "Huckleberry Finn." In the book, Jim is "Nigger Jim," but Archie in the movie wasn't. "I knew the word 'nigger' was out insofar as my friends were concerned," the artist once said. "They would not appreciate it. I supervised and blue-pencilled the script myself, and the word 'nigger' stayed in only once, and that was to establish the unsympathetic character of Huck's father, who said it. Trying to alienate Huck from the Widow Douglas, he says, 'Why, she cares more about that nigger than she does about you,' and then they pan in on me, working out in the yard. The word indicated that Huck's old man is a low person."

McClain and I arrived in time for lunch at Kutsher's, a less grandiose and more relaxed establishment than Grossinger's, twelve miles away, where Rocky Marciano used to train, but on almost the same scale—a Château de Chambord compared to Versailles. It is a large, self-sufficient community, with a main building and recreation buildings surrounded by guest cottages and a golf course. Moore was quartered in one of the cottages, and after lunch McClain and I walked over to see him. As we did so, we found that we were merely a minute portion of a procession that included not only all the Kutsher's guests and about a dozen boxing writers but the chairman and the members of the New York State Athletic Commission, who were about to perform a physical examination on the old gentleman. The Commission doctors—one oldish and small, and one younger and brisker—entered Moore's cottage, and the rest of us remained outside in an agony of apprehension. Would they find the sesquicentenarian senile, his jawbone hyperfriable? I wondered how much they knew about geriatrics. Soon the doctors emerged smiling, as if they had successfully delivered a baby. Dr. Alexander Schiff, the senior, called the reporters about him to announce that disintegration had not yet seriously set in. "He has the reflexes, the arteries, of a man thirty to thirty-two," Dr. Schiff said. "His pulse indicates undiminished recuperative power, and his blood pressure would look good on a kid. The man is a physical marvel."

Relieved, we all retraced our path across the campus to the Palestra, a rustic hall suitable for basketball, dancing, and night-club entertainment, where Moore was to work out in a ring set on a stage, surrounded by the night-club tables. The seasoned performer arrived almost as soon as we did. He wore only ring trunks and a light T shirt—a sign that he would have no trouble making the weight. If weight had still been a problem, he would have been wearing long woollen underwear or a sweatsuit, with sheets of rubber wound around his belly under it. His bare legs were slimmer than I had ever seen them. Most fighters nowadays wear leather headguards when sparring, to protect themselves against cuts over the eyes that might force them to postpone a match, but Moore, with that hundred-thousand-dollar performance only five days off, worked bareheaded. "A headguard is no good," he maintains. "Knowing you can't be hurt, you become careless. Then, in a fight, habit asserts itself and you get hit. Before 1952, when I won my title, I never wore a headguard. Then I became such a valuable piece of property that Charlie Johnston made me put one on." (Johnston was his last contract manager.) "Now I've got rid of Johnston, and I've got rid of the headguard, too."

Moore worked with a tall, very dark boy named Greatest Crawford. ("Greatest swears that that's his real first name," Dr. Kearns, at ringside, said.) Crawford, like Moore, is a cool, fast boxer, who, it was evident, studies the Master as they go along—a learn-and-earn course. He kept moving into Moore, doubtless by instruction, and Moore, in a guard peculiar to him—elbows high, forearms horizontally across his body—moved, swaying, just inside the blows, slipping some with his head and catching others with his elbows, until he saw a chance to counter. They rehearsed again and again the development of a certain situation—a crowder swarming all over a hitter, who tries to spot an opening. Crawford did not rehearse leaving an opening; he did his best to avoid it, and since he is extremely fast, the patriarch had excellent practice. The reason for the sparring pattern, Moore said later, was that before his bout with Rinaldi in Italy he had been told that Rinaldi was a crowder who stayed on top of you. "But he crossed me by non-crowding," he said. "He ran away until all that spaghetti I had been eating bogged me down, and then he put the pressure on. This time, he will expect me to expect him to non-crowd, and therefore he is likely to revert to what I heard was his natural style—namely, crowd. I will be ready for him. He will see more Moore than he saw before."

After his workout, the virtuoso retired into a curtained nook for his rub—a long one—and when he emerged, a dressing gown now swathing him, he led the way back to the cottage and at last gave an audience.

This was McClain's chance, and he said, "I am a drama critic, Archie, and I would like to know how you conceive this role."

Archie said, "I cannot disclose that."

"Have you studied it up?" McClain asked. "Or are you just going to ad-lib?"

"Ad-lib," Archie said. "Ad-lib. You can do a lot of things when you have the props."

Then somebody asked him if he had enjoyed playing Jim in "Huckleberry Finn," and he said that he had. "When I took the test for that part, I memorized sixteen pages verbatim," he said. "I felt I had to play it, because I identified with Jim. All my early life was like his."

"Surely, Archie," I said, scenting a scoop, "you were not born before the Emancipation Proclamation?"

"No," he said, "but all my life has been a long struggle to freedom. It has been a long struggle to express myself."

"Who held you down, Archie?" I asked, for I had never thought that he'd needed a friend to get out a habeas corpus for him.

"Managers," the virtuoso said. "My ability far exceeds the ability of my past managers. I was a chattel. All fighters were chattels. You had a two-year contract, but if you refused to renew, they put you out of work. That was the Boxing Managers' Guild. No other manager would take you, and none of them would let his boy fight you. Johnston was a smart manager, but he didn't understand me." Charlie Johnston, an old-fashioned manager, would have been as hurt at hearing that, I imagine, as an Algerian *cólon* would at being told he didn't understand the natives. I have known Johnston to buy a box of jelly doughnuts for a fighter he liked when the fellow didn't have to make weight. "No one figured a fighter had the sense to talk for himself," Moore went on. "You probably remember how a manager used to come to a newspaper office with two or three fighters, walk them into the sports department, and sit them down on a bench, like dummies, and *he'd* tell the sports editor what *he* was going to do."

"How did you get back on that raft?" I asked.

"I *outlasted* them," the sesquicentenarian replied. "I *outlasted* them."

The next day, I caught Rinaldi's workout at the Eighth Avenue Gym, the place that for thirty-five years before the retirement of its founder was called Stillman's. The Italian, apple-cheeked and without guile, looked juvenile and seemed to be less sure than Moore of making the weight, because he worked, in the sweltering city heat, in a heavy blue sweatsuit bearing on the breast the mystic device "IG-NIS." But he was no *ignis fatuus*; he looked easy to hit. He worked with a good, experienced colored middleweight named Randy Sandy, who cuffed him about handily, but Charlie Goldman, one of the watchers and a sage almost as ancient as Kearns, said, "Sandy is likely to make anybody look bad for two rounds." Rinaldi at least looked uncomfortably strong, and the championship bout would be not at two rounds but at fifteen. "You got to give Rinaldi a chance," Goldman said. Rocky Marciano, his most celebrated disciple, was a strong, rough type, and Goldman, though he esteems artistry, does not, like Archie, consider it a *sine qua non*. Marciano, in fact, once proved to Archie himself that it isn't, by knocking him out in a bout for the heavyweight championship in 1955. Marciano retired after that fight, though he was six or nine years younger chronologically than Archie. He is now a historical character, like Joe Louis or Jack Dempsey, while the sesquicentenarian remains in active practice. "Moore has to go sometime,"

Goldman said. I did not think that the Seasoned Artist was in immediate danger, however, and the evening in Madison Square Garden
bore me out.

The evening, indeed, had about it some of the aura of old-time fight
nights. It drew to the Garden ninety-five hundred paying customers—
almost exactly half capacity—whereas most bouts these days attract a
flesh-and-blood crowd so small that the television cameras, in order to
convey the appearance of a public spectacle, can show nothing more
than the ring and the working press. But this night there were enough
spectators to warm up the great hall and create the illusion of good
times. They paid $46,500—a handsome sum, as gates go now, for a
fight that is not blacked out. Everyone, though, looked old, as at the
fortieth reunion of a college class. Ever since the television blight set
in with the Louis-Walcott bout in 1947, the fight game has hit the slide
of rapid enfeeblement, like the Shreveport I.Q., and there are few new
seconds, trainers, referees, or managers. The fans are old, too—at
least fifty, most of us—because a dying form of entertainment attracts
few recruits. The boy who becomes a fighter in America nowadays is
either a Negro or a Puerto Rican or a romantic. Still, it was a crowd,
and back in the old headquarters.

The preliminaries offered another return to an older age, because
they included a couple of good fights. Rinaldi's manager and trainer, a
bald, gaunt type named Proietti, had taken advantage of the expense
money to bring along as sparring partners a couple of young fighters he
hoped would catch on in America, and he had got them bouts on the
supporting card. I had seen one of these youngsters, named Luigi Napoleoni, box as a member of the Italian Olympic team in Rome last
summer; he reached the quarter-finals, and later turned pro. Teddy
Brenner, the Garden matchmaker, had paired him with an experienced run-of-the-mill pug named Babe Simmons, who looked like the
boys who used to come here out of the West with local reputations in
the twenties and stay on to be bouncers in speakeasies. Napoleoni, a
longilinear type—long arms, long legs, long sideburns—started out
as if he were going the amateur route of three rounds. He boxed with a
speed that had the Babe bleeding and looking faintly discouraged at

the end of the third, but he had apparently forgotten that this was a six-round bout. He ran out of steam at about the same time that Simmons found he could hit him with a left hook to the head whenever he wanted. Now Simmons pounded Napoleoni, who between rounds manifested, with stricken gestures, what torments he was enduring. He stuck it out, though, and finished upright, amid general applause.

There was another grand fight between Greatest Crawford, the sesquicentenarian's research assistant, and a terrifyingly muscled young Negro named Tommy Hough, who swung his arms like scythes. Greatest, a credit to his indoctrination, kept stepping within the arc of the scythes and punching the club fighter's face as if it were a light bag. He is a solemn-looking boy, and as he worked away on Hough he occasionally looked bored, like a young man told to beat a carpet when he would rather be out playing baseball. Hough, meanwhile, continued to swing, his vim unabated. When the referee stopped the fight after the fourth round, on Dr. Schiff's orders, it seemed as though he had turned off Hough's switch. Greatest, the winner, looked solemnly pleased. Hough, protesting, staggered about the ring like a seasick Sunday fisherman just off a party boat. If Greatest, ad-libbing, had stepped aside just once during the bout, Hough might have fallen on his face and knocked himself out.

At last came the moment of confrontation. Because I always like to see what Moore is up to, I had cadged a working-press seat close to the ring; the sesquicentenarian is not one of those fighters with a grand, sweeping style that you can watch from the balcony. His thought is saturated and indirectly expressed; you have to read him closely. His costume and manner before the performance are also significant, being indicative of his mood. Before his Harold Johnson recital, thirty-five professional years ago, he had worn a magnificent mandarin robe, and his air had been Fu-Manchurian, obviously calculated to overawe. And before his epic combat with Marciano, whose anti-intellectualism he had previously decried, he had attempted hypnotism. But tonight his mood was Mozartean, almost *opéra-bouffe*. He wore a motherly white-on-white peignoir, and when his seconds took it off his shoulders he was revealed in a pair of black ring trunks so wide in the waist that he looked to be in peril of losing them. This, I knew, was a calculated humorous effect. Moore, who has a great sense of dramatic fitness, would never want to be found knocked out in pants like that. What he hoped to achieve by them was to accentuate his success in slimming; he is talking of opening a weight-reducing joint. A smile played lightly about his lips, as if he did not think Rinaldi worth the trouble of trying to hypnotize.

Rinaldi, not to slight him, was smiling, too—sincerely. A handsome fellow, his torso—wide at the shoulders, narrow at the waist— was as white as milk. His inverted-triangle face, with pointed jaw, was filled with simple pleasure, as if he thought that all those people were there because they liked him. I remembered, suddenly and with panic, the strange case of Ingemar Johansson, a European whom I had fancied to be equally innocent of talent and who had smiled as fatuously before his first match with Patterson, which he won. In camp at Kutsher's, Moore had looked a hundred years or so younger than he was, but that was different from really being young, and the difference was plain to see when he and Rinaldi stood close together, listening to Ruby Goldstein, the referee. (Ruby, like Moore, was gray now, I noticed. I thought of how black his sleek hair used to be when he was a kid wonder.) I recalled, with disquiet, how Pierce Egan, the Arthur M. Schlesinger, Sr., of the London Prize Ring, had described the Venetian Gondolier, the first Italian challenger for a championship, in 1735: "The Venetian was a man of prodigious strength, possessing an arm not only very large and muscular but surprisingly long. . . . His fame ran before him, and his impetuosity was described to be irresistible." Suppose, I reflected for a panicky moment, that when Moore thought he had been having Rinaldi on in Rome, Rinaldi and his *camorra* had been having *him* on, and concealing the new Gondolier's real form.

The original Gondolier began his London fight by knocking his English opponent clean out of the ring, but Rinaldi showed no such decisive intention. When the gong sounded, he came out and sparred awkwardly; he was in a non-crowding mood. Moore, in his elbow cradle, reconnoitred only. On my program, in the space marked for scoring Round 1, I now find only the accurate notation "Nothing." In the succeeding rounds, the Italian poked a few oddly disarticulated blows at Moore from far out—when he attacked, he started at such a distance that the old man had only to step inside. But when Moore got inside he refrained from hitting; it was early in the fight, and the thought occurred to me that he was taking no chances on spending his strength too soon. An old man can fight himself out very quickly and then find himself with twelve or thirteen rounds still stretching ahead, like a desert traveller whose girl has gone off with his jeep. In the second round, Moore worked a little closer—once he landed a fair uppercut—and my card for the third bears the notation "Stalking." In the fourth, Rinaldi hit Moore a pretty good left hook on the side of the jaw, and this seemed to make up the sesquicentenarian's mind that measures should be taken. Swaying and crouching, he had been working a fraction closer to Rinaldi's body in each round, and now he fought from well within arm's reach, just occasionally jabbing a straight left into Rinaldi's face or whacking a right into his body, and then catching the counter, if any, on elbow or wrist as he swayed away. At this point, he was like a mechanic working under a car—a tap here, a yank there. He could have gone in and smashed away at the boy's strong white belly, but in so doing he would have had Rinaldi's weight on him, and the tension of clutching arms. A body attack *à outrance* is heavy manual work; the attacker has to keep hauling his man off balance and pulling his own arms free to hit again. There were still the desert leagues of time ahead, and Moore could not permit himself such extravagance. But there was a smear of red at Rinaldi's mouth, and other smears began to appear at the boy's eyes as the mechanic tapped.

In the sixth, the ancient began to put punches together—five or six in a sequence. He gave evidence that he wanted to slug, and even fifty years ago, I think, he would at that point have unloaded on a fellow like Rinaldi and left him for dead. He restrained himself, though, probably because he was still husbanding his strength; Rinaldi was proving himself to have stamina, at least, and nothing could be more embarrassing for a great driver in a racing car than to run out of gas and be towed away by a dump truck. In fact, Moore never punched as I had seen him punch against Marciano. He chopped sharply, hooked without his body in it, and jabbed, but he never let the big one go. Afterward, he said he had hurt his metacarpals—a fancy word for the hand bones between the wrist and the first knuckles. So he would tap away, and then for twenty seconds or so in each round he would tear after Rinaldi, hitting freely but within those odd limits. Once, in the eleventh, he hit him a succession of almost-full-strength rights, and the boy's legs buckled, but the old man stopped, as if pacing himself even then, and I jotted "Lost him." In the twelfth, Moore moved Rinaldi around like a man shifting a picture on a wall as he looks for the exact place to hang it. But the hammer never fell; Moore was still undecided at the end of the round. I wrote "Going" in that round, but Rinaldi didn't go, and as the round ended I added "Game." This kind of beating hurts, in the long run, more than being knocked out.

I once knew an old pug who used to say, "Your head is your best hand—there's no glove on it." It is against the rules to butt deliberately, of course, but if your head is so placed that the other fellow runs into it, there is no law that says you may not bring it up to see what damage has resulted. If in so doing you compound the damage, the other party is unfortunate rather than sinned against. An elbow, similarly, should not be a weapon of offense, but nothing short of amputation can stop it from following the hand. Punching in close, if the hand misses, the elbow often won't. No corporation lawyer can play more adroitly with the outer boundary of the law than Mr. Moore. My notation for the thirteenth round recalls that he set Rinaldi up for a knockout with a left hook and then "Lost him again." For the fourteenth, I have "Bang, bang, bang—lost him." In the fifteenth, he did not have Rinaldi in danger. Either he deemed it a pity to knock him out then or he was discouraged.

There was, of course, no doubt about the decision of the referee and the two judges. They voted unanimously for Moore, who had already moved to the microphone dangling above the ring. He felt free to express himself. Don Dunphy, the American Broadcasting Company's announcer, said, "I'd like to ask you about the fight." The sesquicentenarian Thespian grabbed the mike and said, "I'd like to speak first, please, if I may. I'm going to give our wonderful mayor of San Diego,

Mr. Mayor Dell, a three-thousand-dollar check, to be divided as thus." (Archie's wind, after fifteen rounds, was as sound as Billy Graham's.) "I would like very much for one thousand dollars to go to the children who cannot see and the children who cannot hear, the disabled children, in a united fund where all would be involved. Secondly, I would like to give one thousand dollars for the brave little kids going to school for the Freedom Riders." Here, as in many bequests, there was room for confusion; happily, the sesquicentenarian is still with us and has probably cleared it up by now. "And lastly," he said, "I would like to give five hundred dollars to the B'nai B'rith and buy myself a five-hundred-dollar life membership in the N.A.A.C.P." (This will win him few votes in Shreveport.)

While the Seasoned Artist was at the mike, I started struggling toward his dressing room, where I arrived after he did, because he had a police escort through the crowd and I didn't. When I got in, Archie was expressing himself some more, standing on a rubbing table in his undependable-looking trunks and squeezing his waist to show how effective his reducing system was.

"I wore these trunks because they're the smallest in my collection— size 34," he was saying, and then he asked if all the gentlemen of the press were satisfied with his performance.

I was, but my colleagues appeared less enthusiastic.

"I mean," said the Seasoned Artist, "were you satisfied with my performance relative to an old man?"

There wasn't a doubt that *he* was satisfied.

June 24, 1961

Poet and Pedagogue

When Floyd Patterson regained the world heavyweight championship by knocking out Ingemar Johansson in June, 1960, he so excited a teen-ager named Cassius Marcellus Clay, in Louisville, Kentucky, that Clay, who was a good amateur light heavyweight, made up a ballad in honor of the victory. (The tradition of pugilistic poetry is old; according to Pierce Egan, the Polybius of the London Prize Ring, Bob Gregson, the Lancashire Giant, used "to recount the deeds of his Brethren of the Fist in heroic verse, like the Bards of Old." A sample Gregson couplet was "The British lads that's here/Quite strangers are to fear." He was not a very good fighter, either.) At the time, Clay was too busy training for the Olympic boxing tournament in Rome that summer to set his ode down on paper, but he memorized it, as Homer and Gregson must have done with their things, and then polished it up in his head. "It took me about three days to think it up," Clay told me a week or so ago, while he was training in the Department of Parks gymnasium on West Twenty-eighth Street, for his New York début as a professional, against a heavyweight from Detroit named Sonny Banks. In between his composition of the poem and his appearance on

Twenty-eighth Street, Clay had been to Rome and cleaned up his Olympic opposition with aplomb, which is his strongest characteristic. The other finalist had been a Pole with a name that it takes two rounds to pronounce, but Cassius had not tried. A book that I own called "Olympic Games: 1960," translated from the German, says, "Clay fixes the Pole's punch-hand with an almost hypnotic stare and by nimble dodging renders his attacks quite harmless." He thus risked being disqualified for holding and hitting, but he got away with it. He had then turned professional under social and financial auspices sufficient to launch a bank, and had won ten tryout bouts on the road. Now he told me that Banks, whom he had never seen, would be no problem.

I had watched Clay's performance in Rome and had considered it attractive but not probative. Amateur boxing compares with professional boxing as college theatricals compare with stealing scenes from Margaret Rutherford. Clay had a skittering style, like a pebble scaled over water. He was good to watch, but he seemed to make only glancing contact. It is true that the Pole finished the three-round bout helpless and out on his feet, but I thought he had just run out of puff chasing Clay, who had then cut him to pieces. ("Pietrzykowski is done for," the Olympic book says. "He gazes helplessly into his corner of the ring; his legs grow heavier and he cannot escape his rival.") A boxer who uses his legs as much as Clay used his in Rome risks deceleration in a longer bout. I had been more impressed by Patterson when *he* was an Olympian, in 1952; he had knocked out his man in a round.

At the gym that day, Cassius was on a mat doing situps when Mr. Angelo Dundee, his trainer, brought up the subject of the ballad. "He is smart," Dundee said. "He made up a poem." Clay had his hands locked behind his neck, elbows straight out, as he bobbed up and down. He is a golden-brown young man, big-chested and long-legged, whose limbs have the smooth, rounded look that Joe Louis's used to have, and that frequently denotes fast muscles. He is twenty years old and six feet two inches tall, and he weighs a hundred and ninety-five pounds.

"I'll say it for you," the poet announced, without waiting to be wheedled or breaking cadence. He began on a rise:

"You may talk about Sweden [down and up again],
You may talk about Rome [down and up again],
But Rockville Centre is Floyd Patterson's home [down]."

He is probably the only poet in America who can recite this way. I would like to see T. S. Eliot try.

Clay went on, continuing his ventriflexions:

"A lot of people say that Floyd couldn't fight,
But you should have seen him on that comeback night."

There were some lines that I fumbled; the tempo of situps and poetry grew concurrently faster as the bardic fury took hold. But I caught the climax as the poet's voice rose:

"He cut up his eyes and mussed up his face,
And that last left hook *knocked his head out of place!*"

Cassius smiled and said no more for several situps, as if waiting for Johansson to be carried to his corner. He resumed when the Swede's seconds had had time to slosh water in his pants and bring him around. The fight was done; the press took over:

"A reporter asked: 'Ingo, will a rematch be put on?'
Johansson said: 'Don't know. It might be postponed.' "

The poet did a few more silent strophes, and then said:

"If he would have stayed in Sweden,
He wouldn't have took that beatin'."

Here, overcome by admiration, he lay back and laughed. After a minute or two, he said, "That rhymes. I like it."

There are trainers I know who, if they had a fighter who was a poet, would give up on him, no matter how good he looked, but Mr. Dundee is of the permissive school. Dundee has been a leading Italian name in the prizefighting business in this country ever since about 1910, when a manager named Scotty Monteith had a boy named Giuseppe Carrora whom he rechristened Johnny Dundee. Johnny became the hottest lightweight around; in 1923, in the twilight of his career, he boiled down and won the featherweight championship of the world. Clay's trainer is a brother of Chris Dundee, a promoter in Miami Beach, but they are not related to Johnny, who is still around, or to Joe and Vince Dundee, brothers out of Baltimore, who were welterweight and middleweight champions, respectively, in the late twenties and early thirties, and who are not related to Johnny, either.

"He is very talented," Dundee said while Clay was dressing. It was bitter cold outside, but he did not make Clay take a cold shower before putting his clothes on. "He likes his shower better at the hotel," he told me. It smacked of progressive education. Elaborating on Clay's talent, Dundee said, "He will jab you five or six times going away. Busy hands. And he has a left uppercut." He added that Clay, as a business enterprise, was owned and operated by a syndicate of ten leading citizens of Louisville, mostly distillers. They had given the boy a bonus of ten thousand dollars for signing up, and paid him a monthly allowance and his training expenses whether he fought or not—a research fellowship. In return, they took half his earnings when he had any. These had been inconsiderable until his most recent fight, when he made eight thousand dollars. His manager of record (since somebody has to sign contracts) was a member of this junta—Mr. William Faversham, a son of the old matinée idol. Dundee, the tutor in attendance, was a salaried employee. "The idea was he shouldn't be rushed," Dundee said. "Before they hired me, we had a conference about his future like he was a serious subject."

It sounded like flying in the face of the old rule that hungry fighters make the best fighters. I know an old-style manager named Al Weill, who at the beginning of the week used to give each of his fighters a five-dollar meal ticket that was good for five dollars and fifty cents in trade at a coffeepot on Columbus Avenue. A guy had to win a fight to get a second ticket before the following Monday. "It's good for them," Weill used to say. "Keeps their mind on their work."

That day in the gym, Clay's boxing had consisted of three rounds with an amateur light heavyweight, who had been unable to keep away from the busy hands. When the sparring partner covered his head with his arms, the poet didn't bother to punch to the body. "I'm a head-hunter," he said to a watcher who called his attention to this omission. "Keep punching at a man's head, and it mixes his mind." After that, he had skipped rope without a rope. His flippancy would have horrified Colonel John R. Stingo, an ancient connoisseur, who says, "Body-punching is capital investment," or the late Sam Langford, who, when asked why he punched so much for the body, said, "The head got eyes."

Now Cassius reappeared, a glass of fashion in a snuff-colored suit and one of those lace-front shirts, which I had never before known anybody with nerve enough to wear, although I had seen them in shirt-shop windows on Broadway. His tie was like two shoestring ends laid across each other, and his smile was white and optimistic. He did not appear to know how badly he was being brought up.

Just when the sweet science appears to lie like a painted ship upon a painted ocean, a new Hero, as Pierce Egan would term him, comes along like a Moran tug to pull it out of the doldrums. It was because Clay had some of the Heroic aura about him that I went uptown the next day to see Banks, the *morceau* chosen for the prodigy to perform in his big-time début. The exhibition piece is usually a fighter who was once almost illustrious and is now beyond ambition, but Banks was only twenty-one. He had knocked out nine men in twelve professional fights, had won another fight on a decision, and had lost two, being knocked out once. But he had come back against the man who stopped him and had knocked *him* out in two rounds. That showed determination as well as punching power. I had already met Banks, briefly, at a press conference that the Madison Square Garden corporation gave for the two incipient Heroes, and he seemed the antithesis of the Kentucky bard—a grave, quiet young Deep Southerner. He was as introverted as Clay was extro. Banks, a lighter shade than Clay, had migrated to the automobile factories from Tupelo, Mississippi, and boxed as a professional from the start, to earn money. He said at the press conference that he felt he had "done excellently" in the ring, and that the man who had knocked him out, and whom he had subsequently knocked out, was "an excellent boxer." He had a long, rather pointed head, a long chin, and the kind of inverted-triangle torso that pro-

proletarian artists like to put on their steelworkers. His shoulders were so wide that his neat ready-made suit floated around his waist, and he had long, thick arms.

Banks was scheduled to train at two o'clock in the afternoon at Harry Wiley's Gymnasium, at 137th Street and Broadway. I felt back at home in the fight world as soon as I climbed up from the subway and saw the place—a line of plate-glass windows above a Latin-American bar, grill, and barbecue. The windows were flecked with legends giving the hours when the gym was open (it wasn't), the names of fighters training there (they weren't, and half of them had been retired for years), and plugs for physical fitness and boxing instruction. The door of the gym—"Harry Wiley's *Clean* Gym," the sign on it said—was locked, so I went into the Latin-American place and had a beer while I waited. I had had only half the bottle when a taxi drew up at the curb outside the window and five colored men—one little and four big— got out, carrying bags of gear. They had the key for the gym. I finished my beer and followed them.

By the time I got up the stairs, the three fellows who were going to spar were already in the locker room changing their clothes, and the only ones in sight were a big, solid man in a red jersey, who was laying out the gloves and bandages on a rubbing table, and a wispy little chap in an olive-green sweater, who was smoking a long rattail cigar. His thin black hair was carefully marcelled along the top of his narow skull, a long gold watch chain dangled from his fob pocket, and he exuded an air of elegance, precision, and authority, like a withered but still peppery mahout in charge of a string of not quite bright elephants. Both men appeared occupied with their thoughts, so I made a tour of the room before intruding, reading a series of didactic signs that the proprietor had put up among the photographs of prizefighters and pinup girls. "Road Work Builds Your Legs," one sign said, and another, "Train Every Day—Great Fighters Are Made That Way." A third admonished, "The Gentleman Boxer Has the Most Friends." "Ladies Are Fine—At the Right Time," another said. When I had absorbed them all, I got around to the big man.

"Clay looks mighty fast," I said to him by way of an opening.

He said, "He may not be if a big fellow go after him. That amateur stuff don't mean too much." He himself was Johnny Summerlin, he told me, and he had fought a lot of good heavyweights in his day. "Our boy don't move so fast, but he got fast hands," he said. "He don't discourage easy, either. If we win this one, we'll be all set." I could see that they would be, because Clay has been getting a lot of publicity, and a boxer's fame, like a knight's armor, becomes the property of the fellow who licks him.

Banks now came out in ring togs, and, after greeting me, held out his hands to Summerlin to be bandaged. He looked even more formidable without his street clothes. The two other fighters, who wore their names on their dressing robes, were Cody Jones, a heavyweight as big as Banks, and Sammy Poe, nearly as big. Poe, although a Negro, had a shamrock on the back of his robe—a sign that he was a wag. They were both Banks stablemates from Detroit, Summerlin said, and they had come along to spar with him. Jones had had ten fights and had won eight, six of them by knockouts. This was rougher opposition than any amateur light heavyweight. Banks, when he sparred with Jones, did not scuffle around but practiced purposefully a pattern of coming in low, feinting with head and body to draw a lead, and then hammering in hooks to body and head, following the combination with a right cross. His footwork was neat and geometrical but not flashy—he slid his soles along the mat, always set to hit hard. Jones, using his right hand often, provided rough competition but no substitute for Clay's blinding speed. Poe, the clown, followed Jones. He grunted and howled "Whoo-huh-huh!" every time he threw a punch, and Banks howled back; it sounded like feeding time at a zoo. This was a lively workout.

After the sparring, the little man, discarding his cigar, got into the ring alone with Banks. He wore huge sixteen- or eighteen-ounce sparring gloves, which he held, palm open, toward the giant, leading him in what looked like a fan dance. The little man, covering his meagre chest with one glove, would hold up the other, and Banks would hit it. The punch coming into the glove sounded like a fast ball striking a catcher's mitt. By his motions the trainer indicated a scenario, and

Banks, from his crouch, dropped Clay ten or fifteen times this way, theoretically. Then the slender man called a halt and sent Banks to punch the bag. "Remember," he said, "you got to keep on top of him—keep the pressure on."

As the little man climbed out of the ring, I walked around to him and introduced myself. He said that his name was Theodore Mc-Whorter, and that Banks was his baby, his creation—he had taught him everything. For twenty years, McWhorter said, he had run a gymnasium for boxers in Detroit—the Big D. (I supposed it must be pretty much like Wiley's, where we were talking.) He had trained hundreds of neighborhood boys to fight, and had had some good fighters in his time, like Johnny Summerlin, but never a champion. Something always went wrong.

There are fellows like this in almost every big town. Cus D'Amato, who brought Patterson through the amateurs and still has him, used to be one of them, with a one-room gym on Fourteenth Street, but he is among the few who ever hit the mother lode. I could see that McWhorter was a good teacher—such men often are. They are never former champions or notable boxers. The old star is impatient with beginners. He secretly hopes that they won't be as good as he was, and this is a self-defeating quirk in an instructor. The man with the little gym wants to prove himself vicariously. Every promising pupil, consequently, is himself, and he gets knocked out with every one of them, even if he lives to be eighty. McWhorter, typically, said he had been an amateur bantamweight in the thirties but had never turned pro, because times were so hard then that you could pick up more money boxing amateur. Instead of medals, you would get certificates redeemable for cash—two, three, five dollars, sometimes even ten. Once you were a pro, you might not get two fights a year. Whatever his real reason, he had not gone on.

"My boy never got nothing easy," he said. "He don't expect it. Nobody give him nothing. And a boy like that, when he got a chance to be something, he's dangerous."

"You think he's really got a chance?" I asked.

"If we didn't think so, we wouldn't have took the match," Mr.

McWhorter said. "You can trap a man," he added mysteriously. "Flashy boxing is like running. You got a long lead, you can run freely. The other kid's way behind, you can sit down and play, get up fresh, and run away from him again. But you got a man running after you with a knife or a gun, pressing it in your back, you feel the pressure. You can't run so free. I'm fighting Clay my way." The substitution of the first for the third person in conversation is managerial usage. I knew that McWhorter would resubstitute Banks for himself in the actual fight.

We walked over to the heavy bag, where Banks was working. There was one other downtown spectator in the gym, and he came over and joined us. He was one of those anonymous experts, looking like all his kind, whom I have been seeing around gyms and fight camps for thirty years. "You can tell a Detroit fighter every time," he said. "They're well trained. They got the fundamentals. They can hit. Like from Philadelphia the fighters got feneese."

Mr. McWhorter acknowledged the compliment. "We have some fine *trainers* in Detroit," he said.

Banks, no longer gentle, crouched and swayed before the bag, crashing his left hand into it until the thing jigged and clanked its chains.

"Hit him in the belly like that and you got him," the expert said. "He can't take it there."

Banks stopped punching the bag and said, "Thank you, thank you," just as if the expert had said something novel.

"He's a good boy," McWhorter said as the man walked away. "A *polite* boy."

When I left to go downtown, I felt like the possessor of a possibly valuable secret. I toyed with the notion of warning the butterfly Cassius, my fellow-littérateur, of his peril, but decided that I must remain neutral and silent. In a dream the night before the fight, I heard Mr. McWhorter saying ominously, "You can trap a man." He had grown as big as Summerlin, and his cigar had turned into an elephant goad.

The temperature outside the Garden was around fifteen degrees on the night of the fight, and the crowd that had assembled to see Clay's début was so thin that it could more properly be denominated a quorum. Only fans who like sociability ordinarily turn up for a fight that they can watch for nothing on television, and that night the cold had kept even the most gregarious at home. (The boxers, however, were sure of four thousand dollars apiece from television.) Only the sportswriters, the gamblers, and the fight mob were there—nonpayers all—and the Garden management, solicitous about how the ringside would look to the television audience, had to coax relative strangers into the working-press section. This shortage of spectators was too bad, because there was at least one redhot preliminary, which merited a better audience. It was a six-rounder between a lad infelicitously named Ducky Dietz—a hooker and body puncher—and a light heavy from western Pennsylvania named Tommy Gerarde, who preferred a longer range but punched more sharply. Dietz, who shouldn't have, got the decision, and the row that followed warmed our little social group and set the right mood for the main event.

The poet came into the ring first, escorted by Dundee; Nick Florio, the brother of Patterson's trainer, Dan Florio; and a fellow named Gil Clancy, a physical-education supervisor for the Department of Parks, who himself manages a good welterweight named Emile Griffith. (Griffith, unlike Clay, is a worrier. "He is always afraid of being devalued," Clancy says.) As a corner, it was the equivalent of being represented by Sullivan & Cromwell. Clay, who I imagine regretted parting with his lace shirt, had replaced it with a white robe that had a close-fitting red collar and red cuffs. He wore white buckskin bootees that came high on his calves, and, taking hold of the ropes in his corner, he stretched and bounced like a ballet dancer at the bar. In doing so, he turned his back to the other, or hungry, corner before Banks and his faction arrived.

Banks looked determined but slightly uncertain. Maybe he was trying to remember all the things McWhorter had told him to do. He was accompanied by McWhorter, Summerlin, and Harry Wiley, a plump, courtly colored man, who runs the clean gym. McWhorter's parchment brow was wrinkled with concentration, and his mouth was set. He looked like a producer who thinks he may have a hit and doesn't want to jinx it. Summerlin was stolid; he may have been remembering the nights when he had not quite made it. Wiley was comforting and solicitous. The weights were announced: Clay, 194½; Banks, 191¼. It was a difference too slight to count between heavyweights. Banks, wide-shouldered, narrow-waisted, looked as if he would be the better man at slinging a sledge or lifting weights; Clay, more cylindrically formed—arms, legs, and torso—moved more smoothly.

When the bell rang, Banks dropped into the crouch I had seen him rehearse, and began the stalk after Clay that was to put the pressure on him. I felt a species of complicity. The poet, still wrapped in certitude, jabbed, moved, teased, looking the *Konzertstück* over before he banged the ivories. By nimble dodging, as in Rome, he rendered the hungry fighter's attack quite harmless, but this time without keeping his hypnotic stare fixed steadily enough on the punch-hand. They circled around for a minute or so, and then Clay was hit, but not hard, by a left hand. He moved to his own left, across Banks's field of vision, and Banks, turning with him, hit him again, but this time full, with the rising left hook he had worked on so faithfully. The poet went down, and the three men crouching below Banks's corner must have felt, as they listened to the count, like a Reno tourist who hears the silver-dollar jackpot come rolling down. It had been a solid shot—no fluke—and where one shot succeeds, there is no reason to think that another won't. The poet rose at the count of two, but the referee, Ruby Goldstein, as the rules in New York require, stepped between the boxers until the count reached eight, when he let them resume. Now that Banks knew he could hit Clay, he was full of confidence, and the gamblers, who had made Clay a 5–1 favorite, must have had a bad moment. None of them had seen Clay fight, and no doubt they wished they hadn't been so credulous. Clay, I knew, had not been knocked down since his amateur days, but he was cool. He neither rushed after Banks, like an angry kid, nor backed away from him. Standing straight up, he boxed and moved—cuff, slap, jab, and stick, the busy hands stinging like bees. As for Banks, success made him forget his whole plan. Instead of keeping the pressure on—moving in and throwing punches to force an opening—he forgot his right hand and began winging left hooks without trying to set Clay up for them. At the end of the round, the poet was in good shape again, and Banks, the more winded of the two, was spitting a handsome quantity of blood from the jabs that Clay had landed going away. Nothing tires a man more than swinging uselessly. Nevertheless, the knockdown had given Banks the round. The hungry fighter who had listened to his pedagogue was in front, and if he listened again, he might very well stay there.

It didn't happen. In the second round, talent asserted itself. Honest effort and sterling character backed by solid instruction will carry a man a good way, but unearned natural ability has a lot to be said for it. Young Cassius, who will never have to be lean, jabbed the good boy until he had spread his already wide nose over his face. Banks, I could see, was already having difficulty breathing, and the intellectual pace was just too fast. He kept throwing that left hook whenever he could get set, but he was like a man trying to fight off wasps with a shovel. One disadvantage of having had a respected teacher is that whenever the pupil gets in a jam he tries to remember what the professor told him, and there just isn't time. Like the Pole's in the Olympics, Banks's legs grew heavier, and he could not escape his rival. He did not, however, gaze helplessly into his corner of the ring; he kept on trying. Now Cassius, having mixed the mind, began to dig in. He would come in with a flurry of busy hands, jabbing and slapping his man off balance, and then, in close, drive a short, hard right to the head or a looping left to the slim waist. Two-thirds of the way through the round, he staggered Banks, who dropped forward to his glove tips, though his knees did not touch canvas. A moment later, Clay knocked him down fairly with a right hand, but McWhorter's pupil was not done.

The third round was even less competitive; it was now evident that Banks could not win, but he was still trying. He landed the last, and just about the hardest, punch of the round—a good left hook to the side of the poet's face. Clay looked surprised. Between the third and fourth rounds, the Boxing Commission physician, Dr. Schiff, trotted up the steps and looked into Banks's eyes. The Detroit lad came out gamely for the round, but the one-minute rest had not refreshed him.

After the first flurry of punches, he staggered, helpless, and Goldstein stopped the match. An old fighter, brilliant but cursed with a weak jaw, Goldstein could sympathize.

When it was over, I felt that my first social duty was to the stricken. Clay, I estimated, was the kind of Hero likely to be around for a long while, and if he felt depressed by the knockdown, he had the contents of ten distilleries to draw upon for stimulation. I therefore headed for the loser's dressing room to condole with McWhorter, who had experienced another almost. When I arrived, Banks, sitting up on the edge of a rubbing table, was shaking his head, angry at himself, like a kid outfielder who has let the deciding run drop through his fingers. Summerlin was telling him what he had done wrong: "You can't hit anybody throwing just one punch all the time. You had him, but you lost him. You forgot to keep crowding." Then the unquenchable pedagogue said, "You're a better fighter than he is, but you lost your head. If you can only get him again . . ." But poor Banks looked only half convinced. What he felt, I imagine, was that he *had* had Clay, and that it might be a long time before he caught him again. If he had followed through, he would have been in line for dazzling matches—the kind that bring you five figures even if you lose. I asked him what punch had started him on the downgrade, but he just shook his head. Wiley, the gym proprietor, said there hadn't been any one turning point. "Things just went sour gradually all at once," he declared. "You got to respect a boxer. He'll pick you and peck you, peck you and pick you, until you don't know where you are."

March 3, 1962

Fun-Lover

A few days ago, I took a ride up to a resort hotel called the Pines, at South Fallsburg, in the Catskills, to have my first look at Charles L. Liston, the challenger for the world heavyweight championship, who is training there. Early in the spring, Liston and Floyd Patterson, the champion, were sure that the New York State Athletic Commission would let them fight for the title here in late June, so Liston engaged training quarters. Then the Commission barred the match, and it had to be postponed while the promoter, Championship Sports, Inc., picked a site in another state. (It is now set for September 25th at the White Sox ballpark in Chicago.) But Liston had meanwhile started to train, and he decided to continue, as if for two fights; he planned to reach peak form in July and then knock off for a couple of weeks and "slop in," as the fancy phrases it, after which he would go back to training, with not so much ground to regain as if he had spent all the interim loafing. Mr. Liston had been described to me by a colored fight trainer I know as "a big, hard, heavy-handed man," and one who loafs as intensely as he works.

My interest in the contemplated contest is cultural, and has nothing to do with the Commission's reasons for exiling it, which have a political look. There is a gubernatorial election in the fall, and the prize ring has had a bad press lately. Besides, Liston has been called a hard case, although his mother, down in Forrest City, Arkansas, recently told a reporter that he was always a good boy. I was never one to low-grade a mother, so when Mr. Hal Conrad, a press agent for C. S., Inc., invited me to the Pines, I was glad to go. I had heard disparate evaluations of the challenger; one qualified observer had told me he was the best big man since Joe Louis, and another had said he was too slow to compete with the champion, who is less big but gets around faster. All I can say after seeing Liston is that he is as strong as an ox but considerably more agile, and that his stern exterior conceals surprises.

The Pines is a resort of only moderate size compared to the really big hotels in the Catskills; a place called the Concord, which I saw from the expressway going up, looked like the Palace of Chapultepec. I found Liston's training quarters in a split-level pavilion there called the 19th Hole, because of its proximity to a putting course. The lower floor of the 19th Hole is given over to bedrooms, and the upper to a long lounge, with kitchen and lunch counter, which is operated as a canteen in the full summer season. Three members of Liston's faction were on the putting green, trying to talk one another out of putts. They adjourned their game at Conrad's hail, and told us that Liston had gone cycling—a rough test for a bike, since at this stage of his training he weighs nearly an eighth of a ton. Conrad introduced the largest of the three putterers as Willie Reddish, the challenger's head trainer, and I tried to pump him about his principal's disputed talents. Reddish is a big, light-colored, good-natured man who was a pretty good heavyweight himself in the thirties, though never of the top grade. It is often possible to gauge a winning fighter's temperament by his trainer's, which will be just the opposite—a process like mirror-reading. A moody fighter or a worrier does best under an easygoing type, who can make him laugh at himself; the good-tempered fighter needs a martinet to remind him that life is serious.

One reason it has been hard to learn much about Liston is that all but one of his fights since his novice days have been extremely short.

Ten of the last eleven have gone an average of three and a fraction rounds, or about ten minutes, apiece, and two of the victims were pretty good fighters. In the one exception, a highly cautious fellow named Eddie Machen lasted twelve rounds by continuous evasive action, but he left Liston as much of a mystery as before. The ten knockouts showed what kind of a puncher Liston was, Reddish told me—"a couple could have gotten tough, but he made them easy by knocking them out." The fight that went the distance was even more conclusive, Reddish said, because it proved that Liston wouldn't tire: "He went twelve rounds at high speed, chasing a man running away from him, and he finished the twelfth as fresh as he started the first. When a man come to stay, if he got experience, he is hard to take out." I asked him what Liston did best in the ring, and he said, "Everything—short punches, long punches, either hand." The assistant trainer, Joe Polano, a grizzled type in a visored cap, who is an expert at repairing cuts between rounds, said he had never had to perform his specialty for Liston's benefit, because Liston never cut. (In ring language, the verb "to cut" is often passive in sense.) "Still," Mr. Polano said, "you never know when they're going to start." The third putter, a slim young colored man named Ray Munson, said he was the challenger's personal secretary and had no technical information to impart. Liston's faction also includes a sparring partner, Jim McCarter; a camp secretary, Archie Parolli; and a factotum, Ted King. Reddish, Munson, McCarter, and King all sport down-turned pencil mustaches that follow the curve of the upper lip, and when I saw Liston I was not surprised to note that the camp mustaches were discreet copies of his. (This is a practice that began, I believe, when all of Archie Moore's sparring partners sported imperials like his, and all of Ray Robinson's grew long sideburns.)

Conrad and I walked over to the main building, half the distance of the Belmont Stakes, for a dairy lunch, and when we returned, at half past two, Reddish and Polano were laying out the gear for a workout in a gymnasium, with a raised regulation ring, that had been set up under a new small-circus tent. Since it was a weekday and the full resort season had not yet begun, there were only a few spectators—non-paying, like me. The others included the hotel proprietors and a couple of small, fat boys. Reddish had said that Liston wouldn't do much, because it was only his second day of sparring and he had only one partner. The partner, McCarter, now quietly bandaging his own hands, told me that he had played fullback for the University of Washington and had been an alternate on the Olympic boxing team that went to Melbourne in 1956. He had turned professional only lately, and had had eleven fights, winning eight, all on the Pacific Coast. Liston then entered, a big, hard man if ever I saw one—six feet one, with wide shoulders, long arms, big hands, a torso like a tree, and calves stuffed with muscle. He was wearing green tights and heavy sweatclothes, which made him look even bulkier, and he was scowling as if he enjoyed it. If he wins the title, he will be the first scowling champion since John L. Sullivan. He, too, began to bandage his hands, with a care that indicated the amount of power he puts behind them; he used endless yards of gauze bandage, wrapping a small sponge between two layers over the knuckles of each hand.

The two men warmed up with two no-contact rounds without gloves—feinting and motioning punches, which they checked in the air. All I could see was that Liston was a well-schooled conventional boxer, standing even straighter than Louis and using a long left that resembled a thick-bodied snake with a darting head. The man looked ponderous but the hands fast. There was hardly more to see when the men put on gloves and sparred three rounds, conventionally but carefully. Liston gave an impression of power, but he was not trying to hurt, and McCarter was content to keep the big man moving. Often, after a straight left, Liston would drop his body and throw a left hook to the ribs. It was evident, though, that, unlike Johansson, he was a two-handed fighter.

Liston followed the sparring with a long, earnest attack on the heavy bag—nothing fancy, but at times vindictive. The light bag was less in his line. Hundreds of situps followed, then rope-skipping for two sides of a long-playing record. The second selection was "Night Train," and he pounded out the sound of the wheels running through the night, his feet coming up just high enough to let the rope pass under them, as if he were treading a body into the floor. During the rope-jumping, he flared up in mock anger at King, the camp clown, who had been snapping pictures of him. "You fired!" he shouted. "You working for me or for the publicity department? Let them pay you!" King pantomimed despair but seemed not much concerned. He gets fired often, but is always rehired. Liston went on to do more hundreds of situps, with his legs strapped to a board slanting steeply upward, then let Reddish carom medicine balls off his iron torso, and wound up with a specialty—standing on his head and hands, swaying like a bifurcated pendulum, and taking all the weight on the top of his head and the muscles of his neck. Physically, it was a tremendous workout, and he was not breathing hard at the end of it.

When it was over, he put on a heavy robe and motioned to me to approach and ask him questions. He reacted to them as if they were medicine balls thrown at his middle; he let them bounce. I asked him when he first knew that he could knock out a man with a short punch—the great test of a hitter. "When I hit Williams," he said. (Cleveland Williams, on March 21, 1960.) Thinking that he might confess a boyhood doubt, I asked him whether he had ever worried before a fight. He said "No." I asked him whether he had ever worried *during* a fight, and his answer was the same. "It's enough if one man worry," he elaborated. I asked him if he had a model, and he said "Joe Louis." The conversation languished.

Everybody moved over to the 19th Hole lounge, where Liston led me to a seat on a banquette against one wall, and we had tea while he sweated. Members of his faction were on stools strung along the lunch counter, and I heard Munson say to Polano, "Did you give Sonny the two dollars I gave you for him?" ("Sonny" is Liston's *diminutif*.) Polano said "Yeah." At that, there was a roar of animal wrath, and a huge shadow whizzed by my shoulder as Liston rushed toward the cut man. "You lie, you hound!" he shouted. "Gimme my two bucks!" A vast fist shot out, and I heard a tremendous smack as Polano went down, amid a shower of teeth. Pulling a pistol from a pocket of his dressing gown, the challenger, reverting to the alleged errors of his youth, blazed away twice. Groaning, Polano struggled along the floor toward me, imploring protection. Liston aimed again, then, changing his mind, pointed the pistol at me and fired a third time. I threw up my hands and, in doing so, spilled my tea. Everybody shouted happily.

"The man from the Baltimore *Sun*, he run into the fireplace when we done that," Polano said proudly from the floor. "The teeth is white beans. I catch the punch on the palm of my hand, see? That makes the smack."

Liston was jumping up and down as if skipping rope. "It's blanks, see?" he said, showing me the pistol, which was, in repose, a pretty obvious toy.

I told them that they were the best show off Broadway, and Liston, who had stopped scowling long since, said, "You come see us again, hear? You come back!" He had on a broad, unpublicized grin.

Willie Reddish said, "We got to make a little fun so the time pass. That fight seem far away, but it'll be here."

July 7, 1962

The Morest

The city of Chicago is like a friend of mine who often complains about the service he gets in restaurants. Over the last thirty years, I have seldom seen him when he has had no tale to recount of indignity, inconvenience, or what he considers sheer larceny suffered. He orders clams Posilipo and the waiter brings him calf's leever, or a small steak and the waiter brings him a large one—which my friend, a hearty eater, devours rapturously, congratulating himself on having found a restaurant with such generous ideas of smallness. The waiter then charges him for a *large* steak, now irretrievable. My friend says, "I ordered a small steak," and litigation looms. Another waiter, deeming his *pourboire* inadequate, will say "Thank," instead of "Thanks," and my friend, sensitive to such shades, will slowly simmer for days. "I *gave* him fifteen and three-eighths per cent," he will say. "X gave him fourteen per cent, and he said 'Thank you, *sir*.'" The odd thing is that my friend does not hallucinate these disasters. They happen before witnesses. If four or five of us have a drink together, everybody except this unfortunate man will get what he ordered, but if my friend has asked for an Old-Fashioned without fruit, the waiter will bring him a Rob

Roy with an olive in it. If a waiter—even one who has never seen him before—drops soup, it will be in *his* lap. His faith in catastrophe is justified so continually that if he were a betting man he could have by this time parlayed a nickel into a large fortune simply by saying to his table companions at every meal, "I'll bet that my spaghetti will be over-cooked," or "I'll bet that there will be fruit flies in my wine," or "I'll bet that they will have just run out of the kind of cheese I want. Name your cheese from the bill of fare, and I will lay seven to five that if I order it they haven't got it."

Chicago suffers from the same kind of magnetic or inductive pessimism. On my next-to-most-recent visit there, in 1953, Rocky Marciano, the heavyweight champion of the world, was defending his title against Jersey Joe Walcott, from whom he had won it in Philadelphia nine months earlier in a battle that ranks with Mons and Spotsylvania for sanguinary obstination. Before the match, a fellow named Duggan, the Chicago sportswriter and broadcaster then in vogue, denounced it as the kind of bust that was invariably pushed off on Chicago by more sophisticated communities. Walcott, who, Duggan said, had patently allowed himself to be beaten in Philadelphia, would now turn on Marciano and slaughter him instantaneously. It would be a farce. What happened was that Marciano hit Walcott once, and the older hero sat down and stayed there. It was a farce, all right. The fight lasted two minutes and twenty-five seconds. After it, I got aboard a streetcar to go back to my hotel and found myself beside a knowing drunk who reminded me of a fried clam. "Waidle you read the papers tomorrow," he said. "Duggan knew sump'n was up, din't he?" And last week, when I returned to see Floyd Patterson defend the same championship against Charles (Sonny) Liston—a combat to which I had looked forward with lively expectancy—Liston knocked Patterson out in two minutes and six seconds, in a contest that was almost as unilateral as the one in 1953; the chief difference was that Liston hit poor Patterson more often, and I think harder, than Marciano hit Walcott, and Patterson seemed more genuinely dazed. That made two round trips to the Second City to see a total of four minutes and thirty-one seconds of championship prizefighting.

The Cassandra of this latest fight was a columnist (non-sporting) named John Justin Smith, of the Chicago *Daily News*, who said that it would be a third-rate contest. When I read Mr. Smith's column, I took his view to be an unwarranted bit of endemic gloom, but Chicago is favorable territory for Cassandras, as a ballpark with a short right field is for left-handed hitters. Another *News* man, named Bob Smith, who, to judge from his second sentence, has led a sheltered life, completed the Chicago double by writing, after the fight:

> I had a ringside seat, just a few feet from Floyd Patterson's corner. It was the first boxing match I had ever seen. Behind me were 18,894 people who had paid from $100 to $10 for the privilege of watching. I deeply sympathize with each one of them. As I write this, three hours after the fight, I have the overpowering feeling that I have just witnessed one of the super con jobs of all time. (The dictionary lists "deceive, cheat, and swindle," in its definition of the word "con." Never was a word choice more appropriate.) My town had just been suckered into a magnificently designed hoax, and it makes me ill.

His story ran under the headline "Was It a Super Con Job?," but the fight didn't look quite like that to John P. Carmichael, the sports editor, whose column began:

> It was plain old-fashioned murder, so vicious, so devastating, so premeditated that it looked like a put-up job. . . . *The new champion may not only have killed off Patterson but boxing in Chicago, especially at $100 per seat.* A few years ago, Rocky Marciano polished off Joe Walcott in one round at $50 tops at the Stadium, and the screams of disgruntled customers could be heard for miles around. Now they're bound to remember that New York didn't want this fight, that it was "foisted" on Chicago and that it never should happen again.

My own view was in between those of the Messrs. Smith and Carmichael. It wasn't a fake, but it was far from murderous or devastating. Liston didn't hurt Patterson nearly as badly as, for example, Patterson hurt Ingemar Johansson in their second fight, when Johansson was unconscious in the ring for several minutes before being carried away, and the punches that sent Patterson down were not the crisp, spectacular kind that Joe Louis and other conventional great hitters used to throw. He was overpowered by glancing, clublike punches, rather than "taken out" cleanly by classic blows. This made his effort look all the more futile. He kept his chin and jaw—and, except for one punch, the supposedly vulnerable parts of his torso—out of the way, but Liston did not have to land on the classic targets to numb him. The winning punches were the kind that a man might use to beat the resistance out of a boy in a street fight—a pounding blow on the kidney, one good one under the heart, and four ponderous left hooks, like blows of the iron ball that builders employ on demolition jobs. (The kidney punch is technically a foul, if intentional, but when a fighter aims a punch at the other fellow's ribs or belly, and the fellow shrinks in toward him, the blow is sure to land on the kidney; intention is therefore hard to determine.) Each of these left hooks, partly blocked, glanced off Patterson's right shoulder and hit him on the cheekbone and temple. The bigger man was so much stronger, and caused so much hurt, that the champion had no opportunity for offensive moves of his own; it was like one of those saloon fights that end abruptly because the chance combatants are not in the same class. The uppercut under the heart was a peach, but Liston could not have delivered it if he had not been so much the stronger that he was able to pull his arm free in a clinch.

The brevity and finality of the affair were a shock. I, for one, had expected an interesting and probably a great fight, and something like sixty out of a hundred and ten sportswriters had picked Patterson to win. But I and they had made the same mistake as the supporters of Tom Hickman, the Terrible Gas Man, long ago, when they backed him to beat Bill Neat, the Butcher. If two men are of nearly equal celerity and very unequal size, the big one will win nine times out of ten; what fooled me and the sportswriters and the crowd that backed Hickman in 1821 was the difficulty of judging the relative speed of two boxers who have never been in the same ring. The relative size of the contestants is apparent, and the relative strength of two fighters trained down hard is, roughly, in direct ratio to their weights. It is for this reason that in weight-lifting, a test of pure strength, the competitors are divided into classes based on their own body weights, and that the gross weights lifted by the bigger men are heavier than those lifted by the littler. The now ex-champion, I have always contended, has the frame of a light-heavyweight, on which—by exercise, a virtuous life, and an intensive pursuit of sleep—he has packed another dozen pounds or so of muscle. But I had seen him twice beat Johansson, a true heavyweight, by superior speed and by his ability to punch with two hands, while Johansson was effective only with one. The Gas Man's supporters in that early day also had seen him beat less competent big men than Neat by overwhelming them with speed. Patterson himself knew his hopes were founded on speed; when he and his challenger weighed in at the Sheraton-Chicago Hotel on the morning of the fight, a newspaperman asked him whether the disparity in weights discouraged him, and he answered, "It may be that he is stronger but that I am faster." Liston, at 214 pounds, proved as fast as Patterson, at 189, however, and at least as good a boxer. That settled the champion's hash.

I have an idea, after seeing them fight, that Liston is a better hitter, pound for pound. (There is a combination, in hitting, of natural ability and acquired skill.) But even if he were merely Patterson's equal, he would be delivering blows an eighth harder than Patterson's on a body an eighth smaller, and proportionately less resistant, than his own, and Patterson's disadvantage in the clinches would be commensurate. (On the day after the fight, Liston said, with becoming modesty, "I might look as slow as a snail, but in the ring I'm fast as a cat.") His claims to hitting power had been accepted from the start. He was confident when he went into the ring, and I imagine that Patterson was, too. I am disposed to minimize ex-post-facto reports that Patterson "looked like a beaten man" or "like a zombie" when he climbed over the ropes, or that he was frightened. I didn't notice much difference from the way he always looks, and since 1952 I have seen him in seven fights in the flesh and a few on television. In general, I believe that there is more hogwash written about the "psychological" aspect of boxing than about any other facet of the sport. I am sure Patterson became worried when he found that he could neither keep away from Liston nor outbox him, and that Liston's punches, even when blocked, hurt, while his—he landed a tentative couple—didn't affect Liston. Anybody would have worried then. But he didn't quit; he just got licked. It was a pity, in a way, because he is a nice young man—kind to children, socially conscious, conscientious about his work, and ever aspiring to a technical perfection that he has never quite achieved. He has been his own severest critic, rating his performances on a scale based on what he considers his potential maximum. "I was sixty-seven per cent tonight," he might say after a bout. I do not think that he ever gave himself higher than seventy-two. This is unjust, because, considering his physique, he has gone far; he should measure his accomplishments by those of Tommy Burns, a little man early in the century, who won the heavyweight title, as Patterson did, largely because there were no good big men around, and lost it to big Jack Johnson, as Patterson did the other night to Liston.

Patterson was perhaps at his most interesting as a kid of seventeen in the Olympic Games at Helsinki in 1952, when he was so shy that he would lie down under a bench in the gymnasium and pretend to be asleep rather than talk to a reporter. He was fighting at the weight that was natural for him then—167 pounds—and he could afford a wild freedom in his style, which he could not permit himself later, against bigger men and when there were large sums of money dependent on his efforts. The sole begetter of his thoughts then was Cus D'Amato, his teacher and later his manager, who enlisted the interest of a patron, a New York hotel man, now dead. Patterson's early professional career was like that of a young and carefully instructed piano virtuoso. Of late, he has become almost glib; at his training camp, on a Catholic Workers' farm called Marycrest, in Elgin, Illinois, where I attended one of his press conferences a week before the fight, he said, for example, "I hear that in a newspaper the specific statement was made that I definitely would retire after the Liston fight, whether I won or lost. I definitely beyond doubts shall not retire." Asked about his battle plan—one of the silly stock questions addressed to fighters by reporters, as if a fighter, assuming that he had a definite plan, would make it public—he said, "Whether I go back to begin with, or go forward, there will definitely be a fight." There was one foreboding note in the conversation. A reporter recalled Patterson's first fight with Johansson—the only time the champion had ever been knocked out—but Patterson discussed it with charming freedom. "I went in to trade with him," he said, "and in trading that's the last thing I remember."

There is an elegant austerity about Marycrest, where two of the cow barns are named Caritas and Veritas. The press conference took place in a refectory decorated with mosaic portraits of saints; Floyd is a devout Catholic and an ardent ruralist. D'Amato, during the conference, remained in seclusion in an office between Caritas and Veritas and let the new Patterson do the talking. Liston's camp, on an abandoned race track at East Aurora, Illinois, about forty-five miles from the Loop, had a rather different atmosphere. The gym where he worked was set up under the former pari-mutuel shed, and his living quarters were in what had once been the clubhouse. Liston, who was once described to me as a "big, hard, heavy-handed man," was harder but less big than when I saw him begin his training at South Fallsburg, in the Catskills, last June. His weight was down from 230 pounds or so to 215, and for his workout he had discarded his old heavy sweat clothes. His bare legs were thinner and looked longer as he jumped rope (always to a record of "Night Train," which he must consider lucky), but where in the Catskills he had jumped only two records' worth—eleven minutes in all—he now jumped a full four, or twenty-two minutes, without stopping. He jumped with a rapt look, his lips folded inside his mouth, his feet still treading somebody invisible into the ground, as they had seemed to be doing in June. Then he pounded the heavy bag while his trainer, Willie Reddish, an old heavyweight, held it, and afterward he let Reddish slam the medicine ball into him—the same hard, painful routine of the Catskills workout, except that now he did more of everything. He sparred four rounds with two light, fast partners, but without hitting them, for he only simulated his blows. Later, he explained that sparring with light men was a habit he had formed under an early manager who was too poor to hire heavy partners for him to hit. He liked it because it sharpened his speed. He still wore his scowl—I wondered whether it was the June scowl or a clean one—which shifted occasionally into a glare. Watching him, I should have remembered and heeded the admonition of Al Weill, the philosopher who developed Rocky Marciano: "You want to look out for them broken fighters. Them type guys is hard to get outa there." Mr. Liston was broken—which is Weill's version of "broke"—and suffering from a sense of social injustice.

Afterward, the representatives of the world press and the literary cenacles walked over to the dingy ex-clubhouse. The press gatherings before this fight sometimes resembled those highly intellectual *pour-parlers* on a Mediterranean island; placed before typewriters, the accumulated novelists could have produced a copy of the *Paris Review* in forty-two minutes. After a distribution of free Pepsi-Cola, the novelists and the outnumbered sportswriters collected upon undertaker chairs to interrogate Liston, who by this time had put on a bathrobe. The big man's face resembled a moon in total eclipse. Mr. Nat Fleischer, a grandfatherly little man who publishes *Ring Magazine* and the "Ring Record Book and Boxing Encyclopedia," was by common agreement the chief interrogator. But Mr. Liston was not to be drawn on boxing; he says that "newspaper writers ask you is the sun shining when they see the sun is shining," by which he means that they labor the obvious. What he wanted to talk about was the money that he wasn't getting. To secure the match, he said for possibly the one-millionth time since he started training, he had had to sign for twelve and a half per cent of the total receipts, whereas previous challengers, even the least worthy, had received twenty per cent. "Why?" he asked. "I'm de poorest—I need de morest." This smacked of pure Marxism—"To each according to his needs"—and I feared that Liston was getting into pretty deep waters. (Following the fight, he got even more subversive: "The championship belong to all the people." This implied public ownership of a valuable property.) After listening to this attack on the established order, I hastened to get out of the joint before the Minute Men or William F. Buckley, Jr., could arrive, even though I had to leave five novelists behind. But the Scowler's wild words should have given me an intimation of what history had decreed. Ibn Khaldun, the immortal father of rational history, has stated as an immutable rule that when dynasties arise in the desert they are

crude, poor, rancorous, and enterprising. Most important, they are
indignant. After they acquire power, they become urbane, civilized,
charitable, and ineffectual, and are toppled by some new broken sheik
who has been using cobras for skipping ropes and boulders for medicine
balls. In this, though neither knew it, he was in accord with Al Weill.
Nor, says the great Khaldun, can the established ruler (here read
"champion") do anything about it—the historic process of decay began when he dethroned his predecessor. The result of the fight was
therefore ineluctable, and would have been even if Patterson had listened to Cus D'Amato with his pristine attention, instead of visiting
at the White House and hobnobbing with the President of Egypt in a
Cultural Exchange.

At about eleven o'clock on the morning of September 26th, after
history had spoken its hard word, I was sitting in the lobby of the
Sheraton-Chicago Hotel, reading the Chicago *Daily News*, when I
was approached by a tall, dark, large, soberly but elegantly dressed,
and genial gentleman whose face no longer resembled the moon in
eclipse but, rather, a pie intersected by a wide white crescent of teeth.
The corners of his mouth had turned up, apparently for keeps. He
reached out a hand heavy but hearty, and pumped mine as if we had
been old schoolmates. "See you later, fella," he said, referring to a
press conference that he was going to give in the grand ballroom. As he
walked away, I saw him pat a child on the head and then break into a
run to catch up with a panhandler whom he was afraid the hotel detec-
tive would insult before he could give him a large sum of money.

In the conference room, the new Liston presided with the tolerance
of a Mongi Slim and the urbanity of an Archie Moore. Mr. Patterson,
he said, was a gallant and generous fellow, and a good fighter. A couple
of days earlier, when asked whether anything about Patterson's talents
impressed him, he had said, with a bitter laugh, "Yeah, he's de champion," implying that he was a Mr. Scrooge in an Ivy League suit. One
of the novelists, stewed, now rose without being recognized by the
chairman and began an erratic oration. A shocked newspaperman
shouted, from the conservative side of the room, "Throw the bum
out!" The chairman raised a large, affable pink palm and said, "Let de

bum stay!" The novelist babbled some more, and the chairman said, reasonably, "You still drunk." He described, painstakingly, and for the dozenth time since the night's contest, the procedure by which he had implemented history—a right uppercut under the heart and a solid left hook that had induced his generous opponent to seize the ropes. "Then I knew I had him." He deplored his inability to hit Patterson with a jab, too. "I got a funny kind of jab," he acknowledged. "When I hit fighters with it, I can generally hear dem grunt." He was aware of the responsibilities of office, he said, adding, "I will try to prove I am re—" and here he gave the impression that he would say either "habilitated" or "generated." Hesitating as between a hook and a jab, he called on his financial adviser, Jack Nilon, to help him out. "Finish it for me, Jack, will you?" he asked. His money, he said, now alluding to the subject with a mild distaste, had not come easy. "In de ring was easy, but people don't think how much time and aggravation I had to go through before getting *into* it. De newspaper writers—" Here the novelist, trying to reingratiate himelf, cried, "I'm not a newspaper writer!" "You worsen den a newspaper writer," the chairman said. He then gave the national administration credit for making the match. "De President told Patterson make de match," he said. "And if de President had told Patterson go up de top of de Empire State Building and jump off and fly like a bird, Patterson would have did it."

Courtesy, urbanity, good humor, wealth, self-satisfaction, and other destructive elements of civilization had descended upon Liston like the Asian flu, and Ibn Khaldun, that matchless Tunisian diagnostician, would have instantly recognized the symptoms of what is in store for him.

October 6, 1962

The Men
in the Agbadas

In New Orleans, during the winter of 1959, I saw a match between a middleweight named Henry Hank and a light heavyweight named Jesse Bowdry, both colored and both pretty good. Hank, although he was outweighed by ten pounds, won by a knockout in the tenth round. A middleweight must be an exceptionally hard hitter to win at such a disadvantage in weight, so I made it a point to be in Madison Square Garden early this year when Hank came to town to fight another middleweight, a Nigerian named Dick Tiger. This time, Hank, although he hit Tiger some of his best shots, couldn't rock the other fellow at all, and the bout ended with the African chasing the American all around the ring. Hank had shown when he was being badly punished by Bowdry that he was game enough, but there are few dreams worse than the one in which you hit a man without making any impression, and in waking life the situation is even more frightening. The Nigerian, as dark as a Negro can be, had a chest like an old-fashioned black office safe, dropping away to a slender waist, big thighs, and slender legs; he boxed classically, his arms tight against his sides at the beginning of a punch, his savagely methodical blows moving in short arcs and straight lines. A middleweight who can take punches that would knock out a light heavy is even more exceptional than one who can deliver such punches, so when Tiger, a bit later, was matched to box Gene Fullmer, who was recognized as middleweight champion in most parts of the world, I thought he would beat him.

Fullmer, a Mormon mink-rancher from a suburb of Salt Lake City, who is a doting father and a regular churchgoer, is the kind of ringman that Pierce Egan, the Sainte-Beuve of the London prize ring, would have called "a *ruffianlike* fighter! who, disdaining to follow the systematic principles of the art, preferred desperate *rallies* and determined resolution, as the more sure methods to obtain victory, than by any scientific displays of judgment. . . . In all his battles the utmost desperation prevailed, and his *gluttony* [for punishment] was of the most inordinate kind." Continuing his description of a contemporary he called the Old Ruffian, the immortal author of "Boxiana" wrote, "In detailing his contests, one monotonous plan of *milling* was his *forte*, which was so evidently pourtrayed in his encounters that render any further observations unnecessary . . . than merely to state, that Symonds was a truly *bottom* pugilist." "Bottom" in Egan's era meant, as it still does in British horse racing (it has pretty well dropped out of boxing terminology), endurance coupled with gameness. A "bottom" fighter was one who won simply by wearing out his opponents.

"Monotonous" is the key word here in explaining my own aesthetic objection to the *ruffian* approach to the art; it would make me want to see such an anti-intellectual lose, even though outside the ring he brought up his mink on pâté de foie gras and his children on Dr. Spock. The boxer who interests me is the *reasoner* inside the ring. (Whether he learned his art in state prison does not concern me, and still less whether he is going back there.) One of the disturbing aspects of *ruffianism* is that its temporarily successful exponent is popular with the unthinking crowd, and so inspires hundreds of weaker imitators to get the beatings without the glory.

When a Fullmer-Tiger match was set for Candlestick Park, in San Francisco, on last August 27th, therefore, I determined to attend, hoping to see art vindicated. A few days before the scheduled date, I learned that the fight had been put off until September 12th, because the San Francisco Giants, whose park it was, were going to begin a long stand at home on the twenty-eighth of August, and the promoters feared that if it rained on the night of the twenty-seventh their bout would be off indefinitely. The promoters, a fellow named Norman Rothschild, from Syracuse, and a San Franciscan named Bennie Ford, both own restaurants—a common avocation among promoters, who then know that no matter what happens, they will not starve. In September, there was another postponement, because the people who were putting on the bigger Patterson-Liston fight, in Chicago, had tied up the good sites for closed-television showings. The Chicago people apparently thought that the middleweight bout would interfere with the buildup for the heavyweight battle. (Actually, the heavyweight fight was so bad that it helped queer the gate for the middleweights, while the middleweights were so good that they have revived interest in the Sweet Science.)

This time, the Tiger-Fullmer match was set back to Tuesday, October 16th, when the Giants presumably would have finished their season. But the Giants unexpectedly carried the regular baseball season to a playoff with the Dodgers for the National League pennant, and then protracted it again by forcing their World Series with the Yankees to a sixth game, which was scheduled for Friday, October 12th, in San Francisco. If the Yankees took that one, it would end the season, and even if the Giants won, the Series couldn't go beyond a seventh game, which would be played on Saturday. So there was no reason to think that the fight couldn't be fought on the following Tuesday night. I emplaned at Idlewild on the morning of October 12th; I wanted to see Tiger's and Fullmer's last workouts before the fight. It was overcast, as I remember, but not raining, and in California, I had heard, it hardly ever rained anyway, so I hoped that the Yankees would settle the Giants' hash while I was still airborne, and clear San Francisco of baseball fans. Baseball bores me to distraction, but talk about it is even worse. I had made a reservation at a San Francisco hotel, the St. Francis, well before the Giants got into the Series, and I was glad I had done so, because I knew the city would be crowded.

I arrived in the middle of a torrential rain, and the driver of the taxi from the airport said, like the Californians in stories about rain in California, "This is unusual weather we are having." The ball game, of course, had been called off, and the ground was so thoroughly soaked that it was already sure, the driver said, that they wouldn't be able to play on Saturday, either. My room at the excellent but crowded hotel was on a court, and the view from my window was like the tanks at the Coney Island Aquarium, minus the fish. The first news I gleaned from the *News-Call Bulletin*, the sole surviving evening newspaper in San Francisco, was that the fight, too, had been postponed, for a week, since nobody was sure when the World Series would end. I knew the bars would be full of idiots talking baseball, so I sent down to room service for a bottle of Scotch and dinner, and, after trying to read a book about beautiful San Francisco, turned in at about nine o'clock, when it would have been midnight in New York.

It kept on raining, all night and next day, but morning, though hard to perceive, reanimated me, and I called Jersey Jones, who is Tiger's manager, at the Governor, a small hotel on Turk Street, where the challenger's faction was staying. Jersey has been around the fight business for fifty years now, first as a small-time fighter, then as a sportswriter (that ended when Frank Munsey swallowed the New York *Globe* in 1923), and then as a press agent and manager. During all that time, he has never had a "big" fighter of his own, although he has had good ones who never quite made the first rank. He is a small man, who looks twenty years younger than he can possibly be—a graying youngster. Jersey said the Tiger would work that afternoon in the gymnasium at the West Coast Seaman's Union, and I joined the party just before the workout. There were only half a dozen men in the gym besides the Tiger and his people; the onlookers were two deckhands off a tanker and four Mexicans, one of them a fighter.

The Tiger's clan had the air I have often sensed among sporting people who have worked long on a single project, like qualifying a racing car for Indianapolis or readying a horse for a classic: they were in a little world of their own, within which details looked larger than the day's headlines. The tactical chief was Jimmy August, a bald, moon-faced man, short, stout, and anxious, whom I have known for thirty years or so, and who has had the same sort of career among trainers as Jones among managers. August is knowing and painstaking, but has seldom been associated with headline fighters. He once handled an inferior middleweight champion in one fight, and for a while he trained a left-handed light heavyweight who was recognized as a world champion in New York State; these were the high spots of his professional life, although he has spent almost every afternoon since 1922 in fighters' gyms, and nearly every evening, until the small clubs dropped away, seconding run-of-the-mill fighters in neighborhood boxing clubs. As a young man, August sometimes recounts mournfully, he completed one year in the School of Pharmacy at Columbia, and he looks even now as if he would be more at his ease behind a prescription counter than carrying a striking bag. Then, he says, he "had the misfortune to have two amateur fights," took to hanging around gymnasiums, and abandoned pill and pestle forever. There was one sparring partner, a colored middleweight named Willie Turner, from Fresno, and a cheery Chinese-American San Franciscan named Yip, who trained a few boys of his own at the gym and was now acting as car driver, errand man, and volunteer sideline coach. The Tiger, a dark image swathed in sweat clothes, felt his role as the focus of their attention, but he was like a good child, eager to please, and slightly petulant only when August limited his work. He was not letting Tiger do any sparring that day, the trainer said, because he had had him exactly right for Tuesday, and to continue at the same rate for the extra week would bring him down too fine. "But he's superstitious about training," August said. "He feels guilty unless he works every day. 'More, more,' he says. 'More, more.' You'll see when I tell him to knock off. If you left him to himself, he would train down to nothing. And today he is restless because I wouldn't let him run on the road. It's too slippery; he might sprain an ankle."

The Tiger, working on the big bag, stalked it as if it were a man, with short, realistic punches—not the thundering swings that some fighters put in against this happily inanimate target. His face, wide at the cheekbones, was intent, as if he were reading flesh into the leather. When August called him off it, he cried "One! One!"

The trainer finally nodded. "One more round," Jimmy said. "Only one." And the Tiger went at the bag for another three minutes. "None," August said then, and switched him to another exercise.

As the Tiger finished each round, Yip wiped the back of his neck with a rough towel—a kind of ceremonial. "He hates the sweat on the back of his neck," Yip said. The Tiger looked as if he liked the feel of the towel.

August dissuaded the Tiger from continuing, in turn, belly bends, the light bag, and shadowboxing. "One! One!" he would cry, until August said "None." But it was hard to take the skipping rope away from him; he knew that that was the final item in his routine. When August at last, playing the stern parent, pocketed it, the Tiger broke into a wide grin. The play battle was over.

Jones and August said they had never seen anybody take to body punching like the Tiger. Seven years ago, he had come up from Nigeria to England strong but so crude that the manager who paid his passage had given up on him, Jones said. Later, he had done better, with the aid of Maurice Foran, a trainer in Liverpool, who, incidentally, had come over for this fight at the Tiger's expense. "But they don't teach them body punching in England," the manager went on. "If you hit a man below the neck there, the referee is likely to take the fight away on a foul. He had the left hook when he came here in 1959, and he was strong, and had had plenty of hard fights. That tests a man's ticker. But they would be easy fights for him now, with what he's learned. It's the body punching that will kill Fullmer. I wouldn't have taken the match for short money if I wasn't sure he will knock him out."

Mr. Foran, a pale, slender young man with wavy red hair, who had come in a few minutes earlier, said that he had not seen Tiger for three years, and, watching him spar, would hardly have thought he was the same fighter, he was so much improved. "I taught him a bit in England, but he was nothing like," he said. "He's a student—been learning since he first turned up off the boat. He didn't have an overcoat." Foran agreed with Jersey that the Tiger learned thoroughly. He thought it was a Nigerian trait.

Foran and another English Tiger rooter, named Harry Ormesher, had come on by plane, as I had, before learning of the latest postponement, and they were putting up at the Governor with the rest of the faction. Jones said he was glad they had come, because they helped take Tiger's mind off the length of the grind. Talking of old times, they made him laugh. Ormesher, pink, plump, and pawky in a dark pin-striped suit, was a type who would have been recognizable in America, before he began to talk, as a small-city banker or prosperous jobber, but he was in fact the leading bookmaker in a city of forty thousand inhabitants midway between Manchester and Liverpool—both great betting centers, what with football, dogs, and horses. In England, Ormesher had staked Tiger occasionally, I gathered, in the bleak days that followed his landing, when he had lost four successive fights to Liverpudlians who would have to pay their way in to a Tiger bout here. (He beat the two best of them several times each later, at first laboriously and then with ease.)

"This would be a fine, sunny day in Liverpool," Ormesher said, looking out at the downpour as we waited for the fighter to have his rub and shower. Ormesher talked to me about the new public betting shops in Britain, introduced last year, most of which, he said, were operated by the old, established legal-credit-system bookmakers, like himself. He felt a certain reserve about the new shops, although, he said, the volume of play had increased by at least sixty per cent over the old legal *and* old illegal play combined. (Illegal betting, which had continued unchanged from the days of "Esther Waters," dried up when the new shops were opened.) He sounded like an official of an old and dignified bank talking about the new consumers' credit department, or a Morgan partner about selling stocks to shopgirls on the installment plan. He feared that a lot of lads were now betting more often than they could afford. "It's champion for cigarette business, at any rate," he said. "You should see lads in our shop, crowded in shoulder to shoulder, listening to a race on the wireless. Minute it's over, every loser throws his cigarette on the floor—kind of automatic, it is. And every winner, he flips his fag up in the air—he knows he can afford another. We had a posh place when we opened—floor all dark-blue and light-blue squares—and now it's black from gaspers ground into it."

The sound of the rain and the Lancashire accent brought England back about us as we waited, and it was no time at all before Tiger reappeared, now a bit of a fop in a biscuit-colored sports jacket hairy with red threads, and a pair of narrow charcoal-gray slacks. Tiger is not tall for a middleweight—only five feet eight—and the gay clothes hid the menace of his muscles. He moved loosely, with a small suggestion of a jig step. A wide smile serves him in lieu of conversation, and while he answers questions willingly, he cannot be drawn into a lead. Looking at him, I decided that he must already have been asked every question in the world—if it was hot in his country, how many wives he had (he has just one; he is an Episcopalian), what he ate, whether he liked the United States. So I just shook his hand.

All of us—Ormesher, Foran, Jersey Jones, Jimmy August, Tiger, Willie Turner, Yip, and I—crammed ourselves into a well-banged station wagon. With Yip driving, we rolled through the rain to the Hotel Governor. On the way, Jimmy August, who was sitting next to me, said, "I forgot to tell you, he is a very patriotic Nigerian. He wants to win the title for Nigeria, like it was a Nobel Prize. The Nigerian Ambassador and the Minister of Labor and Social Welfare, which includes sports, are coming out here for the fight, with Hogan (Kid) Bassey, who used to be the featherweight champion. Bassey was the first Nigerian to win a world title, and he has a job with the government now, coaching the Olympic boxing team. Tiger would like a job, too." Jones, just behind me, overheard August and said, "Thirty Nigerian students from the University of California are coming to the fight, in their national costumes, and I had to arrange to get an extra row of seats put in on the field, at two dollars a throw, because that is all they can afford, but we want them up front, where they will show up."

When we got out, I asked Tiger about his ambitions, and he said, "Politician is better than fightah. I must get up in the morning to run, but he only read in a book and talk." This is about as much as he has said at one time in our acquaintance.

August and Tiger had adjoining rooms—an arrangement designed to keep the trainer sensitive to his man's morale—and Jersey and Mrs. Jersey had a room on the same floor. It was a familial, almost a patriarchal setup, reminding me of some Arcadian gyp horsemen I used to know who would sleep in the next stall to their horses and fine their apprentice jockeys for swearing. Most fighters, by the time they challenge for titles, think they know more than their handlers—Ingemar Johansson and Sonny Liston, for example, both ran their own training camps before fighting Patterson—but Tiger, a quiet man, has the temperament of a disciple.

The Governor, although comfortable, is not posh; when I went into the Coffee Shoppe and sat down in a booth, the waitress decently warned me that coffee was twenty-five cents there, while at the counter it cost only a dime. I adhered to my extravagance, and Jersey went upstairs to fetch Mrs. Jersey, who is much taller than he is, a Junoesque blonde with a fair, English complexion. She had been out shopping for souvenir teaspoons. They live, as one might expect, in New Jersey—in a town called North Arlington, near Rutherford—and Mrs. Jersey deserts the suburbs only for important fights.

The time passed slowly. Sunday cleared, but the ground was too nearly saturated for baseball. Rothschild and Ford were glad they had announced the postponement, because it was now evident that the town would have no money or time that week for anything but the World Series. A nephew of mine who is studying economics at Berkeley came in with a Volkswagen—the Bay bridge is open now—and took me for a tour of San Francisco, which is accomplished by driving from hilltop to hilltop and looking back at the hilltop you have just left. You then drive across the bridge to Sausalito to look back at San Francisco, and, returning to San Francisco, look back at Sausalito. It is all very pretty.

On Monday, I weakened, and went to the sixth game of the World Series. The ticket man said I was lucky, because many visitors with tickets had gone home, unable to stay away from their businesses past the weekend. So he sold me a good twelve-dollar seat for thirty dollars. I had never seen a World Series game before, or wanted to after 1919, when I went into long pants. The town, however, was so exercised over the event that the church bells audible in my hotel played "Take Me Out to the Ball Game" and, one hour later, "Bye, Bye, Baby," the theme song of the dauntless Giants. The game was of a dullness only cricket can equal. The Giants got a three-run lead in an early inning, which was all they needed; the final score was 5–2. My seat proved to be in a box with a very pretty woman, who was accompanied by her mother. I estimated that the average player, if neither pitcher nor catcher, bestirred himself for about seven and a half minutes in a two-hour baseball game—which for a boxer would be like boxing fifteen-second rounds with three-and-three-quarter-minute intervals. I thought that at that rate Archie Moore would be able to go on into the next century.

Tuesday, I weakened again, just to see how the affair would end. The ticket man told me public interest had risen, and this time charged me fifty dollars. The game was even duller than the sixth. I sat beside a re-iterative imbecile who shouted "Hit! Hit! Hit! Hit!" through the nine half innings when the Giants were at bat, and "Don't give them nothing, Jack! Don't give them nothing!" to the pitcher through the nine half innings when the Giants were in the field. Many windblown foul balls fell near us, but none, unfortunately, concussed him.

The sportswriters tried to read an ex-post-facto thrill into the action by making much of a creditable catch by Tom Tresh, a Yankee outfielder, off Willie Mays, a Giant. Since nobody was on base at the time, or appeared likely to be in the near future, the catch caused only a mild ripple of interest when it occurred, but Willie McCovey, the batsman next *after* Mays, got a three-bagger. The theme of the post-mortem dithyrambs was that if McCovey had been up *before* Mays— which was obviously ridiculous, because the batters appear in prede-termined order—and had been on third when Mays came to bat, Tresh's catch, if he had made it under the altered circumstances, would have prevented a run and created a furor. No one spoiled the dream by surmising that if *anybody* had been on third when Mays came up, Terry, the Yankee pitcher, would have thrown Mays four balls to get at a less dangerous hitter. Mays then wouldn't have hit toward Tresh, Tresh wouldn't have caught anything, and the game would have been even duller than the one I saw. The Yankees won, 1–0, by a run that the Giants had let them have, fearing worse, as a chess player sometimes concedes a pawn, hoping to retrieve the advantage later.

A San Francisco sports columnist I read said that the Giants had lived their finest hour. If the same McCovey, San Francisco's last batsman, had hit the last ball of the game to where a fielder wasn't, instead of to where a fielder was, he implied, things even then would have been different. Baseball is a game that reflects nineteenth-century America, where it was invented and when businessmen went bankrupt annually, consoling themselves with the reflection that they would be in the chips if the town hadn't gone bust. Prospectors overlooked claims that, if they hadn't, would have made them rich. (I had a great-uncle who between 1878 and 1911 barely failed to accumulate, according to his unsolicited testimony, more than a billion dollars in minerals.) Real-estate dealers habitually failed to buy, in their own homemade legends, land at fifty dollars a town lot that if they had bought it would be worth that much a square inch, and my own father loved to tell how he passed up a half interest in the whole movie industry because he thought it was going to be a fad. All these tales are different versions of what would have happened if the fielder hadn't been there. Oddly enough, they made the men who told them happy; they were all baseball fans. (It may be noted here that the Yankees are the least popular of all ball clubs, because they win, which leaves nothing to "if" about.)

On the day after my first World Series ended, I returned, chastened, to the Sweet Science, like an errant husband who has had no fun. Fullmer was training at the Newman & Herman Gymnasium, on Leavenworth Street, a more central and public place than the Seaman's Union. It is the kind of gym that charges admission and has seats for the public, like Lou Stillman's old place on Eighth Avenue. The "name" fighters who come to town train there, and Fullmer, as champion, by an unwritten law had had the choice of gymnasiums for training.

When I arrived, Fullmer was clowning with his three-year-old son, who wore boxing gloves. The champion's face is an advertisement of his style of *milling*—eyebrows built out with scar tissue until they shade over his eyes like porches, a bridgeless nose with ducklike nostrils, and a thin slit of a mouth. It was a figurehead used for ramming, like an ancient galley's. I had not before seen Fullmer in the flesh, but I had watched him in a dozen fights on television. At times, before throwing a punch, he pulls his right elbow back behind his ear, as if he were drawing a longbow at Crécy. At others, he leaps forward with his left elbow ahead of his advance, his fist retracted at an angle of ninety degrees. If the elbow connects, he brings the fist down to complete the demolition, with the motion of an old-fashioned subway guard chopping tickets. Mostly, though, he swings blows from the side, aiming at the ribs and the temples; a tiring opponent, shrinking in toward him, will catch them on the kidneys or the back of the head. They are not proper hooks, because Fullmer does not bend his elbows sharply but throws the blows as if he were beating a carpet, and the striking surface is as often the inside of his forearm as his fist. He exploits these barbarisms by inexhaustible strength, seconded by what Egan called *bottom*, mauling his adversary on the ropes and hauling at his arms until they go limp, like strands of overcooked pasta. In the words of the classicist Dave Shade, who was baffled by Slapsie Maxie Rosenbloom, a Fullmer-like adversary in the nineteen-twenties, "He does everything so wrong that it must be right."

The sources of his strength were visible through the sweat clothes—a torso ropy with well-covered muscle, like a hawser coiled around a bollard, and huge calves, which keep him bouncing long after most opponents' legs begin to buckle. He had a reputation for always losing the early rounds and then coming on to overwhelm the exhausted. This was precisely, I felt, what nobody could do with Tiger; he himself was too strong. The one thing Fullmer had seldom done in a fight was to take out the other man with one punch. The boxer who does that has got to be balanced, though he may be crude. The big-punch man is the only one who can reverse the tide of battle unexpectedly even in the last round.

The prospective battle therefore looked, as Egan would have said, "Lombard Street to a China orange" in favor of the exponent of scientific principles, but Fullmer did not appear to have heard the news. And as I watched him fooling with the child, I began to like him—a sensation as astonishing to me as it would be to find a *Time* writer or an anti-novelist personally amusing, or an atonal musician congenial, or a spray-gun painter good company. After lowering the boy over the top strand of the ring ropes, Fullmer sparred in earnest with a couple of heavy partners; his theory in working with heavier men is to develop strength, I suppose, but strength is what he has the most of. His manager, Marv Jenson, who is a big, Nordic, Chamber of Commerce type, and a community benefactor in West Jordan, Utah, his home town, told me that Fullmer had sparred three hundred rounds or so for the coming match, but I doubted whether any of them had improved his scientific judgment.

When I called again at the Governor, late the next afternoon—I skipped the gym workout—I saw that the Nigerian influence had set in. The Tiger sat at the lunch counter in the Coffee Shoppe, eating a salad out of a wooden bowl, and on the next stool, like a small carbon copy, sat a fellow-countryman—Kid Bassey, the former featherweight champion—eating a steak. Bassey, famous earlier than Tiger, is more worldly, and, as small men often are, rather peppery. The woman behind the counter, with the kindliest intentions, asked him, "And what do you eat in *your* country?"

Bassey answered, "Hu-mon *bee*-ings."

As the waitress hurried to the end of the counter to share this information with her colleague, he said to Tiger, "They think we have tails."

Tiger laughed at this—to him, evidently—new idea. "But we have not," he said.

Both girls returned. The one from the other end, more sophisticated, said, "I hope when you go back you take Jimmy August with you and throw him in the pot."

The inquisitive girl asked Bassey, "What kind of clothes do you wear there?"

Bassey said shortly, "We go neck-ed. In the jungle."

Tiger thought this was going a bit far. "You must not believe him," he said. "He is mischievous."

In between visits, I had picked up, at the promoters' office, a copy of Tiger's record, and some of the early, Nigerian fights interested me. He had beaten opponents named Easy Dynamite, Mighty Joe, Lion Ring, Koko Kid, Black Power, and climactically, Super Human Power. He had out-pointed Super Human Power in eight rounds. I asked Tiger what kind of a fighter Super Human Power had been, and he said, "A good fightah, for Nigeria. You know we take those names to sound big. Like Tigah. There are no tigahs in Nigeria, but it sound great."

Now that the World Series was over, the sports columns had space for the fight. On the two days following the Series, there were still quite a few postmortems, but by Friday, which is payday for a lot of people, the ticket sale had begun to pick up. Until then, the fight's light had been hidden under the Giants' bushel, but now Rothschild, the entrepreneur, began to think it possible that he would not lose money. (Beginning with the onset of the Series, his prayer had become, like the poor horseplayer's, "Please, God, let me break even—I need the money.") He predicted twenty thousand paying customers, and receipts of a hundred and fifty thousand dollars. This, while it was not stupendous, would get him off the nut. A few boxing characters arrived in town, to see and be seen, among them Cassius Clay, the Minnesinger of the Ring, who brought a thin sheaf of verses he had composed on his own forthcoming contest with the Nestor of the Ring, Archie Moore, in Los Angeles on November 15th. Mr. Clay recited for me, in anticipation of the event:

> "He was old, and I was new,
>   And you could tell by the blows I threw.
>   I swept that old man clean out of the ring,
>   For a new broom sweeps most anything."

(The Nestor says he has prepared a punch for the Minnesinger—it is called the Lip-Buttoner.)

Once airborne by his Muse, Clay is hard to stop, and he insisted on rendering for me another poem that he had composed, on the theme of Floyd Patterson's Downfall:

> "Liston was hungry, rough and tough,
>   While the champ had already had enough.
>   As the people left the park you could hear them say:
>   'Liston will be champ until he meets Clay.'"

The Tiger's faction was free of financial cares, because, Jersey told me, he had had to take a flat guarantee of twenty-five thousand dollars, with twenty-seven hundred dollars for total training expenses. This would have been a small percentage of the gate originally expected, but at least it was immune to reduction if the fight didn't draw. The fight was also to be shown on closed-circuit television, but neither Tiger nor the promoters would get any of that money at all; Jenson and Fullmer had kept that deal for themselves. Twenty-five thousand dollars had looked pretty stingy when the match was made, but as disasters accumulated during the promotion, it began to seem pretty good. "What we wanted was the title," Jersey said. "And we're sure to get it." But so many things can happen in the ring extraneous to the pattern of combat—a butt that splits the head, a cut that curtains the eye with blood, an outrageous decision by home-town judges (and Fullmer was a West Coast fighter)—that I knew he couldn't be all that sure, nor could Mrs. Jersey, who was probably planning to redecorate the house in North Arlington.

President Kennedy made his speech on Monday, and again the fight was relegated to dark corners of back pages. Who had time to talk about a prizefight, with the country apparently heading for war? The ticket sale again languished, but there would have been no point in another postponement. Suppose war came? To worsen Rothschild's and Ford's bad luck, fog struck on Monday—a black, almost London brand, which closed the airport against last-minute customers who might want to fly in from Las Vegas or other sporting centers. The fog also promised, to weather-wise San Franciscans, a cold, raw night in Candlestick Park, which is down by the water. The fight drew less than thirteen thousand admissions, including the Nigerians.

The main bout was to go on at seven-thirty in the evening, Pacific Coast Time, so that it could be on closed-circuit television in the East at ten-thirty, and the first preliminary was to begin at six-thirty. I got to Candlestick Park, the scene of the Giants' finest hour, even earlier than that, to find a low, black sky poised just over the ring lights, like a candle snuffer. The working-press seat assigned to me was where I liked it—at the end of a row, so I would have to climb over nobody, and just under one of the working corners, where I could watch the seconds between rounds. Early as I was, several people I knew were there before me. In the first row back of the working press I recognized Mrs. Jersey Jones and the bookmaker, Ormesher, and they were talking to Bassey, the eater of hu-mon *bee*-ings, who was now almost unrecognizably dashing in a sky-blue silk *agbada*, or long cape, worn over sky-blue trousers and soft leather slippers. On his head he wore a red *awo*, or skullcap. He spelled the words out for me. The Nigerians from Washington were just behind the pressmen. Crisis or no crisis, the Ambassador had come on. He was in red and black, and the Minister of Labor and Social Welfare was even more impressive, a vast man in a rose-colored *agbada* and an *awo* that was less a skullcap than a Chinese-mandarin pillbox, embroidered with gold leaf, like naval scrambled eggs, and topped with a tassel. The Minister, mountainous and a light cinnamon, was, I supposed, of a different ethnic group from Tiger, whose people are Ibos, from eastern Nigeria—black and built close to the ground, with great thick necks, corded with muscle from carrying heavy burdens on their heads. The students, as gaily, if less elegantly, robed, were slightly farther back. Tiger had a brilliant cheering section.

There was time for only two preliminaries—an uneventful four-rounder, and then a six-rounder, in which Willie Turner, Tiger's lone sparring partner, engaged a much taller fighter with a mustache. Turner, a bobbing, in-and-under kind of body puncher, did well for four and a half rounds, but in the fifth the bigger man, who was named Sonny Miles, knocked him down and put him on Queer Street. Willie's seconds worked on him hard before the sixth round—he was in my corner of the ring—and his astonishment visibly turned to anger. He went out full of gaiety, as old Pierce would have it, and for two minutes looked like carrying off the decision after all. Then Miles caught him again, with a right to the jaw, and he wobbled. Miles pounded him until he was stopped by the referee, who walked between them as if he had heard the bell for the end of the round and the fighters hadn't. As a matter of fact, he was stopping the bout and awarding it to Miles, with just ten seconds to go. The crowd booed, zealous to defend a boxer's right to receive a full complement of blows.

Next, Tiger and Fullmer entered the ring—Tiger, I was delighted to see, had my corner—and it soon filled with other fighters and famous men of various sorts, a couple in *agbadas* and the rest in Ivy League, natural-shoulder clothes with the Continental look, who were introduced to the public, and who touched the principals' gloves as a form of handshake. Clay, the Minnesinger, was there, a dandified giant, and a fellow I know named Jackie Fields, whom I first saw box at the Olympic Games in Paris in 1924, where he won the featherweight championship. He got bigger and won the welterweight championship as a professional. I will always remember him because he once said, "When I was a kid I used to sleep on my nose so I would look like a fighter." The star of the presentees was Rocky Marciano, the hero of the early fifties, big and fat and, I am afraid, bald. The Tiger, who looked, as he usually does in the ring, polite and noncommittal, was attended by three seconds—Jersey, Jimmy August, and Foran, his old handler from Liverpool. They all looked more concerned than he did.

Now, as the great Egan had it, "the moment became interesting, and anxiety was upon the utmost stretch." The presentees descended from the ring, and the combatants came to the center, where the referee, a chunky old gentlemen, mumbled into the microphone the usual injunctions about wanting a clean fight, which nobody remotely expected. They returned to their corners, and at the warning cry of "Ten seconds!" the handlers left the ring, Jersey clasping the Tiger's right glove in benediction as he dropped down. The bell rang, and Fullmer came out of his corner fast, in accordance with his monotonous mode, his object being to assert his domination from the first by slugging the stranger and shoving him into the ropes. Once he has a man in retrograde, he never lets him get set for an effective punch, and his slaps and chops reduce the victim to steak tartare.

The Tiger stood as firm as a cast-iron black jockey with a ring in his hand to hitch a horse to, and Fullmer found him about as easy to push. The champion lashed out with a couple of sidling swings. Tiger blocked with hands high, then punched to the armored belly with hands low and, coming up, smashed a left hook and a right cross to the impregnable jaw. He "hit Fullmer away," to revert to the historian's idiom, and the crowd, which had seen the champion fight before, howled incredulously. Fullmer came on again, seeking his "desperate *rallies*" and unable to believe in their inefficacy. Tiger's center of gravity was as low as his, Tiger's head was as hard, and Tiger's fists moved on the inside lines, within the arcs of Fullmer's arms.

Sometimes the ruffian, trying to get past this austerely conventional barrier, drove in with his left forearm across his face, throwing his right fist over it, like a man ducking behind a bar to throw beer bottles. The careful notes that at the beginning of a fight I sometimes promise myself I am going to make have turned, as usual, into one-line scrawls, one for each round, but they serve to recall the view from under Tiger's corner. In the first round, I noted, the arms close to the body did the business, and Tiger landed a great right to the jaw, which set the pattern for many to follow. In the second, he employed a good, hurting jab, but Fullmer landed a packet of overhand rights; this, I thought, was the only round of the fight in which Fullmer achieved equality. His smacking blows, though, being all on the outside, were more visible than hurtful. Inside, the calm black continued to demolish him, and by the end of the round it was usually Tiger who moved forward; he had taken the play away.

The first four rounds, Foran said afterward, settled the fight; if Tiger had let the champion get on top, he might never have been able to get started himself. As it was, the pattern soon became clear. In the third, Fullmer's left eye was streaming blood, and in the fourth, brawling desperately to turn the tide, he took a dreadful beating; trying to wrestle Tiger to the ropes, he was himself spun off his feet—a proof of relative strength that must have dumfounded him. In Egan's day, such a fall counted as a knockdown, but in ours it is disregarded.

And now the blows began to take a cumulative effect; Fullmer, like Henry Hank, began to back away. He even awkwardly jabbed—an exercise that in all his previous fights he had scorned as sissy. His ineptitude proved how little he had practiced it. Here the Tiger's limitations—he has them, like all artists—aided Fullmer. Eugène Delacroix once wrote a chapter on the difficulty of knowing when a picture is finished, and the Tiger, like that glorious painter, hestitates over the same point. Come to him and he will murder you, but go away and he will merely follow, implacable, until you recover sufficiently to throw another punch, when he will murder you again. He is a counter-puncher, and must have a lead to counter. (He is, though, the kind of counterpuncher who draws leads by constantly moving forward, and so puts the onus on the other fellow.) Fullmer's normal style was made as if bespoke for Tiger; its collapse gave the Nigerian his only difficulty.

The notion of recapturing the play kept Fullmer in trouble; whenever he mustered up enough strength for self-delusion, he would launch himself at the Tiger again, and the Tiger would punish him and send him reeling back. The first four rounds had been thrilling; the next four were simply grim, illuminated only by the courage of the target. His resolution was as strong as ever, but his imagination as limited. Instead of recovering, therefore, as he might have done if he had stayed on the bicycle—a term unknown to Egan, who wrote before bicycles were invented—he went steadily downhill, like a general who every time he receives a small reinforcement squanders it in a meaningless counterattack. In the ninth round, with the once-invincible legs turning to rubber and one eye shut off by a screen of blood, he looked done—as any less eminent glutton would have been. He was lucky to get to his corner, and in the normal course of events, with a one-minute rest, he would still have been so weak when he stood up that he must have gone down quickly. But the referee, after giving him the full minute (in Egan's time it was thirty seconds), apparently had a fear that should have occurred to him when the previous round ended. He called into the ring the doctor of the California State Boxing Commission, to examine Fullmer's injuries and see if he could safely continue. The doctor was no chamois for agility, and once he reached Fullmer's corner he took his time in forming a prognosis. Fullmer gained another bit of the breath of life with every second that passed. When the doctor discharged him as fit, two more minutes had passed; he had had the advantage of a three-minute rest after a three-minute round—a reprieve that, given his great recuperative powers, cancelled out the damage the Tiger had done him in the last three or four rounds.

I wondered that Jones didn't protest, but his man was, after all, safely ahead on points; he could not afford to have the match end in an indecisive wrangle. When the champion came out again, partly restored, the great moments of the fight were already in the past. Fullmer was now fighting only to go the distance, and the Tiger, though still pursuing, had small hope of knocking him out. The certainty of winning the championship on points may have made him a bit conservative; only an unlucky collision of heads or a broken hand could now endanger him, and cautious well-wishers in the crowd—perhaps people who had bet on him—were shouting, "Steady, Tiger! Watch his head! Take it easy!" And others—disgruntled Fullmer supporters, I imagined—began to boo the champion because he continued to back away. These brave fellows, of course, if they had been in his place, would have crawled out through the ropes.

In the eleventh round, Tiger, angry at not having already finished the evening, paused in his pursuit and, raising his hands, motioned to the champion to come to him again and fight. He had been promised a victory party by the representatives of his government, and he didn't want to keep the Minister and the Ambassador waiting. It was, at that, an impolite gesture, not like the usual Tiger at all. Delacroix may have sounded sharp when a friend like Géricault asked him, "When the hell are you going to finish that picture?"

The Nigerians, chauvinistically impervious to pity, raised their voices.

"Belly, belly, Tigah!" one cried, as repetitiously as the man at the ball game chanting "Hit! Hit! Hit!"

Another, more literary, cried, "What a punishment you are receiving, Fullmer! What an ordeal you are undergoing!"

And now, having recovered a bit, the insatiable glutton returned to the hopeless attack, with the result that near the end of the thirteenth he was again in trouble, the Tiger forcing him back toward his own corner with a flowing sequence of blows from which he could not disengage himself. The glutton sagged, and it looked for a moment as if he really would, after all, be knocked out. But the muddled referee helped him survive again. This time, the referee really thought that the round had ended and that he himself had been too excited to hear the bell. He stepped between the fighters and waved them to their corners—ten seconds too soon. By that time, I was glad.

Tiger's seconds, like horse-race bettors who begin to shout only when they see they have a winner, began to root him home in the fourteenth. "Belly, belly!" I could hear August shouting, and Jersey shouted, "Easy!" But when August clambered down the ladder from the ring after the interval, I saw, to my amazement, that he continued to look anxious.

"How does it look?" he asked, as if he still could not believe what he saw.

"Perfect!" I yelled, but he still looked flabbergasted. Things had worked out too well to be believed—"Like a Leavenworth problem," my old friend Major General Terry de la Mesa Allen once said after a battle that went that way. Not a single unforeseen emergency had developed. The Tiger wasn't even cut.

The Nigerians swarmed into the ring when the bell ended the fifteenth round. They had no need to wait for the decision, which was unanimously in favor of their Tiger. I waited while Tiger came down from the ring, surrounded by bounding wearers of the *agbada*, and headed for the dressing rooms under the stand. Then I joined Mrs. Jones, who hadn't peeped once during this crisis in the family fortunes, and Mr. Ormesher, who was as cheerful as if a 100–1 shot had won the Derby with all the fancies unplaced. We all walked over to the entrance to the dressing rooms and sat down on a bench to wait for the winning faction to emerge; Mrs. Jones, naturally, was ineligible to go farther. We were all going on to the Nigerian party, at the Mark Hopkins, later. I grew impatient after a while, and wandered through a labyrinth of passages under the stand until I got to a shower room, where Tiger stood, like a bit of black basalt, under the stream.

Jersey, waiting outside, said, "He is the first fighter I ever had who did exactly what I told him." He paused a moment, probably musing on the scores of others who would have been champions, too, if they had followed his advice. "He is the first champion I ever made all by myself," he said modestly. August said, lying, that he had never been

worried once, and Tiger, when he came out of the shower, said that
Fullmer had hurt him, but never sufficiently to distress him. The only
marks showing were a few ridges on his cheekbones and temples.
Henry Hank, he said, had hit him much harder than Fullmer, but had
not kept him so constantly at work.

After all of us had joined Mrs. Jones, we headed for the Governor,
so that Tiger could change into his party clothes. While he was upstairs, the rest of us waited in the bar, where a deeply décolletéd lady
pianist was banging out heart-rending old favorites, and a party of
thoroughly marinated baseball fans were still arguing about an event I
barely remembered—the World Series. The "if" legend they had now
set up was that if the runner on third in the Giants' half of the ninth
inning had been allowed by the baseline coach to come home, he
would have scored, tying the game. (He would have been out.) The
Tiger was well liked at the Governor, which now began to seem a
friendly place to me; the bartender bought us drinks, and you would be
a long time waiting for that at a hotel with four stars.

When Tiger came down, he was conservative but magnificent in a
dove-gray *agbada* fastened with small silver pins. He wore a maroon
pillbox. Jimmy August had switched to a knitted shirt with black and
red stripes, but he was slight competition. We hired a pair of taxis for
the drive to the Mark Hopkins, leaving the beat-up station wagon
down on its own level. The social stratum, like the land, rose as we advanced. At the Hopkins, the Minister of Labor and Social Welfare had
laid on a suite worthy of Nigeria's preeminence among African nations. Bar and buffet were well supplied, and the national costume
turned the salon into a garden. The Minister's own *agbada* made him
look like a garden wall covered with rambler roses as he raised his glass
in honor of the modest hero. "To the champion!" he thundered ge-
nially. "*Our* champion! *Your* champion! *Ev*-erybody's champion!"

And the rest of us joined all the men in *agbadas* in singing, "For he's
a jolly good fellow, for he's a jolly good fellow . . . "

It wasn't until I got downstairs, considerably later, that I remembered there might, for all I knew, be a war on.

November 10, 1962

Anti-Poetry

Night

Last February 4th was bitter cold in Albany. Thick ice covered the sidewalks. Cassius Marcellus Clay, the heavyweight poet from Louisville, Kentucky, sat in the witness box before a joint legislative committee that was discussing a bill to abolish boxing in New York State. For this occasion, Clay had abandoned the rhymed form, like

> Some say the greatest was Sugar Ray,
> But they have not seen Cassius Clay,

in favor of a freer medium, in which metaphor took precedence over jingle. "Boxing is at the winter of its year," he said. "In the time when there were great fighters like Dempsey and Joe Louis, nobody talked against it. When there are no great fighters, people lose interest. It's a question of time." Leaning forward and pointing through a window, he said, "In winter, leaves are not on trees, the grass and flowers are dead, the mind is thinking of chili and hot foods. Time is why. But the earth rotates around the sun in three hundred and sixty-five days, and in that *time* there are winter, fall, spring, and summer. ["I thought I'd break that problem down for them," he said the next day.] *Time* makes those flowers jump out of the ground. The trees get leaves, you see people walking the dogs, time changes their mind. They don't want that chili but popsicles and ice cream—their mind changes into light clothes. Time, it takes time. Will man ever get to the moon? In time he will. Will I be the next champ? Time will tell. In boxing's winter, people lose interest, but I am here to liven things up. On March 13th, I will be fighting at the Garden, and it will be a total sellout." A legislator of distrustful aspect asked him if all his seventeen victories had been on the level, and Mr. Clay said pertly, "They say it take a crook to tell a crook." When he stepped down, a faint odor of *hubris*, like Lilac Végétal, lingered behind.

Clay had thus far had a completely successful career, both as a boxer and as a poet. With a flashy, sleight-of-hand style, based on fast footwork and quick reflexes, he had dazzled everybody whom his management had permitted him to fight, "picking and pecking" at his antagonists until they fell, exhausted and bewildered. He had begun his professional career after winning the light-heavyweight title at the Olympic Games in 1960. His first opponents had been men of no fame and the next batch were second-raters on their way down, but in his sixteenth fight he beat the ancient Archie Moore, a great man in his day, who for years had been fooling rivals half his age. Clay was a lot less than half his age (twenty to Moore's official forty-six), and he achieved this victory in just the way that people had been predicting somebody would for ten years—by staying on the move and not letting the veteran pause for a breather. But none of the previous neophytes had been able to carry through; Moore, with his basilisk eye, had always hypnotized them. Although beating the old favorite indicated that Clay had something out of the ordinary, it did not add to his popularity. That idea, however, never occurred to Clay.

Clay's career as a poet began innocently enough when he confided to a couple of reporters a ballad he had composed about the second fight between Floyd Patterson and Ingemar Johansson, in which Patterson regained the title for the United States. The reporters committed the ballad to print, and then colleagues encouraged the boy to recidivate. After that, there was a rapid decline in the quality of Cassius'

verse, coupled with a fatal inflation of its volume. He became his own
favorite subject, as in the Sugar Ray couplet, but he also developed the
brief prognosticative poem, such as

> Jones likes to mix—
> He must go in six.

He started predicting the round in which he would dispatch each opponent, and sometimes he was right. There was a limitless demand for
his verse, which saved sportswriters who interviewed him from having
to think up gags of their own. Moreover, his poetry earned money,
though by an indirect route. The more he bragged in rhyme, the more
of a drawing card he became, although he certainly did not understand
the mechanics of this phenomenon. (Neither, at the time, did I.) Almost from his début, he had said he wanted to fight the champion immediately; it was Floyd Patterson then, before Liston knocked him
out. Later, Clay began talking a Liston fight. After Clay had stopped
Moore, the challenge to Liston began to be taken seriously, from a
money point of view. Once Liston had fought his return bout with Patterson, it seemed there would be no other rival with whom he could
draw a gate. (It is at present taken for granted among the Fancy that
Patterson will not get the title back from Liston, as he did from the
Swede.) Liston has remarked, in his kindly manner, that Clay should
be arrested for impersonating a prizefighter, but Clay's prediction before the legislature came true long before March 13th, the date of his
fight in Madison Square Garden. The house was a total sellout far in
advance.

Typically, Cassius in his testimony did not mention the fellow he
was going to fight, but the latter was a pretty good heavyweight named
Doug Jones. A Negro, like Clay and Liston and Patterson, he had been
a professional fighter for three years longer than the poet and had
fought much tougher men—all the best heavyweights of the second
rank, in fact. But although Jones' potentialities had been more exten-
sively tested than Clay's, his limits were known; in twenty-five fights,
he had lost three decisions, all to heroes of only his own magnitude.
Such is the will in man to seek a demigod, however, that the gamblers

who set the odds had made Clay a 3–1, or at times a 4–1, favorite over Jones. There is a strong human compulsion to go along with an unbeaten competitor, but it frequently arouses irrational expectations. There was an amplitude about Cassius Marcellus Clay, even when he made his first New York appearance, in February, 1962, that impressed his elders. He not only talked big but was. In less than two years since his Olympic consecration, he had grown from a light heavyweight—a hundred and seventy-five pounds—into a two-hundred-pounder, six feet two and a half inches tall. He even had more managers than any other fighter—a syndicate of Louisville capitalists, who ran him like a foundation. They employed a boxing man named Angelo Dundee as a salaried executive vice-president to direct field operations, but the young Cassius didn't let him do much directing. Enjoined to practice body punching in a sparring match I saw, for example, he told Dundee, "I'm a head-hunter. Keep punching at a man's head and it mixes his mind." This was a piece of dialogue that I remembered rather suddenly a few nights ago. Yet all Clay's reported brashness failed to draw paying customers to his Garden début, against a young, equally unknown quantity named Sonny Banks, whom he predicted he would obliterate in four rounds. (He did.) The fight was on television, from which each boxer was guaranteed four thousand dollars, and I wrote in a memorandum at the time, "The crowd that had assembled to see Clay's début was so thin that it could more properly be denominated a quorum. Only the sportswriters, the gamblers, and the fight mob were there—non-payers all—and the Garden management, solicitous about how the ringside would look to the television audience, had to coax relative strangers into the working-press section."

I thought of what a change thirteen months had wrought as I shoved my way through shoals of pedestrians coming *from* the Garden half an hour before the first preliminary to the Jones fight. They were coming away from it because the house was sold out—a report that they had refused to believe—and the cops were chasing them out of the lobby, where they were blocking the entrance. I had to show a ticket to get off the sidewalk; inside the lobby, the public-address system was happily blaring, "This performance sold out. Only ticket holders in the lobby, please." I hadn't seen anything like it since the Louis-Marciano fight in 1951. But Louis was an immortal, making a last stand against a coming immortal, while Clay and Jones had records like semifinalists'. In the jubilant lobby, even the Garden special cops were laughing as they chucked out the gate-crashers, and the life-size bronze statue of Joe Gans, the old lightweight champion, seemed to have broken into a sweat of excitement. I reflected proudly on the drawing power of poetry in an age that had been wrongly decried as one of mediocre culture. Could Paul Valéry have filled the Vél' d'Hiv', I asked myself rhetorically, or Keats Her Majesty's Theatre?

Inside, I was glad that I had come early enough to find my carefully labelled chair in the third row of the working-press section before some photographer from Oshkosh had a chance to put his coat over the label and sit down. Three Louisville reporters were at my left—and it is a one-ownership newspaper town, at that—to cover Clay in detail. Behind me, Desmond Hackett, of the London *Daily Express*, was talking into a telephone to keep the line clear to his paper. Peter Wilson, of the London *Daily Mirror*, was to my right rear, with typewriter and telegrapher. The *Express* and the *Mirror* both have circulations of around five million, and neither was chancing a loss of a million or so through slack coverage of Clay's recital. Of the New York sportswriters, only the five or six from the *Post* would have a chance to write stories, because of the strike, but all the others were present, because they wanted to keep up with history, and it was reported to me that the members of the Joint Legislative Committee on Professional Boxing were in ringside seats, the more closely to study the evil.

Even some of the preliminary fighters were excited by the atmosphere, new to them, of the great arena containing more than a handful of spectators. (They are too young to have pre-television memories, and since on ordinary nights only the main event is on television, the preliminary boys have got into the habit of feeling themselves unwatched. This is as discouraging for them as it is for a writer to go too long unpublished.) A tall matchstick of a Jewish heavyweight named Wipperman, from Buffalo, fought a hard four rounds with a two-hundred-and-seventeen-pound Negro from down here named Reynolds, and beat him on nothing but a long left and a cool head, as in the storybooks, although the big man kept marching in all the time. The crowd applauded briskly, and the heavies, unused to human sounds, looked surprised. Ray Patterson, the ex-champion's younger brother, and a bit chunkier, made his professional début against a suitably crude opponent, and knocked him out in the second round. This Patterson, a highly experienced amateur, had acted as a sparring partner for his famous brother for several years, but Floyd had always deterred him from turning pro. In the fact that he was appearing at last the Fancy detected the old Champion's determination to retire after the Liston fight, which would wash up the brothers' sparring partnership and leave Ray with only strangers to keep him eating. The new Patterson, like Floyd, boxes in the odd, compressed style reinvented by Cus D'Amato, Floyd's discoverer—forearms vertical in front of the face, and blows flung obliquely from the elbow. (It was first developed by Daniel Mendoza, in the late eighteenth century, but Cus didn't know that. It is also true, I believe, that Alexander the Great had a type of submarine. If man remembered everything he invented, there would soon be nothing left to invent.) Young Patterson is a cool customer, as a young man should be who, after years of working with a heavyweight champion and the champion's high-grade sparring partners, is put in with a fellow named Duke Johnson, from Red Bank, New Jersey. He seemed, though, to lack a trifle of what Colonel John R. Stingo calls the divine inflatus; a kindly soul, he showed repugnance toward finishing Johnson off. As the bearer of a famous name, Patterson got well booed. A fight crowd is, above all, democratic.

The semifinal that preceded the great recital was the kind of grudge fight that would normally be the main event at a tough neighborhood fight club, before an impassioned audience of about a thousand. A year ago, two such clubs survived in all the metropolis—the St. Nick, on Sixty-sixth Street, and the Sunnyside Garden, in Queens. Now the St. Nick is going to the wreckers. In the depressed thirties, a dozen neighborhood clubs operated weekly; the free shows on television destroyed them. Nevertheless, the pair in the Garden were club fighters, a breed that would sprout in alleys if there were no clubs at all—tough, brave, unimaginative, and without class, sticking to one or two habitual maneuvers until, by sheer courage and endurance, they arouse the crowd. After six rounds or so, a fight like this begins to resemble one of those flogging matches between Tatars that I have just read about in an old Russian book by Nikolai Leskov. (The Tatars would sit down sole to sole and take each other by the left hand. Then, each with a whip in his right hand, they would lay on alternate lashes until one of them lost consciousness.) It is a kind of prizefight that I would ordinarily go a long way to avoid seeing and yet that exercises a hypnotic excitement when it reaches the Tatar stage.

The Garden semifinal was a "West Side Story" kind of match—a boy from the Bronx with an Italian name, Billy Bello, and a Puerto Rican from East Harlem, Gil Diaz. Both were around a hundred and fifty pounds. They had fought three eight-round matches before, Bello winning the first, Diaz the second, and Bello the third—each time narrowly. Now they were to box ten rounds, the idea being that the two extra rounds would surely exhaust one of them. Diaz, short and muscular, like the understander in a human pyramid, is bald and grave, so he looks old, even though he is only twenty-five; Bello, just under twenty-one, is long, stringy, and freckled. I told Wilson, the London man, that this match would remind him of the Shoreditch Baths, a tough fight arena in the East End, and when it was over he acknowledged that it did.

The men warmed slowly to their work, disquieted by the size of the arena and the audience. Then they set the pattern, from which they did not vary. Diaz would run in with short steps and generally receive a blow in the face, which he would disregard. Arrived in front of Bello, his head about on a level with the longer boy's breastbone, he would throw two sweeping swings that, leaving his shoulders almost laterally, would land on the sides of Bello's head, the point of impact being almost always the underside of glove and wrist. The successive buffets would land with a tremendous noise, and Bello would stagger back. Bello had no plan, apparently, except to wait for the small colossus to exhaust himself; occasionally he hit Diaz a swiping uppercut or a painful jab, but he did not often feel it worth the expenditure of energy. At the beginning of every round, he stood up in his corner with the look of a bather going back into a surf that he did not very much enjoy. But after the middle rounds the surf, as at the beach, began to recede; the waves lost much of their punch. The Puerto Rican pendulum's arms grew heavy, like a kid's in a pillow fight. Mr. Wilson said brightly, "They've run out of ideas." Whitey Bimstein, my friend and frequent preceptor, who was acting as the Puerto Rican's chief second, became exhortative, shaking his fist under his man's nose; he was beyond ear-shot, but from long acquaintance I knew what he was saying: "You're behint on points. Get in there and knock him out"—ornamenting these instructions with adjectives hinting that his chap was less than courageous. When I first met Whitey, twenty-seven years ago, we cal-culated that he had acted as second in fifteen thousand fights. He has certainly added fifteen thousand since, but he gets just as passionate about each one, and the two-dollar mistakes of a mere Diaz affect him as deeply as the lapses of a client like Johansson, which can cost a world's title.

At the beginning of the ninth, the Puerto Rican came out in a blend of a rush and a totter, and the surf bather ran in like a fellow trying to get in under a roller before it breaks. He hit the short man right on the bald spot, and Diaz went out on his face. Whitey left the ring shaking his head; he sometimes feels that he hasn't had a completely satisfac-tory principal since Frankie Jerome died in his arms in the old Garden, on Twenty-sixth Street, in 1924.

The club fight had put everybody in a good humor, like a song of the Gay Nineties. During the last few rounds, the hall had filled to the cracking point as the last few confident holders of ringside seats filed in—an exercise in sang-froid that I have never been capable of, since I fear that if I start out just before the main event I may get caught in a taxi jam and miss it altogether. There were now nineteen thousand spectators in the hall, come to honor Apollo in the person of Cassius Clay, who had had fewer professional fights than Billy Bello. Hardly anybody had mentioned Jones or thought about him during the pre-liminaries to his immolation, but now a susurrus ran through the crowd, commencing at the door of Jones' dressing room and following

him through to the ring, where it became, astonishingly, an accla-
mation. He climbed up the ring steps without visible trace of apprehension—a long, lead-colored, bony, hard, bullet-headed young man
wearing a catfish-style mustache. He was accompanied by his manager, a small, suspicious man named Alex Koskowitz, his face already
wrathful at anticipated chicanery, and by a wide, outwardly placid fellow named Jimmy August, who, like Whitey Bimstein, is an illustrious
second, offering counsel and surgery as required throughout a fight. I
had last seen August in San Francisco, where he seconded Dick Tiger,
who won the world middleweight championship from Gene Fullmer.

A harrowing and at first inexplicable noise attended the approach
of Clay, but long before he reached the ring its import became unmistakable. The crowd was booing him. It was only now, as he mounted
the steps to his corner and jigged as he climbed, that both he and I
understood why the nineteen thousand had come to watch the blithe
minnesinger perform. They wanted to see him killed. A vast "Boo!"
descended from the balcony and mezzanine, another arose from the
arena seats and ringside, and they met in midair and fused. It was the
most emphatic anti-poetry demonstration in American history. Cassius must have wished that he were again at the Bitter End, the Greenwich Village coffee room where he had recently read verse, or at the
Ninety-second Street Young Men's Hebrew Association, where his
fellow-poets often appear. Up to that moment, it had been his opinion
that he was one of the best-loved figures of the decade, but now it was
plain that the public thought he had a swelled head. I suspected that
this might separate him from his aplomb, which is his outstanding
characteristic.

Clay was accompanied by his executive vice-president, Dundee,
and two counsellors of the Bimstein-August strain—Fred Fierro, who
looks like a Shakespearean actor, and Jimmy Wilde, who looks like
Jimmy August. He was wearing a gay white robe with red tabs, white
trunks, and white kid ring boots; he looked like a flower jumping out of
the ground. He is a very handsome boy, of a Joe Louis tinge lightened
by a faint reddish glow, and with small, unmarked features, usually
evenly divided by a wide, pearly smile. That, too, seemed to be a griev-

ance among some spectators. "Bust his face, Doug!" I heard a ringside lady trill. (One of my newspaper friends had just been remarking that Clay had brought the millionaire trade back to the Garden; he hadn't seen so much mink, he said, since the mobsters quit bringing their girls.)

The introductions from the ring were of a chic otherwise reserved for great championships. It is often possible to gauge the class of a big fight by the assortment of eminences introduced before it goes on. When these are merely boys who are going to fight someplace else next week and battered old light heavyweights who held the title briefly, the soirée lacks cachet. For Clay's gala, Jack Dempsey and Gene Tunney appeared together in the ring to shake the fighters' hands and take a bow. This was like Heifetz and Stern appearing together to grace the recital of a child prodigy. When Sugar Ray Robinson, the great fighter of the recent past, walked over and pawed Clay's glove, I could see that Cassius was all right. His aplomb had not been affected by his disillusion—if, indeed, the disillusion had penetrated. He bowed stiffly from the waist, as if being presented for the first time to a potentate, though he and Robinson—never a violet, either—are good friends. The crowd laughed at that. "You gotta admit the bum's a clown," someone behind me said.

The weights were announced—Clay two hundred and two and a half, and Jones a hundred and eighty-eight. The poet towered above his chosen subject, but Jones' iron hue gave him a more durable appearance. The fight itself was close, up to a point. Jones, a straight-up fighter, stands conventionally, moving forward with a straight jab and a following right cross, but he is no body-pounder and does not throw those rapid sequences of punches called combinations. Perhaps his faction had warned him against becoming involved in these flurries, because Clay, who has remarkably fast reflexes, extemporizes rapidly and well. Clay is a circler, working around the other fellow and then leaning in to punch at the head, escaping counters by leaning back and pulling away from them. In the very first round, Jones, going out boldly, drove Clay toward the ropes and hit him as he moved back, knocking him against the ropes with a sharp right to the jaw. The crowd howled, and I had a momentary feeling that the poet might face drastic humiliation; I remembered that Jones had had far more real experience. But Clay came out of it and went into his tried routine, moving, slapping, and stinging. Not all the punches he landed on the small, hard head were easy ones, but Jones takes a punch well. Jones, for his part, was exclusively a head-hunter, too, but he hit less often. When the first round ended, I thought Jones had had the better of it, but not by much, and certainly neither man looked in danger. And so it went—the second round even, and the third, I thought, to Clay, but neither man, it was now apparent, was a tiger. And although the things they did were good, in their way, their repertories were almost as limited as the club fighters'.

The reporters from Louisville were by now asweat. In the last year, Clay has become that city's most important sports figure. The number of out-of-town trips that a provincial sportswriter gets depends on the existence in his city of a competitor of national importance. With a heavyweight champion in residence, an American Association city becomes big time, and trips with the hero can sometimes get a man to Europe. A couple of days earlier, Clay had been talking about licking Liston. Now, it seemed, he would be lucky to win a decision. The crowd's hostility must have further alarmed the Louisville men, because the howl of a crowd has been known to influence judges.

The fourth round began with a paroxysm of derision from the crowd, because Clay had announced a couple of days earlier that he would flatten Jones in that round. ("I'm changing the pick I made before./Instead of six, Doug goes in four.") This looked most unlikely, and as the seconds marched by on the big electric clock on the Garden wall the cheers and the booing increased. The round was a brisk one, and Clay had it, I thought, but he landed a hard right to the head after the bell, and I was afraid that the judges and the referee might take his gain away from him. Now was exactly the time for a young man built like Clay, up against a straight-standing boxer whose noodle was hard to addle with jabs, to begin hooking to the body and then pull the other man in close and bring up a great uppercut, but Clay simply didn't know how to do any of those things. He had been too cocksure to learn. In fact, he showed signs of severe apprehension when Jones, even by accident, got close inside. When this happened, the poet grabbed for him, like an old lady who can't swim. Jones appeared equally inept, and the moments when they should have been infighting were simply pauses until the referee, a fellow named Joe Lo Scalzo, separated them.

All the time that I was watching this quite ordinary fight—just good enough to watch at all—my nineteen thousand fellow-viewers, to judge by the noise they made, were witnessing a vast allegorical struggle between the Modest Underdog and Mr. Swellhead Bigmouth Poet. When Jones landed, they cheered because he had, and when Clay landed, they cheered because Jones hadn't gone down. By the fifth round, Cassius had explored all of Jones' capabilities and was slapping him into discouragement, but in the sixth Jones, exhorted by Jimmy August, landed a couple of fairly stiff punches to the belly, and when the round ended, Freddy Fierro, in the Clay corner, began a violent stomach massage that showed where the trauma had settled in. When the belly is hurt, the legs sympathize; Clay's legs are his fortune, and if they started to go, my Louisville colleagues and I alike feared, Jones might get to him and knock him out. I remembered, gloomily, that Clay was said not to do much roadwork. He is a hedonist.

But we had forgotten youth. Clay recuperated from the body punches in a few seconds and went out gay for the seventh, which, on my card, he won going away. I had the fight all even then, but in the eighth, ninth, and tenth the Distressed Poet got on top and beat Jones to the punch three times out of four, fighting now with a wild confidence. His vanity had been hurt sufficiently, and he has much faster eyes and hands than Jones, who is unlikely ever to be any better than he is right now, while Cassius, if he buckles down to his lessons, can go much farther. It was a fine, all-out finish, with Jones slugging away like a good one, even though he usually missed. The Louisville boys were still anxious, but I ventured to reassure them, and the Messrs. Hackett and Wilson, with their detached, international point of view, were equally certain that Clay had won.

It was then that anti-intellectualism truly raised its ugly head and its still uglier voice. A boxing crowd—and this is one of the nice things about it—always sees the underdog's achievement in direct ratio to the length of the odds against him, so that, for example, if he is expected to be knocked out and instead goes the distance, the crowd is willing to believe that he has won. Its major components are, moreover, stationed at an altitude from which they can perceive no development more subtle than a knockdown. When a crowd has paid its money to see an advertised phenomenon, it will be satisfied only if he *is* a phenomenon, or if he gets killed. If the fellow turns out to be merely a reasonably good fighter, he has antagonized the public two ways. The announcer, a fellow named Johnny Addie, took the slips from the two judges and read them. They both voted for Clay—five rounds for him, four for Jones (which I thought generous), and one even. I thought that it should have been six, three, and one. A vast clamor arose, beneath the first wave of which I barely heard Addie read the referee's card—eight rounds for Clay, one for Jones, and one even. This was a miscarriage of justice—even though it in no way affected the result, since the two judges' votes would have been enough. But eight rounds to one indicates a one-sided bout, which this hadn't been. The second clamorous wave was the loudest I'd heard since I was in the streetcar barn at Donnybrook the night they gave a Frenchman the decision over an Irishman. Here there were massed standees, with choirmasters self-appointed on the spot, shouting in cadence, "Fake! Fake! Fake!" or "Fix! Fix! Fix!" or "Shame! Shame! Shame!" Such are the lengths to which a hatred of poetry can carry people.

Koskowitz and Jimmy August craftily kept their man in the ring until after the poet's faction had left, and then, jerking the loser's hands high in the air, paraded him around under the lights as if he were the victor. A particularly anti-intellectual cantor, who had been leading the choir of dissidents nearest my section, got the goat of a kindly old newspaperman at my right, who picked up a camp chair and was preparing to let him have it. "You hit me with that chair and I'll sue for a million dollars!" the subversionist cried. "I'm a spectator!"

As soon as the aisles had cleared a little—the cops having herded the noisiest demonstrators toward the doors, and the fans who had nowhere else to go having settled down for the postlude bouts—I made my way to Jones' dressing room, where Koskowitz was pretending to have lost his voice from indignation, while Jimmy August sat on a bench laughing bitterly, like a road-company Tonio, and Jones relatives, male and female, surrounded their hero. "Last month in Las Vegas, I had Tiger fighting a rematch with Fullmer, who is a Mormon," August said, "and *after* the fight we find out the referee is married to a Mormon. We was lucky to get a draw, and we killed him. And now this."

From the loser's dressing room, which had the feel of a winner's, I went on to the winner's, which had the atmosphere of a publisher's office after the house novelist has blown the National Book Award. Apollo, unmarked and still as fresh as a jumping flower, was disconsolate; up until that evening, he had thought himself one of the most popular cutups in America. His brother Rudolph Valentino Clay, also a boxer and nearly a twin, couldn't understand things, either. "He win unanimous," he said. "A unanimous decision."

"I'll knock him out next time," the poet said. "I learned his style." But his eyes were sad. He had a grievance. "Why did those people boo me when I whup him?" he asked me. "Why they don't boo *for* me?"

He seemed to feel that the leaves were not on the trees, the grass and flowers were dead. Will he ever be heavyweight champion? Time will tell. Will he learn to punch harder? It is a question of time, too. Will he learn to fight inside? Time is all. A young man's best friend is time.

March 30, 1963

Starting All
Over Again

The evidence of the eye is hard to disbelieve but easy to forget. Last September, I sat in Comiskey Park, in Chicago, and saw Charles (Sonny) Liston win the heavyweight boxing championship of the world from Floyd Patterson by knocking him out in two minutes and six seconds. I wrote then, "It was like one of those saloon fights that end abruptly because the chance combatants are not in the same class." I noted that Liston, the considerably bigger man, was so much the stronger that he was able to pull an arm free in a clinch and hit with it, and that since he was at least as fast as Patterson, these advantages made his victory inevitable. "The winning punches were like those a man might use to beat the resistance out of a boy in a street fight," I wrote.

The contract for the Comiskey Park match gave Patterson the right to command a return bout before Liston could fight anybody else, but I hoped that the former champion would waive the privilege. In the words of the great Tunisian historian and form player Ibn Khaldun, "The past resembles the future more than one drop of water resembles another," and it was inconceivable to me that Patterson could do much with the big fellow. Having watched Patterson since he was a seventeen-year-old amateur, in 1952, I had taken a proprietary interest in him—a phenomenon common to sports fans and opera buffs—and I did not want to see him hurt. When I learned through the public prints of his unfortunate decision to force a return fight, I felt sure that he was making a mistake, and I had no wish to see him take the consequences. But as the months of winter went by and the former champion persisted in his determination, I began to remember how Patterson, badly beaten by a Swede named Ingemar Johansson in 1959, had beaten Johansson just as badly in 1960. I should have equally remembered Khaldun on the fallibility of analogy, but I didn't. I more easily recalled how hopeless Patterson had looked in the 1959 fight, flopping about the ring at the Polo Grounds as the Swede floored him six times before the finish, and how he had seemed an entirely different fighter in the following year, when he flattened the Swede.

In these fantasies I was encouraged by Mr. Cus D'Amato, the manager who developed Patterson, beginning when he was a boy of fourteen and attending a lower East Side school. At the time of the Johansson matches, Cus and Patterson had been estranged—at least partially—for two or three years, during which the fighter had not accepted the manager's advice, although Cus had retained his financial interest in his protégé's earnings. Lawyers and stock promoters from outside the fight game had won away Patterson's confidence from his old Svengali by telling him that he was a grown-up man and should think for himself. This is heady doctrine for a boxer. From the time that these chaps got to Patterson, Cus said, they had had him thinking about everything but fighting, about which they were incapable of advising him. He still believed that his pupil was potentially great, and had, in fact, actually been great twice in his career—against a fighter named Don Grant, in Brooklyn on January 17, 1955, and against Archie Moore, whom he beat for the vacant world heavyweight championship on November 30, 1956. The Grant fight—against a man who rose to no high fame—was in Cus's opinion even better than the triumph over Moore, by now a ring immortal. Floyd knocked Grant out in five rounds. So, in the eyes of a professor of violin, one of his virtuoso pupils may have played the best concert of his career in an obscure town for a small fee. Cus is one of the few managers who care about the techniques of boxing. "The Patterson of the Grant fight would beat even Liston," he said. I did not believe him, but, listening, I thought Patterson might improve on his Chicago performance.

The men were first matched to fight the return bout last April in Miami, and by March I found myself reflecting on the infinite variety of things that could happen in a match between heavyweights, and how silly I would feel if Patterson now did what I had half expected him to do in the first fight, before I had seen Liston at work. The probability was small, but to drop him now made me feel like a deserter. As the date set for the return approached, I telephoned to reserve a ticket. Then Liston hurt one of his knees while swinging a golf club—a confirmation of my theory that boxing is among the less dangerous pastimes—and the fight was postponed. The Miami tourist season ended, eliminating the potential audience there, and the match was remade for Las Vegas on July 22nd. The temperature there at that season is about that of Ouargla, in the Sahara, but the fight would be held in an air-conditioned convention hall. By that time, I wouldn't have missed it for the world.

The twenty-second was a Monday—a day of the week chosen, I imagine, so that the weekend gamblers from California would stay over and, while awaiting the bell, try to win themselves out, to the profit of all the casinos. I got out there on the Saturday, and arrived at the Dunes, my hotel, just in time to attend Patterson's last press conference before the fight. Formal press conferences in dignified surroundings are de rigueur for prizefighters nowadays; I had barely missed Liston's final one, at the Thunderbird, where he was making his headquarters. The sportswriters take turns asking questions, as at a Presidential press conference, and the fighter, at a microphone, answers or says he does not care to. This is a strain on the fighter, who should be concentrating on his business or else playing some simple card game or an intricate practical joke. In the old days, there was division of labor; the managers did the talking and the fighters the fighting, and each excelled in his specialty. Now neither Patterson nor Liston even has an official, practicing manager. Liston has a man named Jack Nilon whom he calls his "adviser," and Patterson keeps D'Amato at a distance while he deals with the outer world through his counsel.

Patterson, shy and almost inarticulate when he won the 167-pound title at the Helsinki Olympic Games in 1952, is now a highly interesting talker, if you are interested in a man who tries to tell the whole truth. A reporter asked him if he hated Liston, and he said that he had hated only one man in his life—Johansson, between their first and second fights. Then, when he saw Johansson unconscious on the floor, his left leg quivering convulsively, he had quit hating him and had resolved never to hate again. This was good Dostoevski, but not reassuring to bettors who were tempted to take the odds of from four to six to one being offered against Patterson. It did not indicate a satisfactory degree of ferocity. Another chap asked the polite young man whether Liston could be knocked out like anybody else, and Patterson said, "Of course he can be." He then spoiled it by adding, "I don't say I'll be the one to do it, but he can be." What he should have said—or, better, let a manager say for him—was "Sure he can be, and I'm going to prove it by knocking him out quicker than he licked me last time." (Managers frequently adopt the vicarious first person.) He then talked for a bit about his trip to Birmingham, Alabama, in company with Jackie Robinson, the former baseball star, to take part in a protest parade. "You feel like an animal walking in a jungle," he said. "It is not like part of the United States." His concern for social justice was manifest, but it did not sound quite like fight talk.

The former champion does not look big in either ring or street clothes—the record book claims an even six feet for him—and his face, with its long, uptilted nose, continues to look boyish, though he is now twenty-eight. After the Chicago fight, as all the world now knows, he made his escape wearing a false beard and mustache, to avoid the humiliation of condolences. A reporter asked him about that, and he said, "If any of you men had been in my position, with letters pouring in on me from all over the country to beat Liston, and then losing as disgraceful as I did, you would have jumped off the roof." In taking the return match, I judged, he wanted to expunge the disgrace. A British correspondent I know who always persuades himself to pick the long shots told me, as the conference broke up, that Patterson was sure to win. "He's been on the road every morning in ninety degrees of heat"—this is the cool of the dawn in Las Vegas—"whilst Liston has been doing his training in a Turkish bath. He's been sweating the pounds off, and his legs show it." Hank Greenspun, the publisher of the Las Vegas *Sun*, admitted that he had bet three hundred dollars on the challenger at one to six-and-a-half. "I couldn't pass up those odds," he said. His paper had an admirable Las Vegas headline that day about a local murder: "GLUE SNIFFER ORDERED TO GAS CHAMBER."

Sunday morning, I taxied to the Thunderbird to reconnoitre the champion's faction. Las Vegas is a taxi-driver's paradise, because visitors use cabs for any distance longer than fifty yards from one air-cooled interior to another. The Thunderbird was built some ten years ago and so ranks as a historic hostelry in Las Vegas, but the action at its craps tables is as lively and the clangor of its slot machines as deafening as those of its juniors. The champion had withdrawn from public contact, but I talked to his trainer, Willie Reddish, a man almost as big and more willingly informative. Reddish is a large, light-colored buffer between Liston and the rest of the world; Sonny, he explains to anybody who will listen, is really a good-natured fellow who just likes to scowl and shout. "He likes to get a man worked up, understand? But in the same time, he'll do anything for you. Now me, I'm just the other way. I seldom holler, but when I do, I'll stay angry the longest time." The champion, Willie said, was in the best shape of his career. "Him and Jersey Joe Walcott are the strongest heavyweights I ever saw," he said. "But he's stronger." Reddish went ten rounds with Jersey Joe back in 1936, when ham and eggs were hard to come by. He does not believe that the whole of the Sweet Science is contained within the ring; like all good trainers, he watches what goes on outside. The first time I met him, a year or so ago, when Liston was training for the first fight, he said that he was discounting young Cassius Clay, the Louisville poet, because Clay was too good-looking. "The women will ruin him long be-

fore he gets up there," he said. "Ugly fighters are the best." When I reminded him this time that Clay looked as though he were "up there"
already—the next opponent for Liston after the Patterson fight—
Willie said, "He came up faster than I thought. In such a short time, it
wouldn't be long enough for the women to get him. But Sonny will
take care of him." Reddish said that they expected Patterson to come
out fighting.

I made inquiries for D'Amato every time I met some member of the
Fancy and sat down for the inevitable glass of iced tea and accompa-
nying anecdote. But I did not catch up with him until late that afternoon, in his room at the Tallyho, a new hotel that has the unique distinction of having no gambling devices on the premises. Las Vegans
other than the proprietor consider this innovation too startling to succeed. Cus has a round head with a snow-white crew cut—the head of
a Roman bust or an elegant Fratellini. He is a nimble man; he jumps
into his trousers with both feet in the morning to protect his joints
against rust. His clothes are sombre but expensive, his language frequently ornate. He is in his mid-fifties now, and full of theories about
boxing, one being that the famous men of old were overrated, which
he loves to demonstrate by showing films of old fights. He used to run
a small gymnasium over a poolroom on Fourteenth Street, near Lu-
chow's, and he still owns it. Cus encouraged neighborhood boys to
box, but he had the gym for many years before he found the one apostle
who could assimilate the style he taught and win with it (or, in the
opinion of some critics, in spite of it) consistently. Patterson was the
kid apostle, and D'Amato and the boy worked their way up through
the minor and the better-class amateurs, and then the professional
shows in small clubs in Brooklyn, with detours to places like Moncton,
New Brunswick, and New Britain, Connecticut. At Las Vegas, Cus
was to second Patterson in the ring, but he was not living at the Patterson training camp—an evidence of their now ambiguous relation-
ship. Mr. D'Amato saw his former protégé as being separated from him
by the sinister intrigues of people with financial designs against both of
them. Last winter, he admitted to me that because of his divided mind

Patterson was no longer "great." Few impartial critics ever conceded that he had been, but they had praised him when he beat Johansson. Cus said that he could be great again if he regained the proper state of mind.

"He has got to be the great Patterson again to get it back," he told me at the Tallyho. "The Grant Patterson, or even the Moore Patterson. He don't have to be any better. Weight is not an insuperable handicap, especially for heavyweights. I've seen plenty of welterweights beat middleweights, which is more serious. The essential is that the little guy have enough punch to take the big guy out, and Floyd has demonstrated the ability against other big guys. Liston is not invincible unless you stand still. Then he throws a lot of punches. But if you keep moving, he gets confused. Floyd stood still the last time. That was the trouble. He had his right glove up by the side of his face, and the guy threw a long left hook and hit him in the temple. That started the series of three left hooks, and Floyd says he never saw the last one coming." This picture of merely tactical defeat was not the one that I retained. "He and I are the only ones who believe it," Cus said, "but you're going to see the great Patterson tomorrow night, and he's going to win."

Nothing of the sort happened in the Convention Center the next night, of course. The bout was set for seven-thirty in the evening, so that it could be on closed television in the East at a reasonable hour. The program was late in starting, but even so it was one of the shortest evenings of boxing that I can remember. The hall, as new as almost everything else in the gambling town, holds a maximum of eight thousand spectators, and there were more than seventy-five hundred present—a striking illustration of how quickly fight fans forget, or how eternally hope springs, or how few people read Ibn Khaldun. The seats cost from twenty to one hundred dollars. The single preliminary ended with a knockout in two minutes and twenty-three seconds. Then Patterson and his faction entered the ring, Cus climbing through the ropes first. Patterson looked in magnificent shape—wide, for him, across the chest, and weighing five pounds more than in Chicago. The booing and cheering were about equally loud. To boo the underdog at a fight is not usual, and I could interpret it only as an expression of contempt. But if the booers thought so little of him, why did they pay to see the fight? Liston entered next, and for him the booing was unanimous and loud, although he is a pleasing fighter to watch and has declined no suggested opponent. His size and his public scowl, perhaps, are the chief counts against him, although the latter is only a professional tool, like a doctor's bedside manner. His competence is also resented, as if it were not quite fair for a man to know his business. At two hundred fifteen and a half pounds, he was twenty-one pounds heavier than Patterson, and had a considerable advantage in height and reach. Old and new boxers were introduced from the ring, where they came to wish the evening's heroes well, and among them was the self-advertising Cassius Clay, a handsome giant. Clay touched Patterson's glove and then, after looking at Liston, vaulted over the ring ropes in simulated terror. This made Patterson laugh so spontaneously that I thought he could not be tense.

But when the bell rang, it was evident that Ibn Khaldun was a voice to be heeded, for the match in Las Vegas was as unequal as the one in Chicago. The inequality became clear even earlier, in fact, because in Chicago Liston had spent the first minute feeling Patterson out; now, having studied the subject sufficiently, he went right to work with a hard straight left to the face, and then, as Patterson rocked, a couple of hard blows to the body. (What most boxing writers now call Liston's left jab is what writers of an older day would have called a straight left—a longer, more jarring blow that is designed to hurt a man as well as throw him off balance.) There was no effective riposte. Liston was on top of Patterson all the time. When the smaller man tried to clinch, Liston hammered him about the belly, and when he bent low, Liston banged his ribs. The tempo was faster than in the Chicago bout, and Liston hit him a great deal more often, knocking him down three times instead of once in approximately the same number of seconds. Knocked out of firing position every time Liston hit him, Patterson got in no effective blow—the one right hand that he seemed to land on Liston's jaw after the first knockdown proved, on inspection of the fight film, to have grazed off. When the referee counted Patterson out, only two minutes and ten seconds had elapsed—a hundred and thirty seconds, as compared with a hundred and twenty-six in Chicago. But, as Liston said after the fight, the hundred and thirty seconds included two counts of eight after knockdowns, so that the fighters were really in action for less time at Las Vegas. Patterson, as in Chicago, picked himself up at the last knockdown one second too late, but it was clear that he could not continue.

The Convention Center, unlike most places where prizefights are held, has a number of ancillary halls and suites, so that Patterson and Liston enjoyed the luxury of two adjoining dressing rooms apiece—one to change in and one in which to give the inevitable post-fight conference. This is a civilized way of doing things, although it may be hard on the boys on the morning papers, who have to wait a few minutes longer to get the deathless words they usually cull from bloody lips. (Still, it seems less like prizefighting.) Liston, as might be expected, since he was completely undamaged, was first out of his dressing room.

He wore a blue denim shirt and slacks, and one of those funny little straw hats with a feather in it, as if he had been spending an evening at an amusement park. The sportswriters asked the customary questions—Had he been hurt at any time? Had the fight been harder than the last one? When had he been sure he would win?—and he answered in the monosyllables, or pairs of them, that are his habitual response to superfluous inquiries. ("A newspaperman will look up at the sun and ask you if the sun is shining," he once said.) He has a concave face, with a bulging forehead and a heavy jaw, and his voice can make "yes" sound like an insult. Then somebody asked him what he had thought when he heard the crowd boo.

"I just thought, well, I'll fix them," he said. Then, "They have to swing along with me till somebody else comes along to beat me." He sounded as if he wanted to be liked more than anything else in the world. A reporter asked him how long it would take him to beat Cassius Clay the beautiful, and he said, "Two rounds—one and a half to ketch him, and a half a round to lick him."

Some of the reporters had wondered whether Patterson would flee into the night, as he had after the Chicago bout, but he didn't. When he appeared in his conference room, with D'Amato at his right hand, he said that he had put the mustache aside forever; he was "through with those things," which, I hoped, included the passion for self-examination that has preoccupied him in these latter years. He blamed nothing and nobody for losing. "I felt inside I could win tonight," he said. "I felt good until I got hit. Liston is just a better fighter than I am—or was tonight." He said that he didn't want another return fight—"I'm out of the picture." But when a reporter asked him if he would now retire, unmarked and with plenty of money, he said, "No, I'm going back to the bottom and start all over again. I love boxing, and if there was no money in it I'd stick to it anyway."

Certainly nothing had happened that night to encourage his love, but a man does not become a good boxer unless he likes to box—a point that the anti-boxing people either don't understand or ignore. And Patterson, at twenty-eight, has devoted half his time on earth to it. "Never mind, Floyd, you're still the greatest!" somebody in the little crowd shouted. As Patterson finished his speech and started toward the door, somebody else cried, "You can train down and win the light-heavyweight championship. Then you'll still be champion."

I found myself next to D'Amato and asked him what had happened. "It was the same as last time," Cus said, again ignoring the discrepancy between the two men. "He didn't move around. We would have said something to correct him in the corner between rounds, but the guy knocked him out before we had a chance. He can still lick anybody else in the world." Patterson and his other handlers headed for the car that would take them back to camp, and D'Amato and I walked out of the Convention Center together. Patterson, if he had won, could have named his own price for a third fight with Liston, and Cus's share would have been in six figures. For a man who had lost all that future money, he seemed oddly cheerful.

We had not eaten yet, and Cus suggested the Tallyho, because, having no gambling, it was quiet. At table, the manager, usually abstemious, had a Manhattan, chicken-liver pâté, calf's liver smothered with onions, and cherry cheesecake. "I am always at my best when the bottom drops out," he said after this dissipation. And I could imagine him packing his bag to accompany the new-model Patterson to Moncton, New Brunswick.

August 10, 1963

Afterword

I doubt whether many of the people who read Liebling's boxing pieces in the *New Yorker*, where nearly all of these essays originally appeared, cared much about boxing. Most of his readers accepted exposure to a brutal and alien sport because they loved good prose, and Liebling could write well about anything. About boxing he wrote superbly. His persistent fascination with the off-beat and the purely secular inclined him toward the demimonde of the ring, with its practitioners' punitive insistence upon art and craft and its milieu of confidence-men, venal promoters, and sage professors, a mixed marriage of sham and shaman. Liebling's early fight pieces went into the books he published before World War II, and most of his boxing essays through 1955 appeared in *The Sweet Science*. This volume gathers Liebling's uncollected boxing essays, including everything he wrote about the sport from the publication of *The Sweet Science* to the second Patterson-Liston fight, which he saw a few months before he died.

In the twenty-seven years since his death, with his work in and out of print and never available at one time in its entirety, A. J. Liebling has been, as he said of Stephen Crane, from time to time "reforgotten." It is bootless to argue that one part of Liebling's oeuvre is substantially better than another. Stanley Edgar Hyman once spoke of "Liebling's amazing variety of specializations." He gave his intelligence and affection to horse racing, the Olympic Games, cockfighting, politics, the press, gambling, Indians, wild horses, travel, food, literature, and what Harold Ross called the "low-life" of New York. No American wrote more lovingly about France, Paris, and the French; his account in *Normandy Revisited* of the liberation of Paris is a magnificent piece of history and a robust hymn of praise to a city and its people. Reading it, one can believe that August 25, 1944, was the happiest day of his life. Concerning the practice of putting writers into categories, which he despised, he wrote of Crane, "The run of the mill critic is a Linnaean; he likes to pop his specimens into plainly labelled phials, and Crane, genus Doomed Genius, went into the one labelled 'Edgar Allan Poe.'" Of himself, he wrote, "There is an old proverb that a girl may sleep with one man without being a trollop, but let a man cover one little war and he is a war correspondent. I belong to the one war category."

Trying to say what kind of writer he was is just one of the difficulties that arise when you look at Liebling and his career. Born into comfortable respectability, he did not want to be respectable. In the twenties he went to Paris to study medieval history and to fall in love with France forever. There he discovered that his best energies ought to go into writing about himself and his adventures in various raffish worlds, life as he curiously found it. Liebling could be urbane, clever, and scholarly in his far-flung erudition and still have a fondness for the rough and dark side of things. He admired the eighteenth-century British writer Pierce Egan, a wide-ranging, wide-liking all-rounder who, like Hazlitt, Cobbett, and Borrow, other Liebling favorites, wrote well about many things. Egan is chiefly remembered for *Boxiana*, his chronicle of the prize ring, but there, as in his other works, what captured his attention is the turbulent world of gamblers, tarts, sharpers, poseurs, bucks, and gentlemen who flourished in Hanoverian England. Liebling relished the expansive life of times past that allowed more room for charming eccentricity, hence his admiration for that champion of chicanery Colonel Stingo, hero of *The Honest Rainmaker*. Stingo was grandiloquent in speech and manner, fleecing the rubes with unfailing panache.

Yet Liebling was anything but a sentimentalist, one of the most difficult things not to be when writing about sports. He did not go to prizefights with the same expectations or desires that Hemingway took to the bullring. There are in both, of course, ritual, drama, beauty, and a performance that is cruelly demanding, but Liebling did not find in boxing a transfiguring metaphor for life and death. He knew that it was, at its best, a passionate fury in which everything is essential.

Part of boxing's great appeal is in providing spectators with a relatively fast decision as to who wins and who loses. In that regard, it is wholly unlike what happens in life. Literature, history, and our own quotidian comedies and tragedies teach that unambiguous moral decisions are rare and no triumph or defeat ever quite final. It *is* final when the referee says "ten" or when the towel flies into the ring (which still happens, for I saw that ancient flag of surrender at a recent bout in Paris). Defeat in boxing is sometimes absolute, leaving the loser a shuffling, punch-drunk wreck, or unconscious, slipping toward death even as the victor prances about him and the ring announcer fumbles for the microphone.

Liebling knew the serious risks involved. His references to Stendhal and other great ironists are not accidental or casual. Like the Russian general in *For Whom the Bell Tolls*, he can joke because he is so serious, as he is at the end of "Poet and Pedagogue," where he describes the beaten and now forgotten fighter who had nearly defeated Cassius Clay and was faced with a lifetime of remembering what might have been. That sad tableau reveals a lot about what made Liebling such a good writer. None of the taints of the sports page are there—hyperbole, hypocrisy, cynicism, or sentimentality. It is heartbreaking, emblematic, and just right.

Abbott Joseph Liebling was born in New York on October 18, 1904, and died there December 28, 1963. He attended Dartmouth College, which expelled him for cutting chapel. In 1925 he was graduated from Columbia University's Pulitzer School of Journalism and went to work for the *New York Times*, which fired him, as he recalled years later, for being "irresponsible." (He once reported the name of the referee in an inconsequential basketball game for which he had no scorecard as "Ignoto.") So he moved on to newspapers in Providence, and in 1926 went to Paris. He returned to work again in Providence, and from 1930 to 1935 he wrote for the *New York World-Telegram*. Harold Ross of the *New Yorker* then hired him, and over the next twenty-eight years he wrote hundreds of pieces for that magazine. He once tried living in Chicago and didn't like it, giving the place its unshakable nickname "The Second City." The only other significant times that he left his hometown were to cover the war in Africa and Europe and during his later travels.

He wrote more than a dozen books and left a vast body of uncollected journalism and a few short stories. By the time of the pieces collected here, the mature Liebling style had become unmistakable, effortlessly allusive, supple, unashamedly personal, his remarkable knowledge and compassion asserting themselves all over the place.

Shortly after Hemingway's death in 1961, Liebling wrote of him, "He also knew that life can be as sweet as the minute between rounds is to a hard-tried fighter; much of his best writing is a catalogue of the things that make it so. Beginning with the intimation that comes to most men late, he was from the start one who looked behind him." Liebling at the fights is often a man doing just that, savoring the past as he uses it to evaluate the present. With an audience he knew would not be put off by his catholicity, he digressed frequently and at length. In "An Old Thuburban Custom," the Roman mosaics in Tunis send him reeling through history. In "A Blow for Austerity," Ingemar Johansson's Lucullan training regimen evokes the fourteenth-century Tunisian writer Ibn Khaldun. Sporting events are rigidly defined, and their outcome admits few possibilities, which is why it is more difficult to write with freshness about a baseball game than a love affair. Liebling's digressions and allusions amplified his accounts, proving his observation that great writing "has the quality that Stendhal attributed to great music. It starts you thinking along parallel and then tangential lines, and reflecting on the inwardness of the meaning of experience." As Stanley Edgar Hyman said of Liebling, "His mind was naturally comparative, perceiving similarity in dissimilars, which Aristotle called the sign of genius." It was never hard to get Liebling started, but, like Scheherazade, he takes his own way home.

He never gives a round-by-round, punch-by-punch transcription, but he does make real the fighters themselves, their handlers, seconds, managers, trainers, sparring partners, friends, and hangers-on. He re-creates the peculiar ambience, the sour antiseptic smell of dressing rooms, the ancient cigar-smoke stink of old arenas where countless young men have gone out under the hard glare of the overhead lights and for money have fought pain, fear, and each other to entertain people who paid for the right to watch and smoke. So much lavender nonsense has been written about boxing in recent years that one wants to absolve Liebling of any participation in some mysterious, arcane masculine theatrical whose metaphorical significance must be decoded before the real meaning emerges. He was too good a student of literature and life not to know that boxing was more than one man inflicting hurt upon another, but in his writing, a fight is a fight, and the people in the ring and in the crowd are people, not prototypes in some cultural drama. What stays with you from a Liebling piece is the feeling of the place, what it was like one night.

Thirty years after Liebling went to Shoreditch Town Hall on London's East Side, I went there, and I found what he had found, "an unmistakable municipal building," smartened up by the scrubbing that much of London has had recently, but still as he saw it, "pretentious, inharmonious, and depresssing," It is Hackney Town Hall now; the borough has been renamed.

Inside, the parquet floor was freshly polished and the vaguely pastoral scenes on the walls were picked out in bright gilt. I crossed the open floor where the ring would have been that night. Liebling had said the hall could hold nine hundred, which seemed about right, but a packed-out tight fit, since the ring would have taken up most of the floor, and most of the crowd would have been put in the balcony. I stood there and looked approvingly at the oddly immaculate arena where Liebling and the small bettors he sat with had watched a mediocre fight-card back in the days when Mrs. Thatcher was a young housewife fresh out of university.

Liebling describes a bit of the fights he saw that night, but most of the piece works to create the feel of a place where unimportant men went to make small bets on fighters whose names cannot be found in *The Ring Record Book.* It was the writing that sent me up Old Street to Hackney née Shoreditch Town Hall, just as another of his pieces sent me to an evening of bouts at the *Cirque d'Hiver* in Paris, where in the twenties he saw Panama Al Brown fight Edouard Mascart, an experience he recalls in *Between Meals*.

In the fifties, when I was still going to fights, his accounts led me to Stillman's Gym on Eighth Avenue. From that scabrous chamber, now long-razed, I eventually wandered to Angelina's on the Rue de Rivoli, Rumplemayer's when he went there, which smells much nicer than Stillman's and has the best hot chocolate in Paris. La Closerie des Lilas on the Boulevard du Montparnasse is now something of a Hemingway shrine, but what made me go there was Liebling's description of it on a night in 1944 when there was still fighting down the way in the Luxembourg Gardens. How does a writer affect one so potently and permanently? What makes you want to carry around pieces of Liebling's diverse, swarming world?

He believed, as he said in *The Sweet Science*, that "the old masters did know something. There is still a kick in style, and tradition carries a nasty wallop." He liked writers whose books gave them plenty of space to exercise and examine their true subjects—themselves. He liked books in which any number of observations and vagrant speculations, the sort of thing Colonel Stingo called "labyrinthine digressions," could be accommodated. He does reach the literal main event in due time, but I wonder if the persistent branching away from the central chronology, and the constant and diverse allusions, are not, in the end, his real concern. If a person wants only to learn who fought whom and who won, then there is always the *Almanach de Gotha* of boxing, *The Ring Record Book*.

Liebling's writing shows why good and bright people loved him, for it is a record of his willingness to be pleased by the world, a quality identified in that phrase by Dr. Johnson, something rarer even than genius. He was one of the lucky few who are willing to risk loving life and who get so much joy in return. Because he was a writer, his pleasures are now our pleasures, the ephemeral as well as the important made permanent by his talent and his devotion to his trade. It is still strangely difficult in this country to evaluate properly a writer who didn't chiefly write fiction, poetry, or plays, and in the academy there are still not many people who know and esteem Liebling's work. How good was he? Well, he once said of Billy Graham, a superb middleweight who never became champion, that "he was as good a fighter as he could be without being a hell of a fighter." There's something of Liebling in those lines, but not all of him. He *was* a hell of a writer, our American Hazlitt, who left behind no novels and no poems, just the passionate record of a large life well lived.

Fred Warner